Wildfire

The Fearless Spread of the Gospel

Ed Waken

ISBN-13: 978-0-9906604-7-7

For further information on Wildfire: The Fearless Spread of the Gospel, free material, spreading the gospel ideas, or booking speaking engagements, contact Ed Waken by visiting www.wildfiregospel.com or email him at wilfiregospelinfo.com

Get Connected:
@wildfiregospel (Twitter)
@edwaken (Twitter)
www.wildfiregospel.com

Wildfire – The Fearless Spread of the Gospel
By Ed Waken

Printed in the United States of America

ISBN 978-0-9906604-6-0 Print

ISBN 978-0-9906604-7-7 Digital

Unless otherwise indicated, Bible quotations are taken from the New American Standard Bible, © 1960, 1962, 1963, 1968, 1971, 1972, 1973, 1975, 1977 by The Lockman Foundation. Used by permission. http://www.lockman.org

Cover design and graphics by Luis Garcia
https://dribbble.com/sweetlou97

Reviews

Wildfire is the most encouraging book on evangelism and discipleship I have read in a long time. Rather than beating his readers on the head, Ed Waken encourages them to get close to Jesus. The closer we are to Jesus, the more we love Him; the more we love Him, the more we want to tell others about Him. Waken makes a strong case for evangelism being the responsibility of every believer, not just a special class of professional Christians. The book is full of illustrations of how to listen to the Spirit's nudging of our spirit to speak into the lives of people we meet everywhere we go. I highly recommend *Wildfire* to any believer who wants to be an effective witness for Christ.

Dr. Dave Anderson
President, Grace School of Theology

I love the title of this book; Wildfire–The Fearless Spread of the Gospel. The title perfectly encapsulates the essence of the entire book. As a long-time Christ follower, I was encouraged and emboldened to pray for daily opportunities to share Christ with those I encounter along the way. For those that are not-yet-believers in Christ, Wildfires is a reassuring testament that anyone can place their trust and their very life in Christ's hands knowing that their eternal, spiritual life is secure, and that they will be guided by the Holy Spirit to confidently share that security with others. Throughout the book, Ed writes that we can be 100% successful, 100% of the time if we will have the courage to speak our faith in Christ out loud to others. What a promise!

Linda Stanley
Retired Vice-President, Leadership Network

If you're looking for a book by a practitioner, this is it! There are plenty of books on evangelism that offer the latest tool or tip. I've read many of them. Ed's voice and experience comes through on every page.

Jeff Reams
Missions Pastor, Dunwoody Baptist Church

Ed's writing is clear and his scriptural points are well made. It was a pleasure to read and left me, encouraged, convicted and motivated. Every Christian should read this to discover a natural and easy way to share their faith with joy.

Stan Fousha
President, Evangelism In Depth Ministry

Wildfire solved the challenges I had with most evangelism methodologies. They depend on formulas and are way too complicated to follow, which gives most Jesus followers an excuse for not sharing Jesus. Waken, a true evangelist, shows how every Jesus disciple can simply share Jesus simply, no matter where they are and with whomever they are talking.

Chris Suitt
Author of *More Than a Sunday Faith.*

Wildfire focuses on the essentials necessary to see 100% success in sharing Jesus with others. I love the focus on relationship not only with the Father, Son and Spirit but how-to live-in way to relate to others through the sensitivity of the Spirit. This book will help energize you to be aware of the success that God gives us when we follow His plan of the Gospel and not a program or preplanned speech. Having worked in ministry in France for over 15 years I see what Ed lays out in this book for effective ministry in all contexts.

Rob Plaster
Church Planter in France with Encompass World Partners.

Ed put evangelism where it belongs - right in middle of everyday life of the follower of Jesus. As someone who has been trained in every conceivable program of evangelism, it is best done in relationship and as conversation. If someone knows you're "witnessing" to them, you're probably not doing it right.

Bob Roberts
Senior Pastor NorthWood Church, Author: Lessons from the East

"So make up your minds not to prepare beforehand to defend yourselves; for I will give you utterance and wisdom which none of your opponents will be able to resist or refute."

–Luke 21:14–15

DEDICATION

The truth and principles found in this book are taken from the Bible. My deepest appreciation is to Jesus Christ as the genesis behind these words.

I would have been unable to complete this project without the full support of my wife and girlfriend for life, Debbie Waken.

My children are an inspiration to me as I have watched them live out their love for Jesus and sharing His good news to many; Jared Waken, Rachel Waken and Bethany Albert, you each amaze me.

I owe a huge thank you to my mentor in evangelism, Juan Isaias. I also want to recognize George Traub and Tony DeRosa who have mentored me in life and developing the concepts found in this book.

Much of my life has been shaped by walking with the following men in life and ministry: Neil Cole, Phil Helfer, Dezi Baker and Chris Suitt.

I want to recognize my editing team. A huge thank you to Merrily Versluis, Monica Meyers and Sam Sacco.

ValleyLife Church in Phoenix, Arizona has allowed me to prove the truths and principles found in this book over the past two decades and I am indebted to them for their grace, love and support.

TABLE OF CONTENTS

INTRODUCTION

Greer, Arizona is one of the prettiest places I have ever seen. A small town in the White Mountains of Arizona, it nestles in a valley where the Little Colorado River flows. In the winter, it is a hub for skiers, snowboarders and snow machine enthusiasts. In the spring and summer, it is a paradise for campers, hunters and fishermen. In June of 2011, two campers left their campfire untended. The Wallow Wildfire that followed roared through this sleepy town, destroying buildings, homes and surrounding forests. A single campfire caused the largest wildfire Arizona had ever known.

Wildfires can destroy and consume. Wildfires are powerful and deadly, but they also give life and cause new growth. They provide new environments and new chances for change. The wildfires that are shared in this book are designed to nudge the reader to step out in the freedom God gives each believer to share the gospel naturally.

The gospel calls people to both leave some ways of living and to live life to the fullest. Inviting friends and strangers to embrace the full life Jesus offers ignites the passion to give His life-filling message to others. This is how spiritual wildfires are started. Wildfires spread by inviting people to follow Jesus and teaching them how to pass on what they have learned. When this happens the landscape of our culture will change.

As wildfires are ignited in the spiritual realm, destruction of old kingdoms and ways of living are inevitable. Spiritual wildfires consume the old ways of living, give life, hope and transformation. They leave room for something much better in the souls of women and men.

The world desperately needs thousands of spiritual life-giving wildfires. Jesus gives every believer this ability to start spiritual wildfires as they simply repeat what God speaks in their soul with not–yet–believers. When believers repeat what God speaks, He accomplishes His purposes in that interaction, whether the interaction is short or long. When believers repeat what God speaks, they can be confident that what God wanted has been done, whether they can see it or not. It doesn't matter if a decision was made or not; they have had the privilege of being part of that person's spiritual journey. This is success–simply repeating what God speaks. This is how spiritual wildfires are ignited naturally, rapidly and repeatedly![1]

The focus of this this book is to provide a biblically-based style of evangelism that focuses on freedom, not on rules. Every follower of Christ should be able to share their story and the truth found in the Scriptures in natural ways.

With this freedom, evangelism becomes fun, adventurous and exciting. If you are looking for methods, programs or rote approaches to evangelism, this is not the book for you. When methodologies or programs become the foundation of our thinking about evangelism, evangelism actually diminishes. Turning salvation into a one-size-fits-all method takes the creative fire out of something so beautiful.

Evangelism is meant to flow naturally, freely, and regularly, not be stuffed into formulas. The story of salvation should be passed along throughout your lifetime.

My life was radically changed when a spiritual wildfire was set in my soul. I was the first one to catch on fire for Jesus in my family. Through God's grace, that fire spread from my life to my father, mother, brother, grandparents, cousins, friends, strangers and many around the world. The fire in my soul for Jesus began in 1976 and is burning strongly today while rapidly spreading wherever I go.

Wildfires are uncontrollable, unpredictable, can jump fire

breaks and spread rapidly. This is due to a supply of dry combustible fuel which creates intense temperatures, driven by the wind to take more ground.[2] Heat, fuel and oxygen are each needed for wildfires to grow and keep building.

Our world is full of *fuel* that waits for us to ignite spiritual wildfires. There are millions of people around the world whom God has prepared to enter the Kingdom of God. Jesus told us that there will always be people who are ready to receive the truth of the gospel and spread it like a wildfire–but we have to lift up our eyes to see where He is leading.[3] Our God continues to draw souls around the world to Himself.

The Holy Spirit lives in each believer. He is the *oxygen* needed to nudge believers to be passionately active in the spreading of the gospel wildfire.

The *heat* for a wildfire to blaze around the world is the believer's heart for God. A believer's heart that is blazing for God will want more of Him. When our hearts for God are growing, we will naturally carry out His purpose. His purpose is to seek and save those who need His salvation.[4]

All the ingredients for a spiritual wildfire (heat, fuel, oxygen) are in each believer once they come to Jesus. What is often missing is a biblical understanding of these truths in the minds and hearts of believers.

God wants the world reached with the gospel, but not by just a few gifted people. He wants every one of His children to be engaged in the mission. And here is the good part. *God has (super)naturally equipped every believer to be 100% successful, 100% of the time when they engage in the mission of giving away the gospel.*

Success, as will be discovered, is simply sharing as God directs. The results of sharing are left up to God. The believer is 100% successful when they speak at God's leading. It is my prayer that this book will help fill the hearts and souls of Christ followers to gain this understanding and ignite wildfires right where they live, spreading to all the world.

This book is written for ordinary people who are handcuffed to unnatural and awkward methods of evangelism. God wants all believers to share the gospel naturally, within their own personality, and with unfettered success.

This book is written for leaders who have been misled into believing that their churches need more programs, more professional evangelists, and better evangelistic events if they want to impact their communities.

This book is written for the world, and all the millions and billions of people who have not yet found a relationship with Jesus. As believers learn to spread the gospel wherever they are, the good news has a chance to spread in places like neighborhood parties, airplane seats, and coffee shops.

The stage is being set for wildfires to ignite. Megachurches may be melting[5] and house churches may be multiplying yet unquantified.[6] Top-down leadership is being inverted so people are empowered instead of being overpowered. Buildings, budgets, and big shots[7] are being replaced with obedience, personal spiritual responsibility and simplicity. Professional and polished leaders are being replaced by authentic, ordinary people.

In these days of reshaping the landscape of church, we also find evangelism being reshaped. If the world is to be overtaken by spiritual wildfires, things must change. We have to rethink our unnatural addiction to canned evangelistic programs that teach us the next right-and-better way of sharing what has happened in our souls. The world needs to be set ablaze with wildfires set by ordinary people everywhere.

In the first section of this book we will explore the *heat* that is needed to move believers from fear to fearlessness in giving away the gospel. Many believers settle for attending meetings to heat up their faith. In reality, investment and sacrifice are needed in their relationship with Jesus in order for their spiritual temperature to rise. This first section will also address the fire extinguishers in the church which unintentionally slow or put out spiritual wildfires.

The second section of this book deals with the *fuel* needed to accelerate the wildfires of evangelism to spread rapidly. It lays out the freedom and confidence given to every believer from the outset of their faith, fueling them to be on spiritual adventures and take risks they have only dreamt about. This section will also deal with how to keep the momentum necessary for a larger and hotter evangelistic wildfire to spread uncontrollably.

The third section of this book deals with the *oxygen* needed to experience the power and passion of the Holy Spirit in drawing souls into the Kingdom. It navigates the Holy Spirit's unconventional leading, empowering ordinary believers to fight forward in the battle for souls. This final section gives Scriptural and contemporary examples of the Holy Spirit sending out ordinary people before they seemed ready. It also explains that a consecrated minority following the lead of the Holy Spirit can have an unexpected influence! And finally, it encourages ordinary people to finish well in their obedience to the heart of God in evangelism.

Wildfire - The Fearless Spreading of the Gospel focuses on Biblical principles every believer will find helpful and freeing. These principles are easy to use and follow for the newest to the most seasoned of believers.

This book is not about modern methods or clever systems that require you to adopt. It is written for the army of ordinary people like you and me who are waiting for the freedom promised throughout the pages of the Bible. Throughout history, the gospel has spread uncontrollably throughout cities and countries. It's time for spiritual wildfires to ignite once again through the freedom, encouragement, and success promised in the Bible.

The world is waiting for you to confidently follow Jesus just as you are, and in your work, school, or city. Every believer can be 100% successful, 100% of the time when they join God in giving away His good news naturally. I want to invite you learn with me how all believers can start spiritual wildfire.

PART 1 - WILDFIRES NEED HEAT

When our souls are heated with a deepening love for Jesus, evangelism will be authentic, adventurous and a way of life. Unintentionally, many leaders have taken away the heart for evangelism and replaced it with methods, programs and professionals. This cools the motivation of ordinary believers to share the gospel with the people around them. Deepening our love for Jesus is necessary to let the wildfire of evangelism once again roar and spread, capturing the hearts of people.

CHAPTER 1: FRESH LOVE

"Love the Lord your God with all your heart, soul, mind and strength." Jesus Christ

What if evangelism was fun, natural and flowed freely out of who you were created to be? What if you didn't have to rely on memorized techniques to share the love of Jesus? What if evangelism made you feel more empowered and used by God rather than restricted, awkward, forcing conversations and embarrassed? What if evangelism was just repeating the words God speaks to your mind and heart for a person to hear instead of reciting a list of questions or a formula to get people to pray a specific sort of prayer? If this is true, sharing Jesus might actually be fun, natural, and flow freely out of our hearts. We might even begin to look for the encounters and conversations that God creates for us to share His deep love with people.

Natural evangelism sounds more like what I read in the New Testament. I don't see anyone in the Bible teaching believer's techniques to share their faith. I do see many believers passionately engaging their friends, neighbors and strangers with the love of Christ on a regular basis. What if evangelism was meant to flow naturally out of who we are? What if every encounter with people who need Jesus is a divine opportunity created by God? Could these conversations move people forward, in small and large steps, toward deciding to follow Him? If any of this is true, it changes everything about evangelism.

Many Christians today have been trained to see evangelism as an event or system of sharing the good news of Jesus with not–yet–believers. There is a programmed feel that has overtaken the concept of evangelism in the modern church age. Recently, a friend of mine went to the Philippines for a two–week mission trip of sharing the gospel in schools. For several months before the trip, Theresa memorized Scripture verses and a lengthy outline to share with the children in the Philippines. As the months led up to her trip, her presentation moved from very rough to almost smooth. She memorized and practiced faithfully the script given to her. Finally, the two–week trip happened. When she got home to the United States, she was thrilled to share that she had given her presentation to 27 schools and had seen dozens of children place their trust in Jesus Christ!

After Theresa had been home for several weeks, I asked her how many times she had shared the gospel since she had been home. Not once, she admitted. When I asked her why, she said she did not have an audience that had invited her to share. Although the result of her experience in the Philippines was amazing, all of her training apparently did not prepare her to share the wonderful news of Jesus in her own context. Her training only focused on sharing the gospel in arranged meetings with strangers whom she would never see again. The memorized verses and truths she learned were helpful, and good practice, but no one had mentored her in how to share the gospel naturally in her hometown.

This type of programmed approach has moved sharing the good news of Jesus from a heart language that flows from our love and experiences to more of a scripted language. This type of evangelism expects believers to memorize a set of questions or Biblical truths and present them to people, mostly in non–relational contexts (like on an airplane, bus, or with a server at a restaurant). Other approaches may include handing out gospel pamphlets to strangers, or preaching on a street corner. These approaches require various types of skills like memorization and speaking in public, and also requires a boldness in larger group settings. Few people feel comfortable with these requirements. (If this type of approach is comfortable for you, keep going!)

Then there is the more generic 'Friendship Evangelism.'[1] Though I don't personally like these modernized, non–relational approaches, I'm not against them. They are definitely better than ignoring the command of Jesus to make disciples.[2] When we do see public evangelism in the book of Acts, it's because the audience invited someone to share, like Paul in Athens[3] or at the synagogue in Antioch. Even in Acts 2 when the Holy Spirit descended on the 120 followers of Christ, the city came together to find out what was happening. This led Peter to preach a message, and over 3,000 people trusted in Jesus and were baptized. The gathering of the people from the city to see what was happening is form of invitation of the audience to learn what was happening.

It is important to note that evangelism does not stand alone in the Scriptures. In the Bible, we don't see our modern focus on the "accomplishment" of getting people to place their trust in Jesus in a one-time deal. We may think of evangelism as an end, but it is only a beginning! In fact, I would say that evangelism is only a part of Jesus' Great Commission to go and make disciples. The normal pattern in a believer's life should flow from faith in Christ, to living out that faith in community and sharing that faith with others.[4] This leads to growing more like Christ throughout life. Alan Hirsch has coined the phrase "Disciplism,"[5] combining the concepts of evangelism and discipleship. We should be nudging people to trust Jesus and to follow His ways of living out that trust. Non–faith to faith to living out and sharing that faith should be seamless, not compartmentalized.

Evangelism literally means the proclaiming or sharing of the good news of Jesus.[6] In the New Testament, sharing the good news of Jesus was deeply authentic. It flowed out of relationships[7] or situations where God strongly impressed on people what to say or do.[8] Believers were motivated to share the Gospel out of obedience and a heart of gratitude, not because of guilt or a seminar they had followed. When evangelism led to persecution, we see that the believers rejoiced instead of trying to find a more effective evangelistic method.[9]

Evangelism and Religion

Many Christians shy away from having anything to do with evangelism. Maybe you are one of them, and that is why you have picked up this book. Everyone who has placed their faith in Jesus is *grateful* that they heard the Good News of Jesus. However, many people who have been evangelized *are not comfortable evangelizing others!* Logically, this makes no sense. When we think of evangelism in broad terms, all of us 'evangelize' others about our favorite restaurants, reality shows, shopping places, or sports teams. We naturally talk about topics with which we are passionate. The gospel is something every believer ought to be passionate about!

One summer evening on the island of Kauai, my son invited me to join him in smoking a cigar. I had never smoked a cigar before (and had never wanted to touch one either). With the sun setting and a warm breeze brushing our faces, I hesitated as my son pulled a cigar out of his travel humidor. He had asked me so many times before. With some curiosity, I took it as an opportunity to bond with my son and experience something he enjoyed so much. I took the cigar and learned how to cut it, light it and smoke it without inhaling (never inhale a cigar). As we enjoyed the sunset and each other's company, my son talked about the finer aspects of smoking a cigar and how it was constructed. He also told me about a local cigar lounge near our home called Fair Oaks.

As the sun set with a mixture of orange and purple hues, Jared shared stories about several men at Fair Oaks. Jared wanted to see his friends at Fair Oaks come to know Christ and he wanted me to join him there. After we returned from Kauai, Jared and I started meeting at Fair Oaks on Monday afternoons for a cigar and conversations with new friends.

One day, I was sitting at Fair Oaks, when Mike walked by. Mike and I had not had many conversations. We were more the "Hey, how's it going?" type of friends. As Mike walked by, I felt a nudge in my soul to tell him that I was praying for him and so I did. Mike kept on walking.

A few weeks later I was having a conversation with a friend at Fair Oaks. Mike, seated in the chair next to us, was able to hear everything we were discussing. After thirty minutes of spiritual conversation with my friend, Mike took his ear buds out and told me how much he appreciated that I told him I was praying for him weeks earlier. This led to a long conversation about Mike's life as he opened up in a very vulnerable way. I shared the gospel through stories from the Scriptures and how Jesus impacts my life. It was natural and flowed out of our conversation led by the Spirit. All of this took place because I told Mike, weeks earlier, that I had been praying for him.

In our culture, it's easy to lump everything related to God under the heading of 'religion.' Religion is an activity full of forms and rituals that must be practiced by people in order to please God. A relationship with God is radically different.

A relationship with God begins by coming to Him honestly with all of our questions, doubts, and fears. When we come to God as we are, we can then choose to switch from going in our own direction to following His direction.

We can follow His direction of life by placing our trust in what Jesus Christ did for us on the cross. When we choose this direction, God gives us the Holy Spirit.[10] God created us in His image so that we would reflect who He is to the world. Because we have each chosen our own path in life (this is called sin) instead of following God's path, we have been separated from God. God initiated restoring us to Him by sending Jesus Christ to repair this separation through His death on the cross, burial and resurrection.

Once we put our trust in what Jesus has done for us, we enter into a relationship where we can freely worship Him and He lives in us through His Spirit. Religion is what we attempt to do to please God. Relationship is what God has done for us so we can connect to Him. It's an ongoing journey of learning how He wants us to live and spread His message of hope, love and restoration to those He brings into our lives.

In the past several decades, evangelism has been "married" to religion in the western church. Evangelism is best lived out of our relationship with Jesus, not out of forms or tactics. Religion is structured, and scheduled. Relationship is a flow of interaction between friends.[11] Jesus is the Son of God, and a Person who wants a relationship with you and me. He offers hope, purpose, significance, and security. I want to introduce people to a relationship with Jesus, not to religion.

Without a deep *relationship* with Jesus anchored in His love for us, evangelism becomes dry, mechanical, and compartmentalized. Then our words may sound more like a stale sales pitch than a story about a life–giving belief that has totally transformed who we were. Memorizing procedural steps may give us a sense of "I've got this," but the power of authenticity and the profound mystery of relationship of inviting people into eternal life is lost.

When evangelism is isolated from our relationship with God, it has all the attraction of a root canal! When we deepen our relationship with Jesus, our love for others will expand. When we love God with everything, and love our neighbors as ourselves, evangelism will come from the heart and not a user manual.

In the past several decades, a variety of evangelistic approaches have been developed. Unfortunately, the emphasis has often been on the technique, while the need is for a foundation. The true foundation for evangelism is a growing love for God (cf. Revelation 2:1-7). Without the foundation of relationship with God being reinforced regularly, a presentation of the Good News can come off stale and wooden. However, with the foundation of a growing love for God, evangelism can be a natural part of who God created us to be. We need to return to the foundation of love as our motivation whether we use a certain approach, a variation of an approach, or a spontaneous conversation.

Evangelism and Love

The Bible says love is meant to be the hallmark of the Christian faith.[12] To push, urge or train people to tell about the good news of Jesus without the context of love is artificial.[13] It may attract people to information but not to relationship. We have all heard stories of people bragging about how many souls they have "led to Jesus" as if this was the ultimate goal. But is it? And does this motivate disciples to see Christ formed in others?[14]

Let's begin our quest to understand Biblical evangelism by looking at one passage that focuses on the foundation and flow of evangelism. It traces sharing the truth of Jesus, out of love for Christ, to those He lived and died for.[15]

> *5 For I am mindful of the sincere faith within you, which first dwelt in your grandmother Lois and your mother Eunice, and I am sure that it is in you as well. 6 For this reason I remind you to kindle afresh the gift of God which is in you through the laying on of my hands. 7 For God has not given us a spirit of timidity, but of power and love and discipline. 8 Therefore do not be ashamed of the testimony of our Lord or of me His prisoner, but join with me in suffering for the gospel according to the power of God, 2 Timothy 1:5-8*

In this passage, Paul is writing to his disciple, Timothy. He instructs Timothy to *"kindle afresh the gift of God"* in his life so he will be strong in sharing his testimony about Christ, and be ready to suffer for Him if necessary. Timothy had seen and experienced this love of God in the lives of his mother and grandmother. There are few relationships stronger than close family ties. It is my understanding that the gift of God that Paul writes about is salvation through relationship with Jesus Christ.[16]

Keeping our relationship with God happens as we regularly interact with Him in conversation all through the day. This is how I keep developing my relationship with my wife. Throughout my work day, I'll send her texts or make a short phone call to hear her voice and hear how she's doing. This regular connection builds a deepening love between us as the years go by. In fact, I can strongly say I love my wife more today than I did when I said, "I do," many decades ago. This is what Paul is encouraging Timothy to do in the passage above. We can keep the fire of our love for God hot by having an ongoing relationship with Him every day, throughout the day. This also builds anticipation to listen for His promptings while reading and pondering the truths in the Bible. As we chew on the principles and truth we have read, we can then commit ourselves to living out those truths.

It's crucial for each of us to take responsibility for developing our relationship with Jesus,[17] especially with our busy schedules. We can develop our relationship through reading God's Word, reflecting on His love for us, and choosing to obey what He teaches us through our interaction with His Word, and appreciating the beauty of His creation. We can also talk with Him about the struggles we are going through, and whisper 'Thank You' throughout our day; simple ways to draw near to the heart of God.

It is hard to cultivate a deepening relationship with Jesus just by hearing sermons, attending Bible studies, or going to some form of a church meeting. These practices are good, but they do not always deepen our personal connection with Jesus. It's tempting to blame our lack of depth on the busyness we allow in our lives. We can easily exchange daily personal relational development with God for group meetings which require little more than showing up and listening. We are often inspired to love God more deeply and spend personal time with Him in these meetings, but without putting the inspiration into concrete action, the relationship grows slowly, if at all. We need to take responsibility for deepening our faith, and become participants, not spectators!

One of the disciplines that I have been incorporating into my life to keep a *kindled fresh* faith is remembering. In the Genesis account of creation, God says He made man and woman "...in His own image...male and female He created them."[18] The word for male in Hebrew is *zakar* which means "the remembering one."[19] It is interesting that remembering is part of being created in God's image. What are we to remember? We need to remember the stories of God working in our lives, and we need to retell these stories to ourselves and those around us. This gives us a vibrant and consistent mindset of staying close to God even when life doesn't make sense or when we are tempted to go off in our own directions.[20]

When Eve was tempted and deceived by Satan in the Garden of Eden, I get the impression that Adam stood by and was silent as he watched the interaction between the serpent and Eve. Did Adam fail to remember what God had done? Because Adam and Eve focused on their own wants, instead of on God and what He had done, sin, death, and decay entered the world. Remembering who God is and what He has done in our lives helps His story to flow from our lives. The sin committed in Genesis 3 not only wounded the soul of humans, it also wounded God because Adam and Eve turned their backs on His goodness.

As we regularly *kindle afresh* our understanding of how much Jesus loves us, we will find a natural flow of sharing our experience with Him in our actions and words towards others. As an example, when we visit a favorite restaurant, we are naturally excited to tell others about the taste of the food, the quality of the service, and the ambiance. When friends come into town, I love introducing them to my favorite places to eat. In the same way, experiencing Jesus should make us excited to share that experience with others. But unless we are in a transformational relationship with Jesus, our evangelism will be dry and dusty.

Keeping the gift of God (salvation) fresh is the charge for every believer. Fires of love are prone to die out or be extinguished by distractions. Fanning the flames of our faith requires a mindset that understands that constant personal effort is essential if we want to stay close to Jesus.[21] When the flames of our faith are fiery and strong, the love of Jesus towards those we encounter will flow naturally. This is the heart of Jesus!

When we find our faith parched and dusty, it is time for adventure and risk! We can choose to leave the comfort of a mundane and sterile faith, and follow the lead of the Holy Spirit into the wilderness of souls that do not yet belong to Jesus. When our faith becomes adventurous, our dependence on and connection to God naturally increases. When we find ourselves in risky situations, our prayers multiply and our expectation for God to come through heightens.

A few years ago, I took Josh, a young man I was mentoring, on a mission trip to India. During the weeks before our trip, we had several good discussions about what we were going to teach and what his role would be. Josh told me he wanted to experience God working powerfully through him. It wasn't my first trip to India, so I could already see a possible problem. From what I had experienced, I knew that Christians who smoked were not respected as teachers within the Indian Christian community. And Josh was a smoker.

Before we boarded the plane bound for New Delhi, India, Josh took his last pack of cigarettes and threw them in the garbage. He chose to honor the Indian Christians and stopped smoking, cold turkey. Once the cigarettes were in the trash, we prayed together. And God chose to honor Josh's decision, and gave him the ability to quit with no withdrawals, which amazed us. During our two weeks in India, Josh's faith went from steady–but–sterile, to off-the-charts powerful. I watched as he spoke with individuals and groups, and didn't let his lack of experience stop him from sharing what God had done in his life. He encouraged believers to step out in faith in ways they had not considered, like leaving old habits behind. He adapted to the culture and listened to the Spirit's guiding. Josh left India a changed man.

On our return, Josh took off on a new adventure to Arizona to make disciples, form community with others, and see people come to Jesus. He hasn't touched another cigarette, not because of rules but because of how God changed him. He has fresh stories to tell of how his love and obedience to Jesus catapulted him to the next level. This is how it can be for every believer who chooses to live adventurously for the King. We move our relationship from dusty to desperate by engaging in fresh adventures that put our faith on the line. If God doesn't come through, we are doomed.

When our love for Christ is our motivation, we will be willing to share His gospel and suffer for Him[22] on a regular basis. The gospel has been placed in our hearts; love for Christ is the only enduring motivation that will consistently move the gospel from our hearts to our words and actions.[23] This is possible because of

16

the power of the Holy Spirit.[24] Part of the suffering Paul instructed Timothy to endure was to live fully focused on Jesus and die to himself.[25] When our focus is fully on Christ, we will emphasize His life and purpose at the expense of ours.[26]

When love is not the foundation of proclaiming the gospel, the heartbeat of evangelism is lost. Sharing the Good News of Jesus as a way of life is the result of love. When love is the foundation, evangelism flows naturally.

Love for Christ and His message is the driving force behind the passionate, purposeful interaction with others.[27] This type of love alerts us to the opportunities that are all around us on a daily basis. Falling in love with Jesus and sharing the love of Jesus informs and feeds each other, and this is the foundation for evangelism. An undying love is what enables us to look into the eyes of those who are lost and suffering and tell them that Jesus is the answer.

The cultivating of this love is an ongoing work. Once begun, never done! Have you ever wondered why some people seem to be full of joy and ready to share the message of Christ with others? I believe it comes from a burning in their soul, birthed out of fresh and ongoing connection with Jesus. Like a married couple who can finish each other's sentences, the more time we spend connecting to God, the more we are going to be familiar with His voice to us. As this familiarity deepens, we develop the heart, eyes and ears of Jesus and begin to see people the way He sees them. The chances to share His love and message seem to explode all around us.

As we love God more deeply, our love for others will flourish. The more we love Jesus, the more His love oozes from our life. When Jesus was asked what the greatest commandment was, He answered, "'You shall love the Lord your God with all your heart, and with all your soul, and with all your mind.' This is the great and foremost commandment. The second is like it, 'You shall love your neighbor as yourself.'" (Matthew 22:37-39) To love your neighbor as yourself certainly includes a deep love and concern for their eternal state. Freely giving away what you have freely received is the result of a deep and flowing love of God in your soul.[28] Loving God and others is linked in both Scripture and how we live out our faith.[29]

One day, I was having breakfast with my friend Eric at a restaurant. I noticed our waitress had some Chinese characters tattooed on the inside of her left wrist, I mentioned I had noticed the tattoo and asked her what it meant. She had to move on to another table, but first she told us that it stood for strength and courage. When she returned, Eric rolled up his sleeve to show her his tattoo of a lion. He shared with her that it reminded him to be strong and courageous. We told her that God wanted her to know that He was aware of the situation that caused her to get that tattoo, and that He wanted to be involved in her life. Our comments brought tears to her eyes. It turned out that those were the exact words she needed to hear at that exact moment.

There is no memorized format that can teach this type of interaction. These observations about her tattoo and the encouragement we gave didn't come from an evangelistic method–they came from a deep love and devotion to Jesus. We were willing to speak the words He whispered to our souls, and they touched this young woman. May Jesus draw her to Himself!

In 2 Timothy 1:5-8, Paul tells Timothy, a young man he was mentoring, that timidity is not something God gives His followers. Timidity often keeps us quiet about our faith, but, as we read in 1 John, "perfect love casts out that fear."[30] Fear leads to hiding the truth and keeping it to ourselves. But when love is our motivation, it releases the life–transforming truth of hope and purpose. When we are not fanning the flames of our faith, silence and apathy rule, and the expansion of Christ's kingdom slows.

We have received a much different spirit from God than fear. Every believer has received from God "...a spirit of power, love and discipline." (2 Timothy 1:7). This spirit of power brings confidence, competence and concern for others. When anyone trusts in Jesus Christ, the Holy Spirit comes on them and takes up permanent residence in them, giving them power to be His witnesses.[31]

Everyone who follows Jesus is (super)naturally empowered to be a witness of everything that Christ has done for them. This power is not a watered–down hope but a supernatural <u>POWER</u> that brings success to our efforts of loving others with the truth! The success is the accomplishment of what God wants to happen in a soul, at that time.

Paul prayed in Ephesians 1:18-20 that the saints would know the greatness of His power towards us, the same power it took to raise Jesus from the dead! We are to walk by the Spirit; by His power and the infusion of His life in us, and not according to timidity or the flesh which is our own natural habits.[32] The Spirit wants to lead our interactions with those around us. When we walk according to the flesh, we are not focused on sharing His good news freely and with power.

This God-infused, supernatural power helps us share about Jesus boldly. It is a power to live differently and to impact those whom God has placed in our lives. God is ready to launch us into the world with His love and truth. He wants us to be successful and knows we need His power.

> *"Such is the confidence that we have through Christ toward God. Not that we are sufficient in ourselves to claim anything as coming from us, but our sufficiency is from God, who has made us competent to be ministers of a new covenant..." 2 Corinthians 3:4-6 ESV*

Not only do we have supernatural power to tell others about Christ, but we also receive supernatural love to do this.[33] This love keeps us sensitive to the Spirit's nudges to share our faith with others. Human eyes are not enough, since we all often pretend everything is fine when we are in desperate need of hope and life.

Love helps us to be in tune to others' needs as directed by the Spirit. The love of God focuses us on others, not on ourselves, and definitely not on fear and silence. The Holy Spirit can nudge us towards actions and words encouragement and truth.

19

In addition to power and love, God also provides a supernatural spirit of discipline.[34] Discipline is necessary if we want to keep growing in maturity and in our relationship with God. As we determinedly focus on Christ and on people, we will see things that a programmed approach to evangelism does not allow us to see. As we become friends with the world as Jesus did, we will gain a reputation like He did when He was here. To be friends with the world means we befriend people and love them. We are not to become friends with the world's systems and desires.[35]

Evangelism and the Reputation of Jesus

> *"For John came neither eating nor drinking, and they say, 'He has a demon!' 19 "The Son of Man came eating and drinking, and they say, 'Behold, a gluttonous man and a drunkard, a friend of tax collectors and sinners!' Yet wisdom is vindicated by her deeds." Matthew 11:18-19*

Some believers may ignore or just overlook the reputation Jesus had in his own time. It can be confronting or uncomfortable, especially if we look at our own nice and tidy Christian lives. But when we look in the Bible, we see that Jesus, the God–Man, connected deeply to sinners, and deliberately surrounded himself with them.

Many believers today have learned to distance themselves from people who have a different moral compass. But Jesus was known to hang out with people with bad reputations. Jesus was also known to befriend people who were considered even worse than ordinary sinners–the tax collectors. Tax collectors were hated and despised by the Jews in Jesus' day because they worked for Rome and often misused their position. For example, tax collectors could walk up to people and tax them for what they were carrying. Jesus became friends with people that other rabbis would never lower themselves to even consider. Besides being a friend of tax collectors, Jesus befriended women, drunkards, prostitutes, lepers, Samaritans, and foreigners. This was unacceptable behavior in the minds of the Jews.

The adventure of acquiring the reputation of Jesus is risky. When we befriend the type of people Jesus befriended, people in the church may criticize us. Some may even *unfriend* us! "Bad company corrupts good character," we may hear. This is a possible danger of loving 'sinners,' but it can be neutralized by mutual accountability with other brothers and sisters in Christ. This is the way Jesus showed us to live as He walked this earth in the company of His twelve closest friends. We can and should follow our Lord's example, instead of worrying that we'll be 'infected' by people who don't live up to church standards.[36]

Second Timothy 2:22 says "Now flee from youthful lusts and pursue righteousness, faith, love and peace, with those who call on the Lord from a pure heart." On our spiritual journey, we can be transparent and accountable to those in our 'spiritual tribe.' Our spiritual tribe is a group of people who are dedicated in their faith, and encourage us. This tribe may take the form of an organized church, a house church, some accountability partners, or a discipleship group.[37] While there are many names for this sort of group, this emphasis on a faith community goes back to Biblical times.

There's a question we can ask ourselves or others when we shy away from befriending people who are not-yet-Christians. Is it worse to take the risk of befriending sinners and falling into the ways of the world? Or to stand before Jesus one day and having Him ask you why you did not befriend those in need of His love and truth? We are to be well pleasing to the Lord and at the same time we are to live and engage the world in a way that will persuade men.[38] Living out the Spirit's leading with His power, love and discipline will startle people both inside the church and outside, just like Jesus did when He walked this earth.

Recently I made a whole new group of friends at a local cigar shop. It would be easy to assume that the customers there are rough, and would sneer at religion or religious people. What I've noticed is they have big hearts that are missing something, and they know it. If I had shown up there with tracts and a prepared sermon about their need for Christ they would ignore or laugh at me. Even if they knew in their hearts that my message was true, they likely wouldn't welcome me. But after telling my story and hearing theirs, I have been accepted for who I am; a follower of King Jesus.

Enjoying cigars or spending time in a cigar shop is not something most Christians would consider to be appropriate. Because I now enjoy cigars with my new friends, some of the believers I know have questioned my choices.

Phoebe is a wonderful friend who is part of our church. At one point, she took me out for coffee and gently discussed with me her concern for my health. I explained to her some of the articles I have read about cigar smoking health risks being much less than smoking cigarettes and that premium cigars do not include the chemicals cigarettes contain. I am not saying everyone should start smoking cigars, but it is something I enjoy and opens up a regular opportunity to talk about Jesus and His gospel on a weekly basis. Phoebe listened to my reasoning and, while not necessarily agreeing that it was a good practice, she promised to pray for the spiritual opportunities I find along the way.

I have begun this adventure into cigar smoking lounges in need of the light of Christ with other believers. I am not going on this adventure alone. Believers who are genuinely concerned for my well–being usually end up saying they will pray for my friends, once they realize I am obeying Jesus' command to love them. But some people misunderstand my motives because religion has muted their ability to have the mind of Christ. I do care about their opinion of my actions, but I'm more motivated by King Jesus' question to me when I meet Him face to face. I'm confident that Jesus is working in the hearts of these men and the transformation I've seen is amazing.

It is comforting to know that Jesus wrestled in life[39] and still kept His love for the Father and others in focus. The Bible says it like this: Jesus was "…tempted in all things as we are, yet without sin"[40] and "…He learned obedience from the things which He suffered."[41] Jesus' life was filled with distractions and desperate people. As our example, He was faithful to the mission of showing us how to interact with God and man in adventurous ways.

Jesus' life was just as difficult as we find ours today, and then some! Jesus knew what it was like to depend on God for His needs to be met.[42] He knew what it felt like to be betrayed.[43] Jesus struggled to balance loving God and people in the middle of problems that competed for His attention and time.[44] Jesus was human in every way and yet without sin. Jesus was busy, had to choose where He should spend His time, and had to get up early to pray when His body wanted to sleep more. I'm convinced that he had stomach cramps after a good meal, and had tired legs at the end of the day. As He walked the earth He walked with a love for God and others ahead of Himself. He needed to eat, sleep, rest, and carry on with life but still maintained His first love for the Father[45]. This let Him see people as distressed, like sheep without a shepherd.[46]

Having a heart for God and others requires a constant fanning of the flames of our faith. Putting our own agendas first creates a more placid faith. We may think, "Life is good, I'm taking care of myself, so all is well." But when a challenge shows up in our life, or in the life of a loved one, we try to snuggle closer to the Father, often until life is good again.

Loving God at the expense of our own comfort is death…which gives life. Love focused on self at the expense of knowing God deeply feels like life…but is actually death.[47] Most have experienced the pain of loving others deeply. To focus on the downcast as Jesus did requires our submitting to the love and will of the Father.

Obedience takes a faith fueled by love for Christ. This helps us to live selflessly so we can help others look to Jesus. Living for ourselves will cause us to protect our own comfort, status, or standing. Selfishness dulls our hearing God's call on our lives. In later chapters, we'll see how the harvest of souls increases when we are motivated by Christ's deep love for the people around us.

Evangelism and Movement

Jesus had an important decision to make early in His public ministry.[48] He had to choose a group of men who would become His students and closest friends. He would show them the way to live and teach the truth so they would believe it and share it. To make this important decision, He spent a whole night in prayer with the Father.[49]

We can learn from Jesus that God wants to be involved in our decisions, whether we think they're spiritual or not. We also learn that when we let God direct our decisions, we are not protected from pain and suffering. The twelve men Jesus chose sometimes disappointed Him. As we read the story of Jesus we hear phrases like, "How long shall I put up with you"[50] and "You men of little faith."[51] The men given to Jesus from the Father were far from the all-star team we might imagine and yet, these twelve men were used by God to *change the world* and begin a movement.

Deepening our love for Christ and obeying His promptings to move towards others can bring change to our world *and* cause us heartache at the same time. Just like Jesus chose His twelve close friends to walk with Him, He also chooses you to walk with Him and influence the people around you. The wonderful news in Jesus choosing you and I to be His spokespeople[52] is that He invites us to invade the world with His purpose.

If you have been a believer for some time, you likely have been taught some version of a gospel presentation. Learning a succinct outline of the gospel is a good thing to do. Often though, these presentations feel just like that; a presentation of facts or truths. Most people aren't interested in listening to presentations, but they would be interested in hearing how your life has been affected by Christ. Or they might listen to other stories that are infused with the truths of the gospel. People want authenticity as we share our faith stories.

Authenticity is often overlooked when sharing the gospel. Real stories, told from a real desire to see God's good news spread, make a difference. But when our sharing is motivated by others' expectations, authenticity is lost and people begin to feel like a project. When our motivation is driven by expectations (ours or others), we will feel pride when we meet the expectations. We will feel frustrated when we don't meet those expectations. Being with Jesus and gaining His heart and mind is a lifetime endeavor with huge rewards.

Some of you may have placed your trust in Jesus some time ago and have not made it a priority to pursue a deepening relationship with Him. No matter how long ago you placed your trust in Jesus, no matter how you may have spent the years since then, you can begin to pursue Him right now. He is also ready to treat you the same way He treated His first twelve disciples; to move them forward in their faith. His arms are always open to you, and He wants to be with you NOW! Do not let your past stop you from pursuing Him today. He will meet you where you are and develop you into a mature believer as you follow Him.

Our understanding of spiritual things matures with time as we get to know Jesus better, but that doesn't change the message.[53] Jesus begins with the end in mind. He wants His followers to know that He trusts them with the message of life from the outset. He trusts you with this message and has made you competent to give it away *from the moment you begin a relationship with Him.*[54]

There is a battle for the souls of women and men, and the King goes with us into that battle. We have His power, confidence, spiritual gifts, and authority to win the day! This most holy fight begins with love for our King and for the souls of people He died to save.

He invites us to remember who He is and what He has done while empowering every one of His disciples to be successful in this fight of love. Paul urges Timothy to be a "good soldier for Christ." The soldiers for Jesus are meant to be fully mobilized for action and success from the outset. We must choose to believe what our commander has said about us, and what He has called us to accomplish for His Kingdom-building pleasure. Do you believe in the Jesus who is King of the world, or the religious concept of Jesus as just a good teacher? Kingdom–building begins with a fresh, fiery love for Jesus. We need to keep this fire kindled afresh because there are fire extinguishers all around us

CHAPTER 2: FIRE EXTINGUISHERS

"The harvest is plentiful but the workers are few." Jesus Christ

Jesus knew that some souls would be white, ripe and ready for harvesting until His return. We must listen to the Spirit to see who those souls are that are ripe for harvesting in our lives. There is always fertile soil, prepared by God, ready to receive the good seed.[1] Our role is to sow the seed indiscriminately until we find the soil ready to receive it and produce a harvest!

Jesus also knew that there would be a lack of workers willing to work in those white fields. At first glance, it seems odd that fields ripe with souls ready to be harvested would be ignored by those instructed to work the fields.[2] In every age, the reason for this lack of workers shifts, and it is no different today.

Today the world's population is expanding with souls faster than ever. As the number of people in the world soars, the number of spiritual workers is diminishing in the West.[3] Many churches and church leaders are familiar with this lack of spiritual workers. This hurts God's heart. He sent His Son to die to welcome people into relationship with Him, and spiritual workers are part of His design.

Since before the foundation of the world, God has had a mission to bring people into relationship with Him.[4] He invites His followers to join with Him on this task, and to do that He has equipped them to be effective.[5] He sent His Spirit to empower the spiritual workers to be successful.[6] He wrote His Word to restore them, and remind them to not lose heart and to keep on sowing the seeds of truth wherever they go. But the wildfire placed by God in the hearts of His children is being suppressed by some people *in His very own church*.[7]

From Passion to Suppression

I woke up one Friday morning in April of 1976 excited about a weekend skiing adventure with some friends. At 18 years old, I felt my life could not have been better. I had a good job, a beautiful girlfriend, a new car, and zest for living. I had the world by the tail... or so I thought. As part of my ski trip preparation, I worked out a plan to steal a case of beer to take with me. Once I had the beer in the back seat, I felt the joy of the liquid in my veins before I had one drink. Grinning, I headed over to pick up my friend Ralph.

It was a cold evening as we headed up to the mountains of Southern California. A light snow hit my windshield. Then, three quarters of the way up the mountain I encountered some black ice on the road. Being a surfer boy from Long Beach, California, I had no idea what happened when my car swerved out of control into the opposite lane. Fear jumped from my stomach into my throat as we headed towards a cliff, and I thought my life was about to end. In the split moment that the car approached the cliff I regained control of my car, slowed down and moved back to the right lane. Just as quickly, it was all over.

As I finally stopped shaking, my friend Ralph asked me a question that caught me off guard. "Ed, what would have happened to you if we had crashed and died?" That brought up flashbacks from my Catholic upbringing, of flickering candles, the smell of incense, and Latin phrases. I tried to joke it off, saying, "Well, if God woke up on the right side of the bed today, I might have a good chance of making it to heaven." Ralph didn't let it go that easily. He surprised me by saying, "Ed, you can know for sure if you're going to make it to Heaven or not." This was something I had never heard before, neither in the Catholic church nor in eight years of Catholic school. I wanted to hear more. Ralph quoted 1 John 5:11-13 which says;

28

*"11 And the testimony is this, that God has given us eternal life, and this life is in His Son. 12 He who has the Son has the life; he who does not have the Son of God does not have the life. 13 These things I have written to you who believe in the name of the Son of God, **so that you may know that you have eternal life.**" 1 John 5:11-13 (emphasis mine)*

That was something I wanted to know, something I needed to know. My attention was on the road and the falling snow, but my heart filled with anticipation to learn more about gaining eternal life. Our conversation about living for Jesus expanded. Without a verbalized prayer or an altar call, I fully trusted in Jesus[8] and was immediately transformed by God's grace.

My heart felt light and I somehow knew that the Scripture Ralph shared with me was true. A few minutes later we arrived at the cabin. I saw a trash dumpster and I knew I needed to do something. The joy of the liquid in my veins was replaced by the joy of Christ. I got out of the car, grabbed the case of beer and threw it into the dumpster. I spent the rest of the weekend sharing what had happened with my skiing buddies and urging them to give their lives to Christ too.

When I came home from this ski trip, I found my girlfriend at my parents' kitchen sink. She could tell that something had happened to me, and asked how the weekend had gone. With joy filling my heart and tears streaming down my face I told her that Jesus had changed my life, and that she and I were going to heaven together.

Debbie couldn't believe what she was hearing. She had become a believer as a child, and had often urged me to trust in Christ too. Throughout our relationship, Debbie would tell me that we could not be married until I became a believer. I had been ignoring this throughout our relationship, but her prayers were suddenly answered in God's timing. The next Sunday, we began going to the church that she had grown up in. Two years later, we were married in that same church.

My new life was so impacted by Jesus that I began reading the Bible daily. I had never opened the Bible before, but suddenly I couldn't close it. I told my parents and brother about Jesus in a way they had never heard before. They saw a radical transformation in my attitude, character and habits. They didn't know who I had become. This convinced them that my new–found faith was true. After several months of sharing the truths of Jesus with them, opening the Bible and having them read it for themselves, my parents and brother trusted Christ on the same day and began going to church with Debbie and me. My passion to share the truth and life of Jesus was a wildfire in my soul.

My grandfather was a devout Catholic man who loved the Roman Catholic Church. He was so proud of me when I became an altar boy and learned the mass in Latin. I had served faithfully as an altar boy, three weeks a month, for several years. After I trusted in Jesus and left the Catholic Church, he was more dismayed than proud of my newfound spiritual zeal.

I often sat down with Gramps to talk about spiritual truth. In one conversation, I began sharing that salvation is a gift and can't be earned by being good enough or by doing certain religious duties. I told him the Catholic Church taught me that salvation was dependent on keeping the sacraments, staying holy, and staying in good standing with the Catholic Church. I used lots of Scripture to back up the truth that salvation was a gift. I showed my grandfather that once you die, you either go to the presence of Jesus or you are eternally separated from Jesus.

I was relentless in fighting for the truth and Gramp's soul. Every time he gave me an answer, I had a counterpoint. Each time he tried to shut me up, I would fan the fire hotter. We were both frustrated after our conversations; he wanted nothing to do with my new–found zeal for Jesus and I wouldn't go back to our Catholic heritage.

As I told my mentor in Christ about my conversations, I was full of excitement and wonder. Jesus had used me to give my grandfather the truth in a mega-dose. I believed in my heart that God's word was effective and that He was pleased with my passion for Him. As I finished telling my story, I was ready to be praised for my faithfulness. Instead, I was scolded.

My mentor told me that I had probably turned off my grandfather to hearing the truth forever. He told me that I was a Bible-thumper with no sense of tact, and that I needed to learn how to share my faith in culturally relevant ways, not just by attacking with Biblical facts. I was told that spewing verses was more hurtful than helpful.

At the end of the scolding I was embarrassed and ashamed, I felt I had ruined my grandfather's opportunity to trust in Jesus. I felt that I was 100% *un*successful at sharing the gospel. After that, I kept my mouth shut about Jesus for a long time, especially around Gramps. I didn't want to blow someone else's chances of getting into heaven. I felt like the wildfire in my soul had just been sprayed with a fire extinguisher.

Troubling Theology on Evangelism

There are many books, articles, websites, and theological themes that echo my mentor's scolding comments. In the book, *Irresistible Evangelism*, the authors begin by stating how Christians with good evangelistic intentions can actually be dangerous to people hearing the good news. They write,

> "Sadly, countless Christ-loving, Bible-believing churches are making the same mistake. We might care deeply about the people who don't yet know Jesus. We might fear for their eternal souls. We may even try our best to correct and warn them. Meanwhile our best intentions are quite literally driving people away from the Lord and even speeding their progress on the 'highway to hell.'"[9]

These writers obviously believe there are 'right' ways to share Jesus and 'wrong' ways to share Jesus.

I understand these men are trying to help believers be sensitive to the people they talk to about Jesus. They believe that being too strong, overt, or harsh when sharing the gospel may turn people away from Jesus. But think about when Jesus confronted the choices of the immoral woman at the well[10] or when He told the Pharisees they were "white washed tombs."[11]

We need to remind ourselves that Jesus lives in us and gives us what to say and when to say it to accomplish His purposes in

31

the hearer's lives.[12] Because Jesus perfectly knows what people need to hear, Jesus may give us hard and seemingly insensitive words so they will have **His** effect in the hearers' lives. I doubt the authors above would think Jesus made mistakes in speaking truth in the above situations. If their point that we are not ever to be condemning or insensitive (as we judge it) is to be taken literally, Jesus had it all wrong, and He had it wrong often.

There are also teachings on evangelism stating some are gifted to be witnesses and some are gifted to do evangelism.[13] Other teachings wrongly say that there is a gift of evangelism and yet others state that only 10% of believers are able to successfully share their faith effectively.[14] One popular mantra is that you have to 'earn the right to be heard.'[15] *You cannot find any of these teachings in the Bible and yet these myths are believed all around the world.* In Ephesians 4:11–16, we learn about the evangelist, whose primary purpose is to equip the saints to do the work of service. In the case of the evangelist, the work of service would be to equip the church (people) to become evangelizers, tellers of the good news.

The main passages that deal with spiritual gifts are found in Romans 12:4–8, 1 Corinthians 12:4–11, Ephesians 4:11 and 1 Peter 4:10. As you look over these passages you will notice that none of them list a gift of evangelism as such; only the Ephesians 4:11 passage mentions the gift of the evangelist.[16] Most spiritual gift tests that mention the gift of evangelism use Ephesians 4:11 as their support. They turn the gift of the evangelist into the gift of evangelism, but this is sloppy theology.[17]

Many have found it difficult to share about their trust in Jesus, even though the Scriptures teach us that every believer is to be engaged in evangelism (Matthew 28:19–20, Acts 1:8, Acts 8:1ff, 1 Thessalonians 1:5–10, 1 Peter 3:15, etc.). Many, if not most, believers are uncomfortable with sharing Christ with others while other believers are very comfortable with it. My opinion is that this is how the concept of a 'gift of evangelism' has emerged. This has led some who create spiritual gifts tests to include the gift of evangelism. The challenge is that this teaching communicates to those who are not comfortable, that they are not gifted to share the gospel, which would lessen their responsibility. As I have said previously, the concept of the gift of evangelism has served to extinguish the passion in many from sharing in natural ways. I would encourage this gift to be removed from spiritual gift tests because it encourages a concept not found in the Bible.

Many of us have believed or said things like: "I don't know enough about the Bible to be effective in evangelism," "I do not have the gift of evangelism," "I do not know what to say or how to say it," "I need more training in evangelism," or "I don't want to mess up someone's chance to come to Jesus." We say these things when we're faced with challenges in evangelism, mostly because we don't know an alternative. As we understand the Biblical evangelistic principles discussed in this book, we will become more comfortable sharing the gospel in natural ways.

The church needs to understand and equip people with what Jesus taught believers about sharing His truth with others. Jesus believes that every follower of His is created to be 100% successful in sharing His truth 100% of the time once their faith in Him has begun.[18]

The New Testament is full of stories of new believers who needed maturity in their life and theology, but still shared the gospel boldly and effectively. In later chapter's we will explore people like the woman at the well in John 4, the man born blind in John 9, the apostle Paul in Acts 9, and the Thessalonian believers. All of these were fresh in their understanding of Jesus, and yet were powerful in affecting whole segments of people with the good news.

Once a person places their trust in Jesus, they are fully competent to share eternal truths adequately because God has placed His Spirit in their lives. It puzzles me that so many leaders across the world believe otherwise.

Recently I learned about the phrase "invest and invite" as it relates to evangelism. In an e–mail conversation I had with a pastor, he mentioned how hard it was for the people in his church to lead their friends and family to place their trust in Jesus. He told me that for him, it was easy. His solution to the problem was to urge the people in his congregation to make friends (invest) and then invite them to their church worship service so they could clearly hear the message (invite). Then he could bring the visitors "across the line" to place their trust in Christ.

His focus was to cast the net of evangelism together to see more people trust in Christ. What this means is that the people of the church would make friends with not–yet–believers, then invite them to church so he could present the message of the gospel. This, the pastor sees, is a partnership between the people's friendship connections and his gifting to move people across the line to believe in Jesus.

It is true that the church should work as a team and cast nets together. Using group events and meetings with an evangelistic theme can be very inspiring![19] However, working together should have the goal of equipping believers to maturity, to take risks for our King, to gain new experiences and develop new spiritual muscle.

Believers should not be relieved from the Biblical truth that everyone should be sharing the gospel. I actually believe that God is sad when we allow some of our Holy Spirit given evangelistic muscle atrophy, so professionals can exercise theirs. This happens too frequently.

The church is thirsty for leaders who will urge people to step out in faith. As people step out, they see the faithfulness of Christ break through as they boldly share the gospel like they have not in a long time. An overwhelming dependency in churches on the "invest and invite" principle reinforces a limiting evangelistic theology. The teaching implies that most believers are unsuccessful–or inefficient–at getting people 'across the line' of salvation.

The Scriptures clearly teach that we are not responsible to change hearts, that is God's terrain![20] When leaders teach that some are better at communicating the gospel than others, it's natural for everyone who isn't a leader or gifted in evangelism to become silent and wait for others to reach the lost. As this happens, the army of spiritual wildfire starters is diminished.

It is no wonder the harvest seems poor. A poor harvest is partly due to the lack of seeds being sown because people believe evangelistic myths instead of Biblical truth. The church today is often focused on multiplying listeners in their meetings. Instead, they could be multiplying communicators of grace in workplaces, gyms, neighborhoods and other 'third places' (bowling alleys, coffee shops, sports bars, networks of all sorts and the like). It shouldn't surprise us that the church is so slow in gaining ground in the West! What the church needs today is a strong Biblical theology about evangelism.

The truth needs to be told, and believers need to be freed to share the gospel with power, precision, and passion as led by the Holy Spirit. It is time for the ordained to tell the truth to the ordinary: God gives every believer authority and power! New believers are often taught a mix of myths and faulty theology when it comes to evangelism, instead of being accurately taught and mentored. What is causing these unbiblical myths to spread?

Two Surprising Reasons for the Lack of Workers

Reason 1: Pastors and Church Leaders

At first, it may shock or surprise you to hear that pastors and leaders may contribute to the lack of workers and a small harvest. We often assume that pastors and leaders are the best at equipping people with a strong understanding of the gospel.[21] Leaders should be praying, teaching and urging believers to be out in the world giving away Jesus' Good News. No pastor or leader intentionally sets out to stifle the gospel wildfires from being spread, but our current structures and practices in the church are in fact doing just that.

Surveys consistently tell us that many churches that grow are doing so at the expense of other churches.[22] Individuals and families choose to leave one church for another, hoping to find something they sense is missing. This leads to 'growth' in one church by subtracting people from another church; the net gain is actually zero.

Statistics have shown for quite some time that the percentage of believers in the West is stagnant, if not in decline.[23] Churches that are growing do not typically see the majority of their growth coming from the harvest of unsaved souls, but from people leaving one church for another.

Many churches advertise in various forms, hoping to attract people to their latest sermon series or high–tech programs. Although successful at times, these tactics reinforce the idea that professionals are better at evangelism. I do not believe that any pastor actually wants to communicate this, but it is what happens.

The practice of churches being 'attractional' is sadly and slowly eroding the number of people igniting wildfires. If we attract people to our churches with impressive worship services and programs, we have to keep up these advancements in order to keep people. Subsequently, we often expect nothing except attendance from church members and the people we attract. We limit discipling to a task for those in leadership, instead of encouraging disciples to make other disciples. When the sowing of seed diminishes, so does the harvest.[24]

Church planting efforts do better at reaching the unreached than established churches. Recent reports tell us 68% of church plants surviving after 4 years have an average attendance of 85.[25] Even with this type of effectiveness in church planting, the truth of the gospel is not transforming entire populations. We need to equip and release more people to impact the culture.

The gospel is stifled behind stained glass windows, fog machines and good sound systems. The wildfire inside every believer needs to be released so it can ignite other souls for God's Kingdom. The life of the church is found in Jesus and He is found in the lives and hearts of ordinary people. *Believers do not need more put in them, they need what God has put in them to be coaxed out!*[26]

There is a whole other dimension of understanding the power of the church when she begins to be scattered out in the world. We must remember that the church is not a location but people; we are always the church. When this is understood, we can see the church influence our workplaces, neighborhoods and surroundings, bringing the integrity and truth of Christ everywhere we go. Wherever we go, the King goes, and wherever the King goes, He has plans to spread His Kingdom. We see this pattern throughout the New Testament, and it needs to be rediscovered, taught, and lived out.[27]

Many churches grow because people who are dissatisfied at one church end up filling a seat at a new one. Too many believers think that the grass is greener in the other pews (or theatre seating). Although the leaders know that many visitors were recently part of another church family, they warmly welcome them and are sure to explain all the benefits of this new church.

Churches rarely ask these people why they left their previous one; this can lead to unresolved issues and stunted personal growth. The churches who surge in numbers feel satisfied, believing that their church is growing and healthy. We need to remember that the church is not our church, nor the pastor's church, but that she belongs to Jesus.[28] *Is it wise or even biblical to measure the health of a church by her size?*

Many church leaders today will cite the proverb that everything rises and falls on leadership. Hosea 4:8, "...like people, like priests," is often cited, indicating that the leadership mirrors the people. Leaders in the Old Testament are a popular source of inspiration when searching for church-growing principles.

One famous Old Testament leader, Nehemiah, had strong qualities of leadership and vision as he led the people of Israel to rebuild the walls around Jerusalem. Pastors often believe that following Nehemiah's example will help strengthen and grow the church. If churches follow a top-down business model in managing their churches (like in Nehemiah), the answer for the lack of workers in the harvest fields must lie at the feet of her leaders. The question that we often ignore is: are we called to manage churches in the same way leaders did in the Old Testament?

Second-Class Christians

Instead of a top-down or CEO style of leadership, Jesus taught a much different way for leaders to follow in the New Testament.[29] Jesus instructed His disciples to teach others to obey everything

He had taught. Part of what He taught was for them to make disciples, be His witnesses,[30] baptize[31] and enjoy communion together.[32] In the majority of churches and denominations today, we do not see 'ordinary' believers confidently baptize, offer the Lord's Supper, or sharing the gospel. These tasks are usually reserved for clergy or elders in the church. This communicates that *some* believers are more holy, or more equipped to share what Jesus has done for them. It also communicates that an ordinary believer is a second-class Christian. Because of our (man-made) traditions, we start to assume that God approves only certain people to initiate communion, to evangelize, or to baptize. *When this happens, an ordinary believer never experiences the joy of obeying Jesus through these holy activities.*

When clergy are the only ones allowed to perform such tasks, it is similar to the tradition of priests in the Old Testament who had to offer sacrifices for the ordinary people. In the Old Testament, priests had the responsibility of being a mediator between the people and God. They were to offer sacrifices for three sets of people; themselves and his family (Leviticus 16:6–11), the people (Leviticus 16:5) and the nation of Israel (Leviticus 16:24, Numbers 15:25). This is much different than the New Testament theology of the priesthood of all believers.[33] In the New Testament, every believer, male and female, are called priests (1 Peter 2:5, 9). Today we know that "…there is one God, and one mediator also between God and men, the man Christ Jesus." (1 Timothy 2:5).

When clergy are the only ones who are allowed to offer baptism and communion, a 'lower class' of Christians is (intentionally or unintentionally) set up. Here again the church leaders and pastors are unintentionally contributing to the lack of workers in the soil of souls.

If 'ordinary' people are not qualified to serve communion or baptize new disciples, how can they ever be trusted to share words of Life with those who need them

In a recent prayer gathering of local pastors, I asked a question. "Which is more important, to baptize or to lead someone to salvation?" The answer was unanimous. Leading someone to begin a relationship with Jesus was more important. I then asked a follow-up question; "Why, then, do many pastors encourage believers to do the more important job of evangelism, yet deny them the opportunity to doing the less important job of baptizing?" Their response was a silent dismissal of the question. This shows the teaching that is prevalent in many churches of 'second–class citizens' and also a fear of engaging change that will release people to be the priests that most protestant churches claim to hold. As a pastor myself, I certainly understand the fear of church leaders to release people in these holy activities. We still need to encourage obedience to the Biblical principles if we want to see the expansion of the Kingdom of God.

Breaking Bread and Tradition

A few years ago, I traveled to New Delhi, India, to visit friends and equip leaders. Two of my Indian friends, Jon and Anna, invited me and a few others for breakfast one morning. As we sat around their kitchen table eating a south Indian breakfast, we talked about family, India, food and faith. Our hearts were drawing closer to each other and to Christ. Jon and Anna were part of a local church and had been for years. As the table was cleared our conversation became more focused. I started sensing that the Lord wanted to encourage Jon and Anna, and that He wanted them to experience Christ more vibrantly.

"So," I began, "I was wondering if you ever share your faith in Jesus with coworkers or neighbors? Jon and Anna glanced at each other. "No." "Not really." I continued, "In your church, do people other than your pastor perform baptisms?" "No… only pastors can baptize people." I could tell by the look on their faces that these questions, maybe uncomfortable ones, were stretching their faith and understanding.

"Are either of you familiar with the Great Commission in Matthew 28?" They gave a characteristic Indian nod–shake, meaning yes, and when I waited, they easily quoted Matthew 28:19–20. "Who had Jesus told to make disciples?" I asked. "Jesus told the remaining eleven disciples to make disciples."

Sensing the Holy Spirit was at work in the conversation, I asked, "And what two things did Jesus tell His disciples they were to do as part of helping people be disciples of Jesus?" Jon responded, "Jesus told them to baptize them in the Name of the Father and of the Son and of the Holy Spirit. He also told them to teach believers to follow everything He had commanded them to do." With a large smile, I responded, "Well done, Jon, that is exactly what Jesus said!"

"So, Jon and Anna, do you think of yourselves as disciples of Jesus?" I nudged. They nodded yes again. "Do you see yourselves as disciple makers?" Jon spoke up, looking ashamed. "Ed, I don't believe I have ever made a disciple of Jesus. I really have not followed Jesus as fully as I know I should." There was something refreshing in the simplicity of his answer. If only more people felt that truth.

There was a quiet pause. When the conversation started again, we flipped open our Bibles to look up passages on communion. I brought up something that had been on my mind for a while, even when in the USA. "Does it say anywhere in the Bible that only clergy or pastors or elders can administer communion?" The obvious answer was no. I then asked Jon and Anna to get some grape juice and naan (Indian bread) so we could enjoy communion, right then and there. With some nervousness, Jon and Anna slipped away. In a few moments, they returned with a very nice plate, a chalice filled with juice, and some naan.

I asked Jon if he would please thank Jesus for the bread and cup, but he hesitated. He had never done anything like that before. A few of us offered to pray but Jon and Anna remained silent. As soon as we said, "Amen," I looked up and noticed that Jon and Anna's eyes were wet with tears. With holy hands, Jon joyfully served each of us the bread and cup. We sang, prayed and worshipped Jesus with passion. As our time of worshipping ended, Anna looked at me with moist eyes and said, "Why hasn't anyone ever told us this before?"

Freedom! This was the beginning of them discovering what Christ had died for them to receive. And it was an unforgettable morning in the trip for me and my friends.

there are workers ready to enter the white fields and harvest souls for Jesus.

Myth #2 The Evangelist is More Persuasive

Some believe that evangelists hear from God in special ways and therefore know the best thing to say at the right time to bring people to salvation in Jesus. It's tempting to believe that they have super–spiritual persuasive abilities to get people to see their need for Jesus. If this were true, then the Apostle Paul would have been one of the great persuaders of history.

When Paul came to Corinth, he says he came without persuasive words, without power and without his renowned human abilities.[41] Paul came in demonstration of spiritual power, not human power or persuasion. This spiritual power, as we'll see later in this book, is for everyone when they share about Jesus.

Starting wildfires is not about human persuasion or power. When a person moves towards faith in Jesus, it is a supernatural act of God, not because of human efforts. God can and does use the most intelligent believers to lead people to Jesus, but He also uses all sorts of individuals to do the same. Both the most intellectual and the most uneducated of believers have several things in common. They both know the truth, they both have Jesus residing in them, and they both can be 100% successful, 100% of the time. The same is true for the richest and the poorest believer, the one who has been a Christian for decades and the one who is a 'newborn' in their faith, the one who is a famous evangelist, and the one who has never dared to talk about God to anyone.

The power or persuasion to see people come to Christ is not in the person or the gift but in the truth, the Word.

> *"For I am not ashamed of the Gospel of Christ for **it** is the power of God to salvation to everyone who believes, to the Jew first and also to the Greek." Romans 1:16 (Emphasis mine)*

The power of God for someone to be saved is not from the person sharing the truth–the power is in the truth itself! Therefore, it doesn't matter who gives the truth or how 'holy' or educated the messenger is. It doesn't even matter if the truth is given through an inanimate object like a billboard or a film, website, or tract. The truth, on its own, is the power of God to salvation.

If anyone could independently persuade another to be saved, certainly Jesus could. And yet we see that not everyone who heard Jesus speak about the Kingdom of God chose to follow Him. Not everyone whom Jesus invited to follow Him did.[42] Not everyone who said they would follow Jesus actually did.[43]

Jesus did not 'persuade' people into the Kingdom. Jesus wants everyone to change their mind in repentance[44] but they will not come by human efforts. They can only come to repentance and belief in Jesus by God changing their minds as they become exposed to the truth. The evangelist is not more gifted at persuading people to come to Jesus than any other believer. God is the persuader, not the gifted evangelist.

Myth #3 The Evangelist is the 'Deal-Closer'

Jesus told His followers that the fields are white for harvest and there needs to be more workers ready to enter the harvest fields.[45] I believe Jesus intended for each of His followers to be out doing the work of the harvest in their daily lives. His audience, context, and the language seem to show that He expected every follower to engage lost souls with the truth of the gospel. Jesus didn't reserve working in the harvest for an elite group of gifted individuals, He was inviting anyone who was willing to jump into the fields and start helping with the harvest of souls. This is, after all, why He came to earth, "...to seek and save those which are lost," (Luke 4:18-19).

Jesus told His disciples that He would make them into fishers of men.[46] He sent them out two by two into every city He was about to go,[47] and told them to make disciples every place they went.[48] New disciples should be taught to baptize the people they lead to Jesus, and to teach those people to obey everything Jesus commanded the disciples.[49] This "...teaching them to obey everything Jesus commanded" then logically includes the command to be fishers of men and sharing the Gospel.

To think a limited amount of gifted people (evangelists) are the main ones who nudge people towards Jesus is a myth and is not found in the Bible. This myth comes with assumptions about 'deal-closing,' slang for getting someone to trust in Jesus at a particular moment. Deal-closing is useful in gauging progress in business deals, but can be risky when applied to spiritual issues. The idea of a deal-closing stands on the assumption that people should make a firm decision at a specific time in a public way to secure entrance into the family of God. The deal–closer is seen as a specialized person, who knows how to move people from indecision to a decision of placing their trust in Christ. In reality, God is the one who changes the heart, whether someone prays a specific prayer or just trusts Jesus for salvation while reading the Bible.

Wrong Assumption #1: "Deal-closing is the hardest part of evangelism, so we should bring people to the evangelist doing the work." This wrong assumption robs believers of confidence to share boldly. It also robs the glory God deserves and shifts it to the 'deal–closer.' It also robs the church from experiencing widespread growth because "ordinary" believers expect to remain passive, not share the Gospel.

Wrong Assumption #2: "Deal-closing takes the right words from a gifted evangelist after long discussions have taken place between a believer and a non–believer." This wrong assumption robs the believer of the confidence that Jesus will give them what to say at the right moment so people will move ahead in their faith journey.

Wrong Assumption #3: "Deal-closing is more important than any other part of evangelism." This is not taught anywhere in the Bible, in fact, the exact opposite is taught to us by Paul in 1 Corinthians chapter 3.

> *"So then neither the one who plants nor the one who waters is anything, but God who causes the growth. Now he who plants and he who waters are one; but each will receive his own reward according to his own labor." 1 Corinthians 3:7-8*

Closing the deal is not what is important here, in fact, it isn't even mentioned. What is important is every believer being empowered to labor in the soil of souls. Every believer can plant and water and beg God to cause the increase. God is the important one in the equation. God uses humans to spread the gospel, but what they do, and where they fall in a faith timeline of someone placing their trust in Christ isn't important. What is important is that each believer IS involved in spreading the seed of the Gospel.

Wrong Assumption #4: "There are some parts of evangelism that the ordinary believer is not able to do well." When you default to a "gifted" person, you automatically reinforce to other believers that they are not able to effectively communicate the Gospel. This stops believers from sharing with boldness, consistency, and power. If people think they can't, they won't.[50] When people understand that Jesus is the one who has already empowered and equipped them supernaturally, a whole new world opens up for them, evangelistically speaking. Amazing things are on the horizon.

Here is a simple illustration showing that every time a person shares a portion of the gospel, God uses the interaction to move a person towards a decision. No one conversation is more important than another.

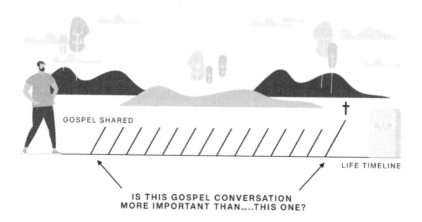

GOSPEL SHARED

LIFE TIMELINE

IS THIS GOSPEL CONVERSATION
MORE IMPORTANT THAN.....THIS ONE?

The Results

Pastors and evangelists have helped to keep the life–giving wildfires from spreading in our communities and cities. This is certainly not intended by anyone. It is however, the truth. The harvest is plentiful, but neglected when churches and leaders focus on increasing listeners instead of multiplying communicators.

We need to redirect our focus to increasing the workers in the fields (missional), not increasing workers in the barns (attractional).[51] When large crowds of people come to hear a good message, and this becomes our focus, we lose the battle. People are not saved just because of a good speaker. When churches depend on evangelists and pastors to fill meetings, buildings, arenas, and stadiums with people (mostly already Christians), they weaken believers from becoming missional good news tellers.

What is also unintentionally communicated is the need for professionals to help believers understand the Bible, instead of teaching them to listen to God and study His Word for themselves.[52] When people mostly hear the story of Jesus from professionals, a lie is reinforced that evangelists or professionals are needed to get the Word into people. We need to hear more stories from ordinary people of how they share Christ with their friends and see people moved towards the cross. We should be equipping all believers to do the work Jesus commanded.

When our passion for multiplying communicators has been reduced to a good program, sermon series, or other events, we have drifted far from Jesus' intentions for His church.

100% Success, 100% of the Time

I began this chapter with the story of sharing Jesus with my grandfather. I certainly felt that I was 100% *un*successful, and the scolding I received from my mentor served to shut my mouth about Jesus for a long time, especially around Gramps. As the years rolled by, I eventually started to share God's truth with him again, because my love for God and for him would not let me stay quiet. We enjoyed many deep conversations about Jesus, which usually ended in my grandfather's reaffirmation of his Catholic beliefs. The years and conversations continued, but then my grandfather was diagnosed with cancer. He was in his mid–nineties when the cancer began to win.

He spent his last few weeks and months in a hospital bed in his living room, visiting with great–grandchildren, grandchildren, his sons and other family members. Near the end of his life, my family and I continued to have conversations with Gramps about life, death, Jesus and where we would each end up once we died. Gramps was also visited by a chaplain who worked for a hospice organization.

The chaplain, we learned, was also a pastor of a local church. Gramps and the chaplain became good friends. They would sit and talk about the sweetness and hardships of life and about things to come. The chaplain was a Bible–teaching man who loved caring for people's souls. As their friendship developed, their conversations turned more and more spiritual. Gramps became weaker and weaker as cancer marched forward, but when death draws near, the walls often come down. And so, it was with my Gramps.

As he and the chaplain continued their visits, my grandfather began to admit that he needed Jesus and that he really never had a relationship with Him. He said he had thought over my conversations with him. He realized over time that my faith was different from his, and he wanted to know God as deeply as I (and the rest of my family) did.

Shortly before my Gramps passed away, he trusted in Jesus for eternal life and surrendered the pride and rebellion that he had held on to for so long. The chaplain held the final conversation used by God to draw my grandfather to Himself, but all our faith conversations were equally important to the process

I once believed that I made a huge mistake in sharing with my Gramps so strongly. I now know that God used my words to begin or continue the shaping process of my grandfather's soul. I was 100% successful, not because of my Bible–thumping ways but because my words were guided by God.

Jesus told His disciples, and us, that there was, and is, a plentiful harvest ready to be reaped, but there is also a lack of workers willing to go to work. The key to harvesting the field of souls is an equipped work force willing to sow an abundance of Gospel seeds throughout the soil of souls. There needs to be a change from leadership attracting listeners, to an equipping and releasing of workers. For this to take place in God's church, there must be a new attitude towards evangelism. This is the topic of the next chapter.

CHAPTER 3: FURNACE

Our real work is prayer. What good is the cold iron of our frantic little efforts unless first we heat it in the furnace of our prayer? Only heat will diffuse heat.

-Mother Maribel

"Brethren, my heart's desire and my prayer to God for them is for their salvation." Romans 10:1

"Seeing the people, He felt compassion for them, because they were distressed and dispirited like sheep without a shepherd." Matthew 9:36

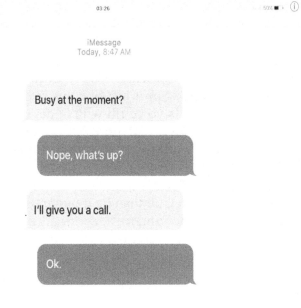

The text conversation above was with my son-in-law, Brian. As soon as I typed "Okay," my phone rang. Brian was at work and felt he had missed an opportunity to share Jesus with a co-worker.

Brian was headed to get a drink when he passed a group of his co-workers taking a smoke break. He said hello to one colleague. At that moment, he sensed the Spirit of God nudging him to say, "Jesus loves you." Fighting the impulse, Brian went in to the break room, grabbed a can of soda, and started to leave. Then he heard God speak to him again, "Tell that man this message, 'Jesus loves you.'" Brian began to stop and repeat what God had told him, but instead he said "See you later," and went about his work.

When his shift was over, Brian drove home a bit defeated. God had told him exactly what this man needed to hear, yet Brian did not repeat what God had spoken to him. This caused Brian to question his connection to God. He was looking to me for insight into the situation. Brian passed up an opportunity to give a friend exactly what God knew his friend needed to hear. Most people have had similar experiences. What would you have said to Brian?

I encouraged him to rejoice that he had heard from God, and that his connection with God was solid. God obviously wanted him to share the good news with his co-worker(s). I also told Brian that because he was drawing close to Christ, that he should expect more nudges of the Spirit just like this in his life. As we talked, I could hear Brian's voice fill with hope. I made sure he knew that God was not upset with him, but wanted to use this experience as a time of learning. He determined that at the next opportunity, he would act with impulsive obedience once he heard the voice of God. Brian's questions showed that he was actually walking closer to God than he thought. Christ was discipling him in obedience and trust, continuing to draw Brian close to Himself. It was a beautiful conversation.

Drawing Near

Jesus' passion for people to have a relationship with God is deep. As Jesus walked through villages, towns and cities, He looked into people's eyes and saw pain and distress.[1] He knew His purpose[2] and it spurred Him to sleep less, pray more, and engage people deeply. Jesus' vision went beyond His life on earth, to eternity, and how His followers could have a positive effect on their spheres of influence as they become more like Him.

Jesus wants those who choose to believe in Him to live just as purposely as He did.[3] The secret to this way of living is found in a new attitude towards purpose. A new attitude only comes through a full dependence on the Father and sacrificing personal wants.[4] This type of passion for the Father's purposes begins with love for God. This passion grows through time spent in His presence, through conversations with Him, and through humble obedience.[5] Jesus wants to start wildfires in souls of His followers. The closer we draw near to the fire (heart) of God, the more we take on the characteristics of His heart.

I met Logan through a mutual friend and over the course of few conversations, he chose to place his trust in Jesus. As Logan told me his story over several weeks, it became clear he had a rough beginning in life. He grew up without a father in the home and a mother who lived depending on others. He had been abused, and his role models had self-indulgent lifestyles. Logan knew that without some big changes in his life, he would end up the same way. He wanted out of living this way.

As I met with Logan, he was using drugs, alcohol, sexual promiscuity, and attention to numb the pain. He felt in his soul that these things were wrong but had no other example of how to handle life. He told me he wanted to break free, but his actions kept sucking him down into a dark hole. Telling him to stop what he was doing would not have been helpful; he was already trying to stop but could not.

Logan and I continued meeting over coffee as we talked about the character qualities of God. We discussed loving others by putting them first and seeing them motivated by the same love God has for the world. We talked about God's holy example and how He hated sin and sent His Son Jesus to give us a way out of self–indulgent living. Deciding to draw near to God and take on His qualities was the answer. Logan started to spend time reading the Bible and praying for his heart to want what God wanted. The pull of living for himself intensified and then began to fade. Today it is still fading and Logan is still fighting.

During the refining process of gold, the heat of the fire burns away impurities and leaves only the precious metal. Drawing near to God throughout life is like going through a furnace where the impurities of self–focus and the world are burned away. For some, this burning away of impurities may seem to take forever. As believers, our goal is to encourage one another in the refining, no matter how slow or fast the process may seem!

As we stay focused in this direction, we are moving and maturing for Jesus. As we draw nearer to the Father, we see our faults and sins begin to rise to the top and be exposed. We can then ask Jesus to remove them. The result is that more of Christ remains, and less of our old selves. As we take on the qualities of God, we begin to impact those who are watching the process. Sometimes this happens quickly, while at other times it takes longer than we would like, but transformation happens as the wildfire of Jesus consumes us.

God's Fire for Souls

God didn't need to create mankind. He chose to create humans so He could share His love with them. From the beginning of mankind, God said he wanted them to be fruitful and multiply and fill the earth.[6] This has both a physical and spiritual reality. He wants His passion for souls to spread fearlessly through every believer and in every generation and culture in ways that He designs for each encounter.

In the Old Testament God chose to spread His desire for people to live for Him through Abraham and the nation of Israel. His blessing on His chosen people is undeniable throughout the Old Testament. In times of obedience and disobedience, God was at work to draw His people to Himself. The chapters of the Old Testament are full of examples of what happens when hearts are fully focused on God.

God's fire for souls in the Old Testament was not limited to Israel. God desires all people to be drawn to Himself. In 2 Kings

4 we see the prophet Elisha was kind to a Gentile (non–Jew) woman and her family, and promised this woman that she would have a son even though "her husband was old" (v.14). Elisha also raised her son from the dead (v. 18-37).

God used the Gentile prostitute, Rahab, to help Israel take the promised land of Jericho.[7] Rahab is listed in the genealogy of Jesus[8] and is mentioned as one of the saints in Hebrews 11.

The book of Ruth is a story about a faithful Gentile woman. God used her to deliver Israel from irresponsible living, to a more obedient way of living for God. Ruth was the grandmother of King David and is mentioned in the lineage of Jesus in Matthew 1:5.

God delivered the non-Jewish Ninevites from destruction when they turned to God after Jonah brought God's message to them.[9] The Old Testament is full of God's promises to include the Gentiles in His redemptive plan, and for them to spread His Good News to all the world.[10]

The wildfire of God's heart to draw all people to Himself is insatiable and unstoppable. His design from the outset is to have relationship with His creation. God empowers, equips and inspires His children to draw near to Him so they will take on His qualities throughout their life and naturally spread His purpose of redemption to those they come into relationship.

Jesus, Our Example

Of course, Jesus is our greatest example of love, sacrifice and passionate purpose to draw people to God. From the beginning of His time on earth, He showed us the burning heart of God for His people. When I think about the birth of Christ, I imagine Jesus in heaven with all of the power, comfort, knowledge and carefree existence that He could have had, only to be transported in a blink of an eye into the womb of Mary His mother. When he went from a complete state of independence to a complete state of dependency, he showed His passionate love and commitment to His creation.

Jesus' example of becoming a man and laying down His life for relationship with women and men is inspiring. It is also painful! Philippians 2 teaches us that we are to have the same attitude that Jesus had about sacrificing for the Gospel. Jesus existed in the form of God (a spirit form of existence) and laid that perfect existence aside; He emptied Himself to become a man. Imagine the painful change that the Trinity experienced as Jesus became human. They knowingly experienced that pain for you and all the world. Jesus allowed Himself to become fully human, while maintaining undiminished deity, to the point of death on the cross, something He did not deserve. He went through that pain so that we could have relationship with Him.

Jesus is now exalted and sitting at the right hand of the Father. Though Jesus is now in heaven, He will always have a glorified, resurrected body which is both similar to and yet very different from our human form and limitations. Jesus chose this eternal change in His form for you and me![11] Before he entered the womb of Mary, he existed in a spirit form and now He forever will have a glorified body. Though glorified, it is a unique form different from his former Spirit form before He became God in the flesh.

Because of Jesus' painful yet powerful example of love and sacrifice, "...EVERY KNEE WILL BOW, of those who are in heaven and on earth and under the earth, and that every tongue will confess that Jesus Christ is Lord, to the glory of God the Father" (Philippians 2:10-11, emphasis mine). This is the ultimate goal of Jesus: that every person will in one way or another admit that He is Lord of all.

While on earth as fully human and while being fully God as well, Jesus lived among ordinary men and women, teaching and showing them how to live in a way that will spread His Gospel throughout all the earth. Knowing that His time on earth was limited, He gave truth and life to His followers and instructed them to invite others to follow Him. He completed His task of paying the sacrifice to satisfy God's justice.[12] God's plan is to use us to spread His truth. When we come nearer to God, He gives us the passion to share the wildfire with others.

Raising Our Temperature for Mission

As we draw close to the Father, more of His heart becomes ours. Our agendas decrease and Jesus' life in us increases. With His last words to His disciples, Jesus assured them that He would be with them, and told them to make disciples. This focus for their lives increased the passion in them that He had been stirring throughout their years together.

This passion was to carry out His mission as they worked, raised their families and enjoyed relationships. This is Jesus' desire for all believers. Jesus showed humanity how to live on earth in a way that put God's priorities above all others. He also directed His closest friends to go about their lives with the focus of starting wildfires of spiritual transformation in individuals and communities. This is the heart of the Father for His creation.

The goal of the early believers was to become more like Jesus[13] and to help others to live like this too. Most believers do not have this focus. They believe they are not yet at a level of faith to be able to carry out this purpose, but that is not what Jesus believes. It is certainly not what Jesus believes about you! Jesus gave His closest followers a fresh understanding of their ability to impact those they interacted with.[14]

Second Corinthians 5:14 says we are to be controlled by Christ's love.[15] This love will give us a deep sense of mission to draw all people to Christ through our actions and words. Every believer is made fully capable to share His good news with others. The understanding of this ability increases as we are controlled or motivated by His love for others. Our faith becomes intoxicating and catapults us to take risks for His gospel. Keeping our faith to ourselves no longer becomes a viable option as we draw closer and closer to the heart of Christ. This fresh understanding and attitude means that we will live less for ourselves and more for Him. Our life is no longer ours;[16] how can we live otherwise?

John 17 is said to be the most powerful prayer recorded in the Bible. In John 17, Jesus is praying for all believers in all generations, including us. He understands the dangers and fears that His followers would face and goes to work interceding for us to overcome them. Jesus prays that we will have His joy to the fullest by taking risks for His Gospel. This joy includes carrying out His mission as we move into relationship with the Father, Son and Holy Spirit. It is this joy that is a stimulus to naturally and freely share the gospel. It is a result of drawing near to God.

Jesus states that He has given us His Word and because of this, the world hated Him![17] His prayer tells us that we are not of this world, it is not our home. We were created for greater things than just living for our own comfort or purposes. Jesus raises the stakes by asking the Father to not remove us from the world.

Jesus expects us to influence even those who fight against His good news. Our love for God and others can influence them towards becoming part of His team of gospel receivers and givers. Jesus desires us to be in this risky position of engaging the world, and prays for us to be protected from the evil one in the meantime.[18]

As we draw closer to Jesus, we are constantly being made more like Him by knowing His word and living out what we learn.[19] The maturity of our faith is not measured by what we know about God and His word, but how we put it into practice. This needs to include a Biblical understanding of drawing near to God and sharing our faith with others.

Jesus then gives all believers their marching orders; "As You sent Me into the world, I also have sent them into the world." (John 17:18). Remember, Jesus is praying for all believers of all time in all cultures and levels of maturity. A fresh understanding of this prayer is that each one of us is to live out the Gospel passionately as we bring it to the world.

Jesus gave Himself entirely to the Father so His purposes could be carried out. He is our ultimate example in this. Again, He was not praying only for His closest followers but for believers of all time when He prays, "I do not ask on behalf of these alone, but for those also who believe in Me through their word; that they may all be one; even as You, Father, are in Me and I in You, that they also may be in Us, so that the world may believe that You sent Me." (John 17:20-21).

As we embrace this fresh understanding of Jesus' purpose for our lives, our willingness to live on mission rises. Jesus lived out a passion for souls and fulfilling His Father's purposes. Armed with this understanding, we will be free to follow the nudges of the Spirit as we engage the world.

The new believers of Thessalonica understood this, and they made a huge impact in their region. The apostle Paul spent only three Sabbaths (Saturdays, the worship days) with these new believers.[20] When he wrote them a letter, he made an amazing statement. Paul remarks that "For the word of the Lord has sounded forth from you, not only in Macedonia and Achaia, but also in every place your faith toward God has gone forth, so that we have no need to say anything." (1 Thessalonians 1:8). How could such a new community of believers be so influential? What did they learn in three or four short weeks of instruction that caused them to be so effective?

The verses preceding gives us the answer; "You also became imitators of us and of the Lord, having received the word in much tribulation with the joy of the Holy Spirit, so that you became an example to all the believers in Macedonia and in Achaia." (1 Thessalonians 1:6-7). These brand-new believers actually followed through on all that Paul had taught them. They imitated Paul's example and the example of Christ they had been taught in a very short time. They had captured the understanding that they could make a difference through their lives. Their wildfire(s) was undeniable.

Constant Prayer and Action

We can't catch the wildfire of God's heart for the world just by learning more information. Our faith must include sacrificial action. In the church at Thessalonica, Paul reasoned with them from the Scriptures, "…explaining and giving evidence that the Christ had to suffer and rise again from the dead, and saying, 'This Jesus whom I am proclaiming to you is the Christ.'" (Acts 17:3). Acts 17:4 reveals that many did in fact place their faith in Jesus, "And some of them were persuaded and joined Paul and Silas, along with a large number of the God–fearing Greeks and a number of the leading women." (Acts 17:4). They believed but they also joined Paul and Silas. The women and men of Thessalonica became followers of Jesus through the teaching of

Paul and Silas. But they didn't just become listeners; they became fellow disciples of Jesus who also made disciples.

In Paul's letters, he often invited disciples of Jesus to imitate him as he imitated Christ.[21] You cannot imitate someone just by gaining knowledge; you watch how they live and follow what they do. In short, you learn by doing. Too often believers learn or are inspired to give away their faith but there is rarely accountability to see if they follow through. Knowledge without application leaves us ignorant and apathetic; spiritual knowledge with application leads to wildfires!

In Thessalonica, imitating Paul and Silas would have included many practical things for the believers; praying for people to believe in Christ, serving in the community, placing others people's needs above their own, and learning how to follow the Spirit and speak truth to others. The combination of learning and imitating meant that the young Thessalonian believers spread the gospel thoroughly in their area. They spread it so well, in fact, that Paul had full confidence in their ability as he moved on to the regions of Macedonia and Achaia. Their actions, plus their prayer, resulted in a wildfire in Thessalonica.

Prayer is vital to drawing near to the heart of God. Prayer is the constant communication with the Father. It is also times of deep intense interaction with the concerns of our lives and hearts. It is often in prayer that God shapes a heart to be more in tune with Him and His purposes.

Through the Gospels, we often see that Jesus was in prayer[22] in order to hear from His Father and move forward on His mission.[23] Paul prayed for the souls of his countrymen[24] and carried the sacrificial heart of God for those souls. He prayed or wished that if it were possible, he would be cursed and cut off from Christ for the sake of the Jews.[25] Of course this was not possible, but it did reflect his heart and concern for his fellow Jews. Paul was ready to sacrifice in how he lived and in prayer, with an understanding of how important it was for them to be in relationship with God.

I have spent many nights in prayer with others until the sun rose on a fresh day. We have agonized with God for our hearts to align with His heart for our city and for individuals. This kind of prayer dramatically changes our hearts. After that sort of prayer, it becomes easier to go through life with the eyes of Jesus for the lost. Prayer–walking through neighborhoods, begging God for insight on how to connect with others, is another way to gain a God–soaked heart for people. Keeping a list of individuals who do not yet know the Savior and bringing those souls before Him daily keeps our focus in line with the focus of our King.

The Scriptures are clear that as we pray in accordance with the heart of God that He will hear and surely answer.

> *"These things I have written to you who believe in the name of the Son of God, so that you may know that you have eternal life. This is the confidence which we have before Him, that, if we ask anything according to His will, He hears us. And if we know that He hears us in whatever we ask, we know that we have the requests which we have asked from Him." 1 John 5:13–14*

God's heart is for the people of His creation to believe in the name of the Son of God. Prayer is a powerful way for our hearts to catch the sparks of God's wildfire.

Many Christians quote Jesus in Matthew 21:21-22 "…all things you ask believing, God will do…" and assume they can have whatever they want in life. The larger context of Matthew 21 describes Jesus bringing in His Kingdom. The will of God in this passage is for believers to gain the heart of God for Jesus' Kingdom to spread among people. God desires you to be praying for your friends to come into relationship with Christ. He promises to respond to this kind of prayer, and sometimes answers in surprising ways!

Peter teaches us that "The Lord is not slow about His promise, as some count slowness, but is patient toward you, not wishing for any to perish but for all to come to repentance." (2 Peter 3:9). God wants everyone to realize they need to turn from their way of living and come to God's way of living. This happens when they place their trust in the person and work of Jesus Christ.

One foundational teaching of Jesus on prayer is found in Luke 10. Jesus taught His followers that there are always people who are ready to come into the Kingdom of God as we go through life, "The harvest is plentiful..." (Luke 10:2). Prayers and seeds of truth (the Word of God) have been sown in the hearts of people you know. God has unique ways to show people His love, power, grace and presence. These seeds have been sown by you and others whom you may not know. Some of these seeds have germinated and are ready to be harvested while others are waiting for more watering. They are right in front of our eyes, but we need to be looking for them.

Jesus continued on in Luke 10:2 telling us there is a problem; "The harvest is plentiful but the workers are few." His solution to this problem is simple, clear and concise. We need to pray, begging the Lord of the harvest to send out workers into the harvest (Luke 10:2b). We are those workers who are sent out. We again see the need for prayer for God to gather souls into His Kingdom.

The 10:2b Virus

Since 2001, I have been infected by a virus that has changed my life and outlook. It is a spiritual virus, not physical, and I would like to pass it on to you. I call it the10:2b virus, from Luke 10:2b. I have set an alarm to go off every day at 10:02 am to remind me to pray that we will experience the plentiful harvest. It doesn't matter who I am with at 10:02 am; when the alarm goes off, I invite them to join me in my call to prayer. My prayers are for the good of the community, and for God to raise up women and men who will be bold to share the good news of Jesus. I also beg God to set my heart on fire with the things that set His heart on fire. Why not put this book down right now, and set your own alarm for 10:02 am or a time that is convenient for you?

I am amazed at how direct Jesus is on this topic of a ripe harvest and the need for us to pray for more workers. I am also amazed at how many believers and church leaders do not follow this command of Jesus on a daily basis. When we obey His instructions, we make room in our hearts for His wildfire for the souls of friends, neighbors, and even strangers.

Action

Prayer and action are both vital, and should go hand–in–hand on our faith journeys. God responds to our prayers for souls to come into His kingdom in both direct and subtle ways, so if we pray, we should be ready to act on opportunities!

I recently challenged a group of believers to ask God to give them a few souls to sow into and harvest for His Kingdom. "Beg God," I urged, "and don't stop until He answers!" A few weeks later when this group met again, one of the men shared that he took my challenge seriously and began praying. After a few days of begging God to bring people into his life who were hungry for him, nothing happened. He began to think that praying the same thing, over and over again, wasn't getting any results, but he kept on praying.

A couple of days later his neighbor came across the street to chat, so he followed the lead of the Spirit and shared his story and asked some spiritual questions. That's when he learned that his neighbor had been seeking a fresh spiritual direction. The next day, one of his co-workers admitted that he had been away from God for years and wanted to reconnect, but was not interested in the commercial side of church. You could not stop this man in our church from beaming. It required prayer, conversation, and acts of love, but he finally saw results. These men have begun to meet together to discuss the Word, admit their mistakes, and pray for others to join them in pursuing Christ. I believe that a new church is about to start!

In my conversations with believers around the world, I have learned that a large percentage of them do not have friendships with non–believers outside of work or family. Many believers do not have dinner with not–yet–believers or enjoy a ball game, go bowling or have them over to swim or play cards. This lack of interaction with the world has a wide range of reasons from strict separatist theology[26] to fear of getting the message wrong, busyness, or feeling awkward in discussing issues of spirituality.

These reasons mean we fall short of our Lord's example and those of the first century believers.

Jesus is clear that every one of His followers needs to engage with people who don't know Jesus yet. When Jesus called the first disciples, He told them, "Follow Me and I will make you become fishers of men" (Matthew 4:19). That is an invitation to action.

When Jesus choose the twelve Apostles, He *"...called them to Himself so they could be with Him and so He could send them out..."* (Mark 3:13-15). Another invitation to action! When Jesus cast a legion of demons out of man, the suddenly freed man wanted to go with Jesus. Surprisingly, Jesus said no. *"...He did not permit him but said to him, 'Go home to your friends and tell them how much the Lord has done for you, and how he has had mercy on you.'"* (Mark 5:19). Action was the first step of obedience that Jesus asked of this formerly demonized man.

Jesus' last instruction to His disciples before being taken up into Heaven was to, *"Go therefore and make disciples of all nations..."* (Matthew 28:19). Jesus clearly expected His followers to take initiative towards those not yet in relationship with Him. _Action_ was His first invitation[27] and His last command![28]

Jesus Himself set the example of continually befriending and interacting with not–yet–believers, setting the prime example for all believers to follow. When Jesus initiated interaction with Peter, James, John, Andrew, and the rest of the twelve, they did not yet understand His message or what it meant to follow Him. They quickly found out that His message required action towards the world.

As Jesus set out on His public ministry, we find Him immediately engaging the lost, speaking to them[29] and healing their infirmities.[30] Jesus also did the unimaginable by speaking with a single woman in the taboo land of the Samaritans.[31] After Jesus' interaction with the Samaritan woman, he healed an official's son.[32] Jesus also healed a Gentile woman's daughter,[33] ate in tax collector homes,[34] ate in Pharisee homes,[35] attended a wedding,[36] healed a Roman centurion's servant,[37] and allowed a sinful woman to wash His feet.[38] Jesus invited not–yet–believers to relax, celebrate, heal, and discuss deep spiritual truths.

Few of the people Jesus engaged with chose to follow Him, but that didn't change the way He treated them. He was also true to His ministry and offered them His message of life. As Jesus connected with people, He was constantly seeking the Father's advice on how to act towards them. Jesus saw in the people the trouble life had dealt to them, and had compassion on them as He traveled through their villages. He saw them as harassed and helpless, like sheep without a shepherd,[39] and His heart was broken for them.

Sheep without shepherds are vulnerable. They may think they are safe when they are actually in danger. There are wolves in the world seeking to devour sheep, especially those without a shepherd. Jesus came to be that shepherd, to bring the sheep into the safety of His Kingdom. With a heart for these lost sheep, Jesus tells His disciples that "...the harvest is plentiful..." (Matthew 9:37). Jesus wanted His disciples to understand that there are people everywhere who are ready to step into His Kingdom. They are all around us, we just need to open our eyes and have a willing heart to share God's love with them.

Matthew 9:37–38 reveals that the harvest is plentiful, *"... but the workers are few."* I understand this to mean that many (maybe too many) followers of Jesus are not in tune to the hearts of men, nor the heart of the Father. This may be a reason why you are reading this book. Many of us are focused on the things in this world instead of on the harvest that Jesus tells us is ready. The Father sent His Son, Jesus, and He is constantly on a search and rescue mission for these people.

It is a strong belief of mine that the Father is always creating fresh ways for us to engage not–yet–believers. He creates natural ways that dovetail with their personalities, abilities, interests, families, and neighborhoods. When we listen to the voice of Jesus as we look into the eyes of others, we give Him the space to show us how to connect with them. A chance may come as you chat with your neighbor about the weather. It may be when you listen to a co–worker's challenges with their children. New opportunities may show up when sharing your life story, or listening to someone else's life story.

Because the Father has designed special ways for us to interact with the people we come in contact with, the options are endless. The ways to engage not–yet–believers are customized for us by God–what freedom! To be aware of what God has for us in these conversations, we need to be constantly talking with the Father. We see this in the Gospels. And, like Jesus showed us during His earthly ministry, we also need to be constantly praying for those around us who are not yet connected to Christ.

Another thing we see in the Gospels is that Jesus told His followers that imitating Him will be costly.[40] It requires sacrifice of self, comfort, and control to follow the lead of Jesus in our relationships. The message of Christ is worth the sacrifice. This looks counterintuitive to those around us. When we sacrifice our agendas to put others first, they can tell that they are important to us.

Jesus said we are the salt of the earth (Matthew 5:13). Life without salt is bland. When we are salty, we add dimensions of both flavor and preserving souls for the King. Flavor adds a dimension of attraction and anticipation for the next bite. The salty flavor of our lives often puts a desire in others for more of the Christ in us. Salt also has a preserving quality. In the time before refrigeration, people would use salt to extend the life of meat and keep it from spoiling. Our faith keeps the morals and focus of life more in line with how God wants us to live. The preserving qualities of salt adds balance and security. Being in Christ is a place of safety for our souls. When our lives are salty, we offer the eternal safety in Christ to others when they place their faith in Him. We also offer the flavor the world is craving.

In Luke 15, we see Jesus set a beautiful example for us to follow. "Now the tax collectors and sinners were all drawing near to hear Him. And the Pharisees and the scribes grumbled, saying, 'This man receives sinners and eats with them.'" (Luke 15:1–2). Because Jesus' life was full of flavorful salt, all kinds of people were drawn to Him and His words. As you connect with those who don't know Jesus yet, don't be surprised if some people grumble about you connecting to them, just like the Pharisees did. Instead, make the most of the opportunity, like Jesus did.

Surrounded by 'sinners' as well as His disciples, Jesus told three parables. The parables of the lost sheep, the lost coin and the lost son remind us how important it is to be with not–yet–believers.[41] Disciples of Jesus can seek out the lost sheep, not leave them to the dangers of the world without a shepherd (Luke 15:1–7). We can drop our own priorities and search out for the valuable people, and throw a party of rejoicing when the lost soul is found (Luke 15:8–10)! We can keep a hopeful eye towards the lost son who might return to the safety of the family (Luke 15:11–32). Jesus invites us to a life of action, not passive waiting, and that includes relationships with not–yet–believers.

Remaining Diligent in Action

One of the best ways I have found to remain diligent in a life of prayer and action is to join a like–minded group. Every week, for over 20 years, I have met with small groups of men who are committed to keeping our hearts in line with the desires of Christ. We read large amounts of the Bible, share honest dialogue about the areas of our life where we struggle, and pray together for our friends to come to Jesus.[42] I have found that these habits, or spiritual disciplines, have kept me from being isolated from not–yet–believers. They also keep my heart connected to the heart of Jesus for the world He died to redeem.

Recently, two other believers and I met together with a plan to discuss life, the Word of God, and to pray for the lost, but we did not get to too much of what we set out to do. As we sat in our circle of chairs in a local cafe, one of the men we had been praying for to come to Jesus came over and greeted us. Our Bibles were open and our conversation had begun, but that didn't seem to bother the 'intruder,' who pulled over a chair and sat down.

Our 'intruder' began to make small talk and we learned about his past experiences as a war veteran. He told about times where he found himself in harm's way behind enemy lines; days when life and death wrestled in front of him. Captivated by his stories, we asked questions, forgetting we were in the middle of a coffee

69

house and our small group time. Instead of an intruder, he became our guest. As his stories came to an end, I could hear God whispering a question for me to ask. "How do you deal with dangers in your soul?" He sidestepped the question, saying that he was an atheist but appreciated all faiths. The conversation in the group turned to the need for faith in general, but then landed on the difference that faith in Christ offers.

Our guest commented that he didn't disagree that Jesus had existed, but had serious doubts about His claims to being God and rising from the dead. His answer to the idea of the risen Christ being seen by over five hundred people at one time[43] was that there was a group delusion. Then someone asked him why some of these five hundred people, who were so sure they had seen Jesus alive again, chose to be (gruesomely) martyred instead of deny Him. His answers began to unravel. He did not surrender his life to Jesus at that time, but he committed to read more about the topic, both in the Scriptures and in history.[44] The end of his story has yet to be told.

Drawing near to God through His Word, prayer and action towards the not–yet–believers is a furnace of purification. Knowing God better purifies us to pursue and care for people on an ongoing basis. Pursuing God with small groups of like–minded people is crucial for accountability, strength and courage to carry on in our faith. As we move closer to Christ, we become better at recognizing the Spirit leading us to connect with others who need to know Him.

The next chapter begins to unpack how Jesus leads us into these relationships and gives us the right words so others can move closer to Christ. Jesus guarantees when we choose to follow the Spirit's lead that we will be 100% successful, 100% of the time. Remember that success in sharing the gospel just means repeating what He speaks to you. Spreading the gospel fire by praying for the recipient or reminding them of the message over time count as success. They accomplish their purpose–God's purpose, at that moment in time, even when we don't see immediate results. *People responding positively to the gospel is not our responsibility.* That is fully the responsibility of God.

May your soul be freed to share radically, passionately and start more wildfires.

PART 2 - WILDFIRES NEED FUEL

When we fuel our lives with God's truth and passion for Him, we find freedom to spread the Gospel. When we embrace the evangelistic power given to us, we become fearless in our faith and actions. When we fuel the wildfires with our obedience, we will be more fruitful wherever God leads us.

Understanding the truth from the Scriptures is essential so every believer's soul is fueled to start wildfires. A fearlessness in our faith and actions will grow into more obedience and fruitfulness.

CHAPTER 4: FREEDOM

The Ph.D. vs. the B.A. in Bible

A church in eastern Pennsylvania had tried several evangelism programs over the years. Like many churches, they found that these programs were unsuccessful at stimulating ongoing evangelism. This church and I came into contact through a mutual friend who recommended they talk to me. As our conversation turned to using Biblical principles instead of memorized programs, they became intrigued and invited me to come for a weekend of interaction on starting spiritual wildfires.

Travel from my home to the church would take a full day of travel, which meant that I would have time during the flights to look over the material I would present. When I boarded the last plane, I was happily surprised to find the adjacent window seat was vacant. With no one sitting next to me, I could focus fully on my work during the flight. I pulled out my computer, Bible, and teaching syllabus, placing them on the seat next to me and put away my backpack. As I grabbed my Bible and settled in to study, the flight attendant made an announcement that this was a full flight and for the passengers to quickly find their seats for an on–time departure. I couldn't help relaxing. No distractions this flight.

As I heard the clunk of the cabin door being closed and locked, I looked down the aisle and saw the last passenger striding towards the back of the plane. Surely, she had a seat somewhere else than the seat next to me. At least I hoped so. She wore a nice business suit, had short dark hair and walked with confidence. As

73

she came down the aisle I pulled my Bible up and held it closer to my face. I supposed I was trying to communicate something like "Danger, a religious fanatic is sitting here. Do not sit next to me or you may be spiritually harassed." This tactic often works to stop people from sitting by me on airlines where there are no seat assignments. This plane had assigned seating, but I tried it anyway.

As the Bible rose to cover my face a very judgmental thought ran through my mind; "This woman looks like a radical left–wing feminist." I know, I know, that is terrible. I did confess my sin of judgement, but as it happened to be, I also was right.

Of course, with all the seats already taken in front of me, she stopped two feet away from my seat and said in a loud voice, "Hello, I have the seat next to you." I lowered my Bible, as if I was surprised to see someone speaking to me and politely gathered my syllabus and computer from her seat and got up to allow this lady to sit. As I placed her luggage in the bin over our heads, I thought, "Oh boy, she will want to chat and now I'll never get any work done." I took my seat and hoped I would be left alone. God had different plans.

My new seat mate introduced herself as Laura and I politely asked her why she was headed to Washington D. C. She said that she was presenting to a professional group at a University. So, I asked her what line of work she was involved in. She was the Department Chair of English at a highly–acclaimed university. Laura went on to say that she was the editor of several academic periodicals. When I heard her impressive credentials, I let doubts and insecurities cloud my thoughts.

I wondered how our conversation could ever possibly turn spiritual. Here was a Ph.D. department chair sitting next to me. At the time, I had a B. A. in Bible from a now defunct institution that was never accredited. Then she asked, "So, Ed, what kind of business are you in and where are you headed today?" My mind raced as I thought about telling Laura, "I'm making some last–minute preparations for a presentation and I really need time to study. So, thanks for the conversation but I need to get back to my Bible, err, book…."

The next second felt like forever. In that second, God reminded me of a couple of truths. First, every interaction when the gospel is discussed is a supernatural event that He arranges so He can be glorified.[1] Second, He reminded me that I was competent to talk with this lady and share with her His good news. Third, God reminded me that He was going to use this conversation and put His words in my mouth to accomplish His purpose.

God's Word had taught me I am a competent minister of the new covenant, no matter how I felt.[2] I may have been no match intellectually, but I remembered that God had not only set up that appointment, but He also had made me sufficient to share the good news with 100% success, no matter whom I was speaking to.

I told Dr. Laura that I was presenting on how the Christian faith was designed to be organic and decentralized, and that it was meant to push people to make positive differences in culture. I briefly outlined my thoughts on how Western Christianity had taken Jesus' principles and truth and turned them into institutions that served to cause a co–dependency between the clergy and laity. And that needed changed, I added.

Laura looked intrigued. "Go on." Encouraged, I talked about how Jesus' teachings empowered women and inspired the early church to be sacrificial in how they lived and how they served others. I mentioned the Biblical stories from Acts where the early church shared their resources to meet the needs of people around them–to "anyone who had need." [3] I also shared how our church community was attempting to imitate their example. This caused my new friend to comment that I sounded like I embraced strong notions of socialism. Apparently, she had found some common ground to continue our conversation.

Laura commented on how conservative the mainstream media was and how this had negatively impacted our culture. I have a much different view! Our conversation then turned towards the subject of abortion. Laura spoke strongly of this "basic right of women" and how it needed to be protected at all costs. My head was spinning. Somehow, she assumed I was a sort of neo–socialist who also embraced abortion as a basic right of women.

All I could do was pray for wisdom and the right words to show what I really thought on those issues.

While Laura laid out her arguments for abortion, God reminded me of the one and only logic class I had taken in junior college. As Laura presented her arguments, the Holy Spirit nudged my memory so I could challenge many of her arguments that were not logical. When I made counter–points, Laura even agreed with me several times. It was an amazing experience to see God at work, several thousand feet in the sky.

As the plane began descending, my new friend admitted that I had caused her to rethink her position on abortion being a woman's right to terminate an unwanted fetus. Maybe my view, that abortion is murdering unwanted human beings, wasn't as archaic as she had first thought. It took a bold trust in God's ability to assist me in a technical conversation with an intellectual like Laura. It caused me to learn a deeper dependence on the Spirit of God to give me the exact right words at the precise time, to cause the effect He wanted to have in this unique woman's heart. My fear was overcome by trust, and her fallacious arguments were overcome with the truth. Laura and I have had a few e–mail conversations since that flight, and I still pray for her. I'm confident that my voice was added to the chorus of voices God is using to speak truth into Laura's heart. I pray I will eventually see her in eternity worshipping at the feet of Jesus.

Being Ready to Give a Defense

In a culture that values control and success more than mystery, the following verse has often been incorrectly taught and misunderstood.

> *"...But sanctify Christ as Lord in your hearts, **always being ready to make a defense** to everyone who asks you to give an account for the hope that is in you, yet with gentleness and reverence," 1 Peter 3:15 (emphasis mine)*

This verse begins by instructing us to sanctify, or set aside, Christ as Lord in our hearts. Christ is to have the first place in our hearts. This is a deliberate decision we are to make and maintain as we follow Jesus. As we make Him King of our lives, we should be constantly prepared to defend and explain our faith. The question is: how do we get ready to defend and explain our faith?

The word for "make a defense" in 1 Peter 3:15 is apologia (from which we get apologetics). Apologia means 'a verbal defense.'[4] The meaning can be refined to include an intelligent or well thought out response. A popular view is that apologetics starts with a sufficient religious education for refuting questions or accusations against Christianity. With this understanding of *apologia*, most believers will feel inadequate. How can ordinary believers ever know enough to deal with the many complex issues out there?

Many books have been written on the topic of apologetics to help believers become better equipped at defending their faith.[5] A glance at just the table of contents in these books may seem too complex to pursue further. Apologetics can be a very intellectual topic. There is just too much to know for most believers to give a well thought out response to the endless list of questions people can ask about our faith. With this understanding of *apologia*, few people will feel competent and confident enough to make a defense to everyone who asks. It serves to silence the majority to get ready to give a defense.

I believe there is a better way to approach this verse or the concept of 'apologia' that works well for all believers and fits well with the words of Jesus and the examples we see in the New Testament. To always be ready to defend your faith means that you are ready to depend on God for the right words at the right time during interactions. To trust that Jesus will do what He has promised and give us what to say at the right time to say it is something anyone can do.

To give a defense (apologia), we simply talk about the "hope that is within" us. We do not have to be ready to refute every doctrinal, theological or philosophical argument! We only need to share the hope that Christ has given us when we place our trust in Him. We don't have to debate people with the goal of crushing their opinions; we can respect that they are made in the image of God but don't know Him yet.

In the opening story of this chapter I had a long conversation on an airplane with Dr. Laura. There is no way I was humanly prepared to engage her intellectually. On top of that, I was insecure and judgmental. God still allowed me to be instrumental in sharing His love for her. God is gracious to include us in His work in people's lives as He also shapes our hearts to be more like Christ.

My conversation with Dr. Laura covered areas where she was an expert, or at least more educated than me, and yet, God gave me the precise way to interact with her in the moment. The only preparation I had for that conversation was depending on the Holy Spirit to bring to my mind what she needed to hear at that time; and He did! In every interaction where the Gospel is either hinted at or the central topic, God is at work. He will give the believer the right words at the right time to accomplish His purpose in the heart of the not–yet–believer. That brings freedom. First Peter 3:15 does not instruct us to know the *best* response; it tells us to 'always be ready' to give an account for the hope already in us.[6] God makes us ready when we rely on Him to give us the necessary words. The person we are talking to is the important one in spiritual conversations. *Evangelism is not about us, it is about what God is doing in the other person in the moment!*

Are you skeptical about the last paragraph? Let's begin to walk through the Biblical guarantees given to all believers so we can be *100% successful, 100% of the time* as we share portions of the good news.

100% Success, 100% of the Time

The best way to be ready to give a defense of the hope in you is to depend on Christ to tell you what to say and how to say it. To do this, we need supernatural 'intel' and a commitment to follow that information, trusting that God knows what He wants to accomplish. As we learn to follow the nudges of God, freedom will rise in our hearts and our appetite to follow the Lord will increase. Let's begin in the Gospels.

"Behold, I send you out as sheep in the midst of wolves; so be shrewd as serpents and innocent as doves. "But beware of men, for they will hand you over to the courts and scourge you in their synagogues; and you will even be brought before governors and kings for My sake, as a testimony to them and to the Gentiles. "But when they hand you over, do not worry about how or what you are to say; for it will be given you in that hour what you are to say. "For it is not you who speak, but it is the Spirit of your Father who speaks in you. Matthew 10:16–20

Jesus plainly told His twelve disciples that when they brought the Gospel to the world they would face difficulties. These difficulties would, in part, take place because they followed Jesus' instructions. We know now that the Twelve were arrested, beaten and brought before rulers, and some were even martyred. This warning was directly spoken to the twelve closest friends of Jesus, but the principle of being surrounded by opportunities and difficulties is for all believers.[7] Although it is dangerous for sheep to be surrounded by wolves, we can be confident that the Great Shepherd, Jesus Christ, always goes with us.

Commenting on this passage, Charles Spurgeon said,

> "Though primarily addressed to the Apostles, it seems to me that our text relates, in its measure, to all who have any talent or ability for spreading the Gospel and, indeed, to all the saints so far as they are true to their calling as the children of God. They are, all of them, more or less as sheep in the midst of wolves, and to them all is the advice given, 'Be you therefore wise as serpents, and harmless as doves.' Let us hear for ourselves as though the Lord Jesus spoke individually to each of us."[8]

Jesus instructed His twelve disciples to teach those who come after them to *"...obey everything I have commanded you..."* (Matthew 28:20). The instruction from Matthew 10:16–20 was part of what He commanded them to do, and is to be passed on to all generations of Christians. To push the importance of this concept further, we find Jesus praying about the principle of every believer engaging with not–yet–believers in all future generations. Here is a part of Jesus' prayer from John 17:

> *"15 I do not ask You to take them out of the world, but to keep them from the evil one. 16 They are not of the world, even as I am not of the world. 17 Sanctify them in the truth: Your word is truth, 18 As You sent Me into the world, I also have sent them into the world. 19 For their sakes I sanctify Myself, that they themselves also may be sanctified in truth. 20 I do not ask on behalf of these alone, but for those also who believe in Me through their word; 21 that they may all be one; even as You, Father, are in Me and I in You, that they also may be in Us, so that the world may believe that You sent Me." John 17:15–21*

There are a few principles to highlight in this passage. The first is that Jesus asks the Father to not take believers out of the world. We have a purpose here, or He could easily take us up to Heaven whenever He wanted. Jesus asks the Father to keep believers from the evil one while they are left in the world. We need God's protection. In verse 18, Jesus also prays that the Father would send believers into the world, just as He was sent into the world. In verse 20, Jesus includes all believers in these principles when He says, *"I do not ask on behalf of these alone, but for those also who believe in Me through their word."* This extends to all believers for all generations, which includes you and me. Our purpose for being left in the world and being sent into the world is that the world may believe that the Father sent Jesus (John 17:21).

Opportunities Given

So, what guarantees does God give believers as they follow the lead of Jesus? The first guarantee is that every believer will be given opportunities to speak about the hope of the Gospel. Spiritual conversations may be with family members, friends, co–workers, neighbors or strangers. God designs these encounters so that His Word will be spread as widely as possible. It is our responsibility to be aware of the opportunities, both obvious and subtle. God will create opportunities that will fit with who He has designed you to be. These interactions with the people around us may nudge them forward towards placing their trust in Christ, whether we are aware of "progress" or not. Pray that God brings people into your life every day and follow His lead in how to engage them.

Because of the fire extinguishers discussed in chapter two, many believers today do not believe they are able to competently share the Gospel. This has kept them from noticing the opportunities that are all around them. But Jesus is clear, if you are one of His followers, there will be people who need to hear His good news from your lips.

What happens once we recognize the opportunities Jesus brings into our lives? Jesus again is extremely clear. He tells us we are not to worry about what to say or how to say it. This is a truth that needs to be emphasized in evangelism to provide confidence and freedom to all believers.

Do Not Worry

One of the biggest problems people tell me they have about evangelism is fear or worry.

People are concerned that they do not know what to say, that they might get the message wrong or they are afraid they will be ridiculed, ignored or persecuted in some way. Some of us also worry that we will be outsmarted, just like I worried with Dr. Laura. But Jesus says we are not to worry. He knows worry is our natural inclination. Many believers find themselves in situations where they feel inadequate to answer others' questions about the Gospel. When we have no idea what to say, this should force us to cry out to Jesus for the words we need. If we are not supposed to worry, what should we do? We should trust Him as we step into the opportunity He has created for us.

The Precise Words

Remember Jesus says, *"...do not worry about how or what you are to say; for it will be given you in that hour what you are to say."* (Matthew 10:19). Jesus says you will be given precisely what the person or people you are speaking to are to hear at that exact moment.

We get a sense of Christ's purpose for coming into the world in Luke 4:18–19, when He quotes the prophecy from Isaiah 61:1, 2 which He fulfilled. *"The Spirit of the Lord is upon Me, because He anointed Me to preach the gospel to the poor. He has sent Me to proclaim release to the captives, and recovery of sight to the blind, to set free those who are oppressed, to proclaim the favorable year of the Lord."*

The theme in these two verses is bringing life to the people of the world. He wants His message to spread like a wildfire through each of His followers on a consistent basis. A sure way of getting His message out is to give His followers the right words at the right time so they will confidently share what others need to hear. This supernatural promise frees us.

Hearing the voice of God is an art form that may take some practice. It will also be somewhat different for each person. The key is practice and a willingness to stumble at times in our listening for His words. How else do we learn how to run? As babies, we first learn to roll over, crawl, walk with assistance, walk on our own and finally we learn to run–though a little clumsily at first. To practice repeating what God speaks, you have to listen. You have to be aware that God is always speaking to us.[9] He may speak through a whisper to your heart, or through an impression on your soul, or through a thought that pops up in your mind.

When you become aware of these thoughts, the key is to go with them. It will feel awkward at first, and maybe awkward for a while, but repeat the idea or concept you sense may be from God. Once the words flow out of your mouth, notice the response of the person you are speaking with. Often you will see "the lights come on" about what you just said. At other times, there may not be a response just then. Be confident that God is more concerned about the person you are speaking with to understand His love for them than you are. You may not see any response or results, but you can be sure God is eroding their opposition or growing their interest. You may even see visible opposition.[10] Again, the key is to follow the nudges of the Spirit in your mind to repeat what God speaks to you in the moment. Trust Him to know what the person needs to hear from you in that conversation. You will grow in this discipline of listening as God customizes how the message of His grace is to be delivered. Don't forget to have fun in the adventure of learning to hear and repeat what God says to you. Your faith will increase as you practice!

Jesus gives us the right words at the right time, but He also wants to cultivate in us a dependence on Him for those words. Jesus says that He will give us the how and what to say "in that hour." He may not give you the words until *the interaction has begun.* He doesn't promise to give us what or how to speak leading up to the conversation. He gives the words to us at the moment of need. This keeps us tethered to Him. It pushes us to keep our spiritual ears open to His voice in our souls.

Words from God to Your Mouth

I wrote this section while at Fair Oaks Cigar Lounge. As I was writing, an acquaintance sat down nearby and greeted me. I had my earbuds in and was listening to music as I wrote but that didn't stop Jerry from interrupting.

Jerry started telling me about his shoulder pain. It had bothered him on and off for months and he wasn't able to sleep well because of the pain. He then told me a long meandering story about his new doctor and how great the office was. He was debating whether he should go and see his doctor about this particular nagging shoulder issue. During his drawn-out story, I thought, "Jerry, I really don't want to hear about your shoulder pain now, I'm in the middle of writing!" As those thoughts passed through my mind, my eyes focused on Jerry. Then the Spirit of God nudged me to begin praying for Jerry's shoulder to be healed.

A few minutes later, Jerry stopped speaking to make a phone call to his doctor for an appointment. After he hung up, he told me he could not see his doctor for another five days. At that moment, God nudged me to tell Jerry I had prayed for his shoulder to be healed by God so that he would not need to see the doctor. I knew Jerry was an agnostic, but I told him what the

Spirit of Jesus put in my heart anyway. Jerry's response was brief silence, followed by a comment that he hoped the doctor could help him.

This story may sound anticlimactic, but it's just a part of a larger story where I and others have spoken into Jerry's life many times about how God loves him. I fully believe that God used that short interaction to nudge Jerry a 'baby step' closer to seeing God's great love for him. What if he told his wife about that interaction when he got home? What if that spurs further conversations? What if the Spirit leads another believer to say something similar during the next five days? We may not know how it will all turn out when we follow His lead, but God does. Tomorrow is a memory for God.

In Matthew 10:20, Jesus tells us, *"For it is not you who speaks, but it is the Spirit of your Father who speaks in you."* The words I spoke to Jerry, or the words you speak to a friend, when it is any portion of the Gospel, are from the Spirit of the Father speaking in us! If the Father gives you what to say at the precise moment, how can those words ever be the wrong ones, or useless? The Father never makes mistakes. The Father knows exactly what each person needs to hear at any given moment to move them closer towards believing in Jesus so why would we hesitate to repeat the words He puts in our mouths? This guarantee makes every interaction when we share God's love, a supernatural interaction; exciting and enjoyable!

It amazes me that so many evangelistic methods do not equip people with this freedom. In almost all evangelistic training, the scripts that are given result in people actually sharing less because using man–made systems are awkward and restricting. The Father takes all the worry out of the way. He gives us exactly what to say at the precise time to have the effect He wants at that moment. That is freedom.

Do Not Worry Beforehand

When giving presentations on evangelism, the most common question I am asked is, "Well, if you don't have a method, what do you say to people?" My answer is, "Just listen." Listen to what the person is saying, listen for their pain, listen for their questions, listen to their story, and also listen to the whispers of God in your heart. God promises to share with us what the person you are talking to needs to hear, but what He has you to say may not always make sense to you. God has a way of keeping us depending on Him so we learn to trust Him more deeply.

Many people struggle with knowing how to hear the whispers of God in their heart. Are the thoughts we might consider being from God our own desires or thoughts? How can we tell the difference? My answer to this type of question is to first remember that no matter the motivation (God's words or your desires), when we point people to Jesus with our words based on the Scriptures, those words will always have a positive impact![11]

Second, there is a need to practice. We practice by repeating what you hear from God to the person you are talking to. As we become aware that Jesus wants to use our conversations with people to nudge them towards placing their trust in Him, we will begin to discern His words over our desires. Then we will be able to tune into His voice and ignore the noise of our own thoughts. Because God speaks to each person individually and creatively, the only way to learn is to repeat what you think He is saying to you in the moment. Without practice, you will never know. Remember, however, if your words are leading them in the direction of Christ, they will always have a positive impact even if you don't see it (Isaiah 55:11).

One day, I was waiting for a package that I needed to complete a project I was working on. The delivery driver finally arrived with a load of boxes, but I was only really interested in one of these boxes. After helping unload the boxes and moving them into the office, I realized the one box I needed was not there. The driver checked his manifest. The box had been put on the truck, and he had not yet delivered it to any other address. He was confused as to where this package might be. We headed back to the office to check the boxes again. It wasn't there.

As we were walking back to the truck, the driver tripped over a crack in the cement. At that instant, I felt a nudge from God telling me that I needed to say to the delivery driver that he was tripping into hell and needed Jesus. I quickly dismissed this thought as something inappropriate to say given the situation. After all, I rationalized, I really don't know this person. He may even be a believer for all I know. I did not follow this nudge from Jesus as we returned to the truck.

The delivery man climbed back into the truck and rummaged through more boxes, looking for the missing package. He commented that he would be reprimanded for losing a package. As I saw him worry, I again felt a nudge from God telling me that I needed to stop looking and invite this man to pray with me for God to show us where the box was. I thought this was an odd nudge by God again, but the feeling was so strong I had to act on it. I looked up to the driver and said something like, "I know this might sound weird, but I believe God wants us to stop looking and pray that He will show us where the package is so you don't have to worry about being reprimanded." I immediately bowed my head, closed my eyes and started praying for God to show us where the box was. I don't know if this guy joined me by closing his eyes, or just rolled them at my suggestion. I just prayed.

No sooner had I said, "Amen," and opened my eyes, when the driver blurted out, "How did you do that?" We were both amazed to see the package sitting off to the side. We had looked there and did not see it before. Now I don't know if God caused the package to materialize or if He pulled off some cloaking device from the package, but there it was! "I didn't do it," I said. "God did it to show you how much He loves and wants to have a relationship with you." I then spent the next several minutes sharing the message of redemption with this driver as he listened intently. He thanked God for the miracle, and thanked me for praying and sharing, and then he drove off.

I had no idea what to say to the driver before he arrived. I wasn't even thinking about sharing Jesus with this man. I just wanted to find the package I needed to finish the project I was working on. However, God knew exactly what this man needed to hear right then. He needed to hear that God loved him and would take care of him. God put this driver on that route on that day so he would hear it. No amount of planning would have prepared me for that sort of interaction.

In the Gospel of Mark, we find a parallel passage to the one in Matthew 10, but with a different perspective and emphasis.

"You must be on your guard. You will be handed over to the local councils and flogged in the synagogues. On account of me you will stand before governors and kings as witnesses to them. And the gospel must first be preached to all nations. Whenever you are arrested and brought to trial, do not worry beforehand about what to say. Just say whatever is given you at the time, for it is not you speaking, but the Holy Spirit. Mark 13:9-11 NIV

This passage's primary instruction and application is for Jesus' immediate audience, His twelve disciples. The application for us today is that when we find an opportunity to speak for Jesus, that we can rely on Him to give us the words to say. Mark's account of this passage adds some dimensions the Holy Spirit wants believers to understand. There are several nuances that Mark brings to the light as we think a bit deeper on not worrying about what to say when sharing the Gospel.

Jesus tells the Twelve that they would be brought in front of governors and kings as witnesses to them. The application for all believers is that you may find yourself engaged with several levels of people in society; politicians, professionals, those in authority, blue-collar and white-collar employees, more and less fortunate people, etc. These interactions are all arranged by God so they can hear some part of the Gospel through you. Jesus states in verse 10 that the Gospel must be brought to all the nations. In other words, the Gospel will go out to all people groups through His followers throughout history. When we find ourselves in these opportunities, we should be in prayer knowing something amazing is about to happen in the hearts of the people we are talking to.

Jesus again is concise and clear. When we find ourselves in relationships with people, doors for sharing truth with them about the Gospel will swing open. It may just be an ember of truth that we share, but embers start wildfires all the time. Jesus tells us to not worry beforehand about what to say. The emphasis in this section of Scripture is not to worry *beforehand*! This highlights our dependence on God, not our own thinking. We don't need to worry about outlining our thoughts and presenting them logically and persuasively. To do that puts the pressure on us to get things right. Many of us are not good at thinking on our feet; when stressed, we often stumble over our own words and thoughts. Instead, Jesus tells us to "Just say whatever is given to you...." Jesus offers us relief from having to know what to say in our own abilities.

Notice *when* the embers of truth are given to you to speak, "...at that time...!" We may not be given the words that are needed before or in the middle of the conversation, but they will be given to us at the precise time they are needed. This forces us to rely deeply on God to provide the right words at the right time. It strengthens our faith and our ability to hear His voice. Waiting for God to give us the right words at the right time helps develop the ability to not worry about what to say. Jesus wants us to be confident that God is active in every conversation that moves towards discussing Him or His attributes. As we practice this holy waiting, we become attentive to the voice of God in our hearts to speak what He gives us to say.

In Mark's account of Jesus' instructions to His followers, he tells us that they are not the ones speaking. Every encounter we have with not–yet–believers where spiritual topics are introduced, God gives precise words to His followers that the hearer needs at that time. The One who is speaking is the Holy Spirit in Mark's account. We know that the Holy Spirit does not make mistakes. He gives us what to say at the right time to have the effect He wants in the listeners' hearts. Our responsibility is only to repeat what we hear in our souls.

Following this pattern of relying on God for the words to speak takes away the stress of evangelism. We don't have to be concerned about the 'best approach' in our sharing. We can relax, and even enjoy the process of sharing our faith, knowing God has the results under control. There is no worry about making an error. There is no pressure to secure a decision. There is no guilt that we might miss something. There is a guarantee that we will not fail in the attempt. We are assured of 100% success, 100% of the time, because God is the one giving us the right words to accomplish His purpose in the hearer's heart.

As I have taught these simple principles to people, I begin to hear both simple and sensational stories from others as they learn to follow the voice of God and repeat what He speaks.

Monica works for a government agency in Arizona and is a friend from our network of organic churches. She is a wonderful follower of Jesus who has learned to speak as God directs her. In her office, she has a white couch that the Lord has often used as a place for spiritual conversations as she and colleagues or friends sit and talk. One of these "white couch" moments took place with Stephy.

Stephy is an intelligent woman in her thirties. Monica told me, "God opens up Friday afternoons for Stephy and me to get into deep conversations." One day, Monica felt God nudging her to share about how she came to forgive her ex–husband. "God had to take me to a very raw and real place of examining my own heart and admitting to my part in the failure of our marriage," Monica began. "Once I realized I played a pretty significant role in it, over time, I repented and felt God's grace and forgiveness in my heart. About a year later, God opened up the opportunity for me, quite unexpectedly, to say I was sorry, and ask for forgiveness from my ex–husband for my part in the failure of our marriage." Stephy got tears in her own eyes, and moved to the edge of her seat as the story continued. "All that guilt, hatred and judgment... gone. I am free," finished Monica. By then, both friends needed tissues.

Monica wasn't sure why God had wanted her to share that story until a few weeks later. During another Friday "white couch" moment, Stephy shared with Monica about her parents' very difficult and unhappy marriage. Stephy's father had been an alcoholic for the first twenty years of their marriage, which tore at the soul of her mother. For the last ten years, her father had been sober. Instead of the husband's sobriety being a cause of celebration, her mother couldn't forgive him for the past. And

Stephy asked Monica for advice on how to help her mother work through her bitterness.

As silence settled in the room, Monica prayed in her spirit for the words to say. "Stephy, the only way I could forgive my ex–husband was to understand how much I had been forgiven by God–and how much grace Jesus had had on me. When I realized in a fresh way how much I was loved by Christ when I was so unlovely, I wept." Monica then shared the message of the cross, how Jesus loved her so much that He died for her.

As Monica spoke, she could feel the Spirit leading her and giving her the words Stephy needed to hear, both for herself and her parents. Monica told me later, "I felt I spoke eloquently, when normally talking about Jesus to a non–believer is really hard for me! I was emotional and humbled. When I finished talking, Stephy told me, 'Monica, I wish you could see your face right now! I've never seen such genuine belief. Your words were not what I was looking for, but it is what I've needed to hear. It really hit me in the heart!'" In that moment, Jesus affirmed to Monica in her soul that she had shared just what He wanted her to share. And that wasn't the last of the weekly "white couch" moments for the two women.

Monica walked in the truth that God would give her what to say and when to say it. Monica's humble transparency turned into an opportunity to share the good news of Jesus, spread over a few weeks. Monica did not plan it or set it up; how could she? She simply repeated what God spoke to her heart.

Make Up Your Mind Not to Worry

In Luke 11, we read that Jesus had just finished criticizing the Pharisees (the religious leaders of the Jewish faith) for being hypocrites and misleading people.[12] Instead of repenting, they turned hostile and began plotting against Him. It was under these circumstances that thousands of people crowded around just to hear Jesus' wisdom or be healed by Him. Instead of speaking to the crowd, Jesus turned His attention to His disciples.

He assured them that God knew the Pharisees' hypocrisy and that they will be accountable to God, so the disciples shouldn't fear them.[13] He then told them to respect God (as opposed to the Pharisees) because they were more valuable than any of the other creatures that He cared for.[14] Jesus chose his words to help his disciples; He wanted them to know how much He cared for them in all areas of life.

> "When they bring you before the synagogues and the rulers and the authorities, do not worry about how or what you are to speak in your defense, or what you are to say; for the Holy Spirit will teach you in that very hour what you ought to say." Luke 12:11-12

Jesus then discussed the ministry of the Holy Spirit in the believers' lives when it came to starting wildfires of faith. He told His disciples that they would stand before leaders of all sorts but they should not worry. I imagine that the disciples were uncomfortable, maybe even shocked, when Jesus told them this. How could plain fisherman and despised tax collectors adequately share their faith when faced with rulers and intellectuals? Jesus told His disciples that in every environment, they were not to worry about how or what they are to speak in their defense. Jesus promised that the Holy Spirit would teach them what to say in that very hour of the opportunity given to them. The Holy Spirit, being God,[15] gives the right words at the right time for His purpose. Jesus is calling His followers of every generation to rely on the Spirit's wisdom and words as He goes before them.

As we learn to listen for what to say from God in every situation, we begin to understand that as we repeat His words, we can defend and explain the Gospel in ways the hearer needs. This is possible because the Holy Spirit adjusts the presentation of the message to the need of the hearer. He uses our experiences, intellect and ways of relating to adjust the message so it feels natural for us and relevant for the hearer. This makes starting spiritual wildfires in the souls of people fun and adventurous. It also gives us the confidence to know God has our back when we choose to follow His leading and speak what He whispers in our souls.

"But before all these things, they will lay their hands on you and will persecute you, delivering you to the synagogues and prisons, bringing you before kings and governors for My name's sake. "It will lead to an opportunity for your testimony. "So make up your minds not to prepare beforehand to defend yourselves; for I will give you utterance and wisdom which none of your opponents will be able to resist or refute. Luke 21:12-15

The last parallel passage from the Gospels is found in Luke 21. Here, Jesus began to discuss future events with His followers. In Luke 21:12 Jesus warned them that, before all these end time events happen, they will be given opportunities to share the Gospel (Luke 21:12). For His immediate disciples, the opportunities included hardships of persecution and even prison and death for some. For followers of Christ today, we can understand from this passage that opportunities to share the good news of Jesus, will be given to us.

We may only share one small part of the gospel, like, "God really loves His creation and longs to see it restored to the beauty He intended it to be." We may also enter a longer conversation where we discuss with a friend that the world we live in is broken and everyone chases their own self–centered priorities (sin). Because of this brokenness, God provided the solution by sending Jesus to pay the penalty for our wrong choices (sin). Now that we understand that the world is broken and every person sins against God's standards, we can choose to place our trust in God's solution, Jesus Christ. When we place our trust in Christ, we are freely given salvation from what we deserved, eternal separation from God.[16]

Whether the opportunities come during hardships, or happens over coffee with a friend, Jesus has some more encouraging words for us. We are told in this passage to *"make up our minds not to worry beforehand to defend yourselves." (Luke 21:14 NIV).* Jesus' words assume His followers will intentionally interact with people who need to hear His good news. Unfortunately, many people shy away from sharing the Gospel because they worry about not saying the right or best thing. This often leads people to avoid spiritual conversations. Others fall back to inviting people they interact with to a church meeting so they can hear a 'professional,' instead of trusting that the teachings of Jesus are true. And when we assume that all meaningful spiritual conversations happen in a church or with a professional, we miss the opportunities God creates around us every day.

These passages from the Gospels instruct us to be determined to share the Good News as God provides the opportunities. It is our right, privilege and responsibility to take advantage of sharing with people the message of our King and His Kingdom.[17] *Our excuses are taken away*. We are promised that God will give us the exact words needed in any conversation about the Good News.

In the parallel passages from the Gospels we have explored, there are three phrases I want to string together to emphasize how much God supports us whenever we choose to share any portion of the Good News of Jesus with people who need to hear.

Don't Worry (Matthew 10:16-20)

Don't Worry Beforehand (Mark 13:9-11)

Make Up Your Mind Not to Worry (Luke 21:12-15)

The message from God to His followers is clear–don't worry when it comes to evangelism! God wants His message to get out as broadly as possible and He has entrusted every single one of His followers with this task. God not only entrusts you and me with the honor of speaking the Gospel to the world, but He guarantees that He will give to us precisely what the hearer needs to hear in every single interaction. This means that you will be successful to accomplish His purpose in every evangelistic encounter as you repeat what He gives you to say.

The Trinity is Involved

In these passages, we also see that the <u>Trinity</u> is committed to our success when we share the Gospel. Notice who Jesus says will be the active agent in providing what to say and how to say it in each interaction where we are sharing the good news;

*"For it is not you who speak, but it is the Spirit of your **Father** who speaks in you. Matthew 10:20 (emphasis mine)*

*"Just say whatever is given you at the time, for it is not you speaking, but the **Holy Spirit**." Mark 13:11 (NIV, emphasis mine)*

*"**I** will give you utterance and wisdom which none of your opponents will be able to resist or refute. Luke 21:15 (emphasis mine)*

The Father, Son and Holy Spirit are all active in providing us with the approach and words needed to accomplish Their purpose in each and every interaction. The complete Godhead is committed to our success.

As we repeat what God speaks to our souls, God will affect the heart of the hearer(s) in unique ways. All of this will draw people towards placing their trust in Jesus, and what He has done for them. I believe God is constantly creating opportunities for us to experience His deep commitment to making us 100% successful, 100% of the time. We need to believe and act on God's guarantees to give us all we need in each encounter. As we do, our trust increases, our faith expands, and our boldness swells. All of this will result in an abundance of wildfires set in the souls of people to reach His purposes through you!

A Wildfire Story

Stephen grew up in a strict sect of Christianity, forced to attend church meetings multiple times a week while growing up. From the people around him, he heard a steady stream of rules and expectations. "Don't drink alcohol, don't go to the movies, don't do drugs or have premarital sex. Be at church every week, read your Bible daily, have a prayer journal." The religion he saw around him was a set of laws instead of relationship with God. All of these experiences just calloused him to the sweet love of Christ's message.

Eventually, Stephen rebelled. He left that sect of Christianity and went as far as he could in the other direction. He had been told that tattoos were wrong, so he chose to ink his body. He had been told that piercings were sinful, so he gauged his ears and pierced his nose. He chased sex and drugs and everything he had been warned away from. Things that were sure to bring happiness, he thoughts, since the rules did not. But the things that promised freedom trapped him. Soon he found that he had to use prescription drugs to feel normal. He depended on sleep medications to get any sleep. Anger and isolation followed him even when he got married and started a family.

As Stephen sank into depression, his wife Laura and children needed relief. Laura found a house church within our network of churches and began to participate regularly. It was a loving community of Christ–followers who, through the course of several months, heard her story and prayed with her. After a while, Laura invited the church to gather at her home. Stephen didn't object, but stayed in his bedroom while the people worshipped Jesus and discussed the Bible. Laura had prayed for God to soften and heal Stephen's heart for some time without seeing results.

One day, Stephen and Laura were talking about this new church experience and Stephen's anger rose to the surface. "I thought we had an agreement that we would let our children figure out religion for themselves. Why do you get to teach them about the God of the Bible but I can't teach them about how I see God?" The normally soft-spoken Laura told Stephen boldly, "No one is stopping you from sharing your idea of God. Why don't you teach them what you think?" Stephen was stunned. He knew he did not want to infect his children with his dark thoughts so he did nothing.

Time passed and Mother's Day approached. Stephen wrestled with the things Laura had said. He loved her deeply, but he also wanted to prove that her new church was just as restrictive as the one he had grown up in. Stephen decided that his gift to Laura for Mother's Day would be to go with her to a church gathering.

I had met Stephen once before at a birthday party for one of their family members. When he walked through the entrance of our gathering place, I immediately greeted him with a hug. He told me later that he was startled by the hug; in his experience, church people didn't act like that. He found the interactive nature of the gathering to be calming, inviting and weirdly peaceful.

During the evening, the church celebrated the Lord's Supper. Stephen's oldest son, Brandon, invited him to join them to take the bread and cup with them as a family, but Stephen chose to watch instead. He looked around the room as the others worshipped had remembered what Jesus had done for them. Throughout the next week, Stephen found himself looking forward to joining his family again at the church gathering.

The next Sunday evening, as the bread and cup were celebrated, Brandon invited his dad to join them, but he said no again. This went on for several weeks. Stephen was intrigued by this new community. He was puzzled because all that he expected; the judgement for how he looked, the disapproval for how he had acted, never happened. He listened intensely during the evenings, and even found himself making comments during discussions. "What is happening to me?" he thought to himself. In this community, there was no hint of the type of church experience he had as a young man. One day I felt the nudge of Jesus to invite him for coffee to hear his story. Again, startled, Stephen agreed. He couldn't believe someone wanted to hear his story.

Stephen came to my house and we sat out on my back patio and shared our stories. We spent hours talking about life, our experiences, disappointments, pain and deep questions. At one point, Stephen asked if he could smoke a cigarette. (Later, Stephen told me that he was testing me to see where the "rules" would come in.) He was pleasantly surprised when I said, "Sure!" During that long conversation, birds sang in the background as Stephen poured out a lot of his pain and asked a lot of questions. It was the beginning of a new friendship.

Each Sunday evening, Brandon would ask his dad to join them for communion and each Sunday Stephen refused. He was resisting the call of the Spirit and kept fighting the nudges of God. He also kept coming to the Sunday gatherings. He kept listening, and interacting with people who shared God's love in a way he hadn't seen before. New friends from the church stepped up and offered to loan a car when Stephen's family needed one. Laura and others kept praying for Stephen.

A few months after his first visit, Stephen could no longer resist the drawing power of the Spirit and agreed to join his family to share the bread and cup together. When I looked over, I saw that they all had tears in their eyes as they shared the bread and cup and joined in a circle for prayer. During that prayer, Stephen placed his trust in Jesus Christ. Instead of returning to a religion full of rules and expectations, he entered into a relationship with Christ.

God used ordinary conversations and questions, prompted by the Spirit, to stream His love into Stephen's life. He used the prayers, the tangible help, Brandon's persistent offer to join during the Lord's Supper, and even a simple invitation of, "I want to hear your story, can we have coffee?" After Stephen placed his trust in Christ, he began to pray for his neighbors to know Jesus and he joyfully started to join in with the house church each week. A few months later, Stephen and his family began their own house church and invited other friends to join. All of this was because God gave words, prayers and conversations to people; it was natural and even fun.

As we saw in Stephen's story, God gives us opportunities and the words to speak so that we are 100% successful, 100% of the time. The more we understand this, the more fearless we will become in spreading the Gospel throughout our lives. Let's look at the guarantees God gives about spreading the Gospel.

CHAPTER 5: FEARLESS

Moses

We find the history of Moses in the book of Exodus. He grew up as royalty in the palace of the Egyptian Pharaoh, was well-educated[1] and had all the rights and privileges of being a son of Pharaoh's daughter.[2] Josephus, a first–century historian, wrote in his *Antiquities* that Moses was also a general in the Egyptian army.[3] While the Bible does not tell us details about his career or responsibilities in the Egyptian court, it does tell us about a dramatic turning point in his life. At the age of 40, Moses saw one of his Israelite brothers being mistreated by an Egyptian; Moses killed the offender.[4] The murmurs of this event spread throughout the Israelite slaves, reaching the ears of Pharaoh. We find in Exodus 2:15 that when Pharaoh learned of Moses murdering an Egyptian, he wanted to kill Moses, but Moses had already fled.

Once the son of royalty, Moses, found himself running for his life. He settled in the land of Midian and married a woman named Zipporah. He spent the next 40 years of his life as a shepherd pasturing the flock of Jethro, his father–in–law. Moses had been demoted from royalty to a shepherd. He became an ordinary man with a family.

Moses' years in the wilderness had transformed him from a prince who gave orders to a shepherd who cared for his flock. He may have learned to be a leader in Egypt as an adopted son of Pharaoh, but he learned also to care for flocks and people in Midian as a family man and shepherd. After 40 years living as a shepherd and family man, I imagine he was comfortable in his role in Midian, even if he longed for the more elegant life he left in Egypt. At 80 years old, he had likely settled in his ways, and wouldn't welcome a new assignment.

I can relate to Moses at this stage of his life. Sometimes I live passively, resigned to the situation I find myself. When I am comfortable, going through the motions of life, my heart is not really concerned about hearing God's voice or being aware of His directions and assignments. Safety and security become strong motivations in these times of predictable comfort. However, the good news is that God is still very much *for* me and will allow circumstances to jar my heart back into alignment with His passion and purpose. As I draw closer to Him, my ability to be flexible, fearless and to hear His voice, increases. God is always creating ways for us to be closer to Him as we follow His directions, just as He did in the life of Moses.

God Draws Moses Close

Back in Egypt, the Egyptians continued to increase pressure on the Israelite slaves and their cry for help rose up to God. God heard their groaning and began to act on their behalf to deliver them from Egypt. We have no record of Moses repenting of his murder in the Scripture, and we don't know if his heart was closely aligned with God while he was a shepherd. We do know that God was about to get his attention in a special way and assign him the task of freeing his countrymen. Unless a person is drawing close to God and hearing His voice, following His will is difficult, if not impossible.

One day, as Moses tended the flock in the wilderness, he noticed something he had never seen before. A bush was on fire but not burning up. Moses went over to get a better look. God drew Moses closer, and as Moses approached the burning bush, God called out, "Moses, Moses!" I imagine that Moses was shaken by a voice out of nowhere calling his name, but he replied, "Here I am."

Once God had drawn Moses close, He spoke to Moses again and said, *"Do not come near here; remove your sandals from your feet, for the place on which you are standing is holy ground."* (Exodus 3:5). Having Moses remove his sandals showed God's desire for humility and obedience when people draw near to Him. The presence of the Lord made the interaction holy; in fact, every interaction we have with God is holy.

God continued, *"I am the God of your father, the God of Abraham, the God of Isaac, the God of Jacob."* (Exodus 3:6). Moses hid his face when he heard this, afraid to look at God.[5] He understood that he was in the presence of his holy Creator. God wanted to shape Moses to become a fearless leader, leading through humility and dependency on God. There was more work to be done in Moses to get him there.

It had been 40 years since he fled from Pharaoh. Moses may have forgotten the situation of the Israelites but God had not. The Lord told Moses, *"I have surely seen the affliction of My people who are in Egypt, and have given heed to their cry because of their taskmasters, for I am aware of their sufferings"* (Exodus 3:7). Moses had seen first–hand the harsh treatment of his fellow Israelites. This statement by God shows that He was aware of their suffering and was concerned! Despite their long slavery, and Moses' long exile, here was a chance to see the ongoing shepherding, care, and love God had for his countrymen and his own life.

Then God revealed His plan to Moses. *"I have come down to deliver them from the power of the Egyptians, and to bring them up from the land to a good and spacious land, to a land flowing with milk and honey..."* (Exodus 3:8). God was going to do something amazing in releasing the Israelites from their taskmasters. The Good Shepherd was going to free His sheep and bring them to a new home.

Drawing Close and a Missional Heart are One

The next words Moses heard from the midst of the burning bush changed his life. *"Therefore, come now and I will send you to Pharaoh, so that you may bring My people, the sons of Israel, out of Egypt."* (Exodus 3:10). I wonder how much time passed before Moses responded.

I imagine him thinking something like, "Wait, you said that YOU were going to deliver them, but now You are sending me? Why would You want to use me to bring the Israelite people out of Egypt? I am no general with an army. I am a shepherd who killed an Egyptian and ran for my life. I deserted my people and Egypt. I am neither capable nor worthy of such a task!" And then there was the fear Moses most likely felt. Much time had passed but surely the Egyptians remembered what Moses had done and would kill him if he showed up to take the Israelites out of Egypt. Not to mention…he was 80 years old!

Whatever Moses was thinking, he replied, *"Who am I, that I should go to Pharaoh, and that I should bring the sons of Israel out of Egypt?"* (Exodus 3:11). Moses couldn't possibly have been prepared for what God said next. *"Certainly, I will be with you…"* (Exodus 3:12a). God would be with Him? If God was to be with Moses, that would mean forgiveness, a second chance! Could he suddenly be so close to reconciliation and restoration?

God was in the process of breaking through Moses' concepts of how a person is made worthy. God was pulling Moses into the truth of who he was created to be; a child of God. God doesn't forget His children. God was restoring Moses while simultaneously calling him into action. But Moses was not done questioning God's grace and call.

Moses continued the dialogue at the burning bush. He wanted to make sure he was hearing correctly. In Exodus 3:13-22, Moses asked how he was to go about this task of delivering the Israelites from the Egyptians. He (possibly sarcastically) asked God if he was supposed to just walk into Egypt and tell the sons of Israel that God had sent him to deliver them. God replied that that was exactly what he was to do. "Go to the sons of Israel and tell them that, *'I AM has sent me to you.'"* (Exodus 3:14b).

There are at least three truths that all believers can learn from this encounter as we think about setting wildfires for God in our midst.

First, we learn that God wants every one of His followers to be close to Him, no matter how we may have resisted or run away from Him in the past. God is about restoring the most broken people to be made powerful for His purposes. When we choose to be humble, repentant and obedient, opportunities will blossom in our lives. We have to surrender to Him if we want His heart for carrying out His mission.

Second, we learn that moving close to God does not have to be a long, drawn–out process as we respond to Him moving in our souls. Moses interacted with God at the burning bush. He was forgiven, and then given an assignment of historic magnitude in virtually the same breath.

Because of grace, we do not need to earn our standing with God. We may still need to grow in some areas, but our ability to be put into action for our King is all about what He has done for us. Stories like the ones about Jepthah[6] or David with Goliath[7] show that God can quickly change circumstances and empower us to carry out His will.

Third, we learn that drawing close to God requires having a missional heart so that we bring the restoration that we have experienced to others. No matter what the storyline of your life is, God wants you to be close to Him, to restore you, and to make you powerful for His glory. God does not redeem us without giving us missions to carry out so His Kingdom way of life becomes our way of life. One mission that every believer is given is to be engaged in helping others become like Jesus.[8] That alone is a grand mission! Embrace that truth and walk it out courageously throughout your life!

God called Moses to meet with Him in order to send Moses on mission. The mission seemed impossible, but God promised to give Moses all that he needed for it. He promises the same for you and me in the assignments He gives us. God told Moses exactly what to say to the Israelites, and promised to be with Moses along the way. God knew that Moses doubted God's mission for him, just as the Israelites would doubt Moses could be their human rescuer. God's instructions were, in part, designed to (re)build Moses' trust in God. God was teaching Moses to be humble yet fearless.

Humility and fearlessness grow in our lives as we learn to depend on the One we serve. When we know who He is and who we are, we become humble. When we know what He can do as we follow Him, we become fearless.[9]

This encounter between God and Moses leads me to understand that Moses needed to move from being fearful to fearless and from resistant to humility. God wanted to comfort Moses with His presence, His forgiveness, His mission and His success.

We learned in the previous chapter that the Trinity is fully involved with us when we share His gospel at His guidance. God provides the opportunities, the words, and the way to share the Gospel when we need them. This is how He has moved through the centuries on women and men when they are on mission for Him. I see the consistency of God in walking with us as we repeat what He speaks throughout the Bible. For example, we see God's interaction with Jeremiah (Jeremiah 1:4–9, 12), Isaiah (Isaiah 6:1–10), Jesus (John 5:19), Peter and John (Acts 3), and all believers (Revelation 12:10–11). And there are many others!

In Exodus 3:18, God promised Moses that the Israelites *"...will pay heed to what you say..."* They would pay attention to Moses because he would be speaking the words God knew they needed to hear so they would follow Him.

A full reading of this story in Exodus shows us that these promises of God did not happen immediately or without struggle. The ten plagues show that sometimes it takes time. Moses had to believe God's words to Him and follow through even when he experienced resistance from Pharaoh.[10] Always believe and follow God's Word, even when things do not seem to be working or do not make sense; He always keeps His promises!

God also promised that He would give Moses and the elders of Israel what they should say to the King of Egypt.[11] God also told Moses about a special confirmation that they were following God's will; the Egyptians would be open–hearted and give the Israelites articles of silver, gold and clothing.[12] *"Thus you will plunder the Egyptians."* (Exodus 3:22).

God is with us when we speak His message to people and nothing can stop us from accomplishing His purpose under His direction! The missions God assigns to us may not be as elaborate as Moses', but every mission God sends us on is important to accomplish His purposes. We can trust His involvement, even when, or especially when, we don't trust our own skills.

Rooting Out Fear

You and I are like Moses in many ways. Even with all the guarantees from God, fear quiets us. Chapter four of Exodus begins with more questions from Moses that were rooted in fear. *"What if they will not believe me or listen to what I say? For they may say, 'The Lord has not appeared to you.'"* (Exodus 4:1 emphasis mine). If I had this long drawn out conversation with God, and witnessed a miraculous burning bush, I hope I would be confident to face anything in my future. But I might also react just like Moses did, afraid that God wasn't capable of doing exactly what He told me. God spent a lot of time assuring Moses that He was with him. He also showed him several miraculous signs, like turning his staff into a serpent, and causing his hand to be leprous and then restoring it.[13] God addressed every fear Moses had, and yet Moses came up with even more excuses to not follow through on God's mission!

So far in Moses' encounter with God, he had heard the voice of God, seen the burning bush, received the promise of giving him the words to say, seen the staff becoming a serpent, and experienced his hand being leprous and then restored. Yet Moses' main excuse was that he would get tongue tied and not know what to say. *"Then Moses said to the Lord, 'Please, Lord, I have never been eloquent, neither recently or in the time past, nor since...I am slow of speech and slow of tongue.'"* (Exodus 4:10). Those words sound so much like my thoughts when I met Dr. Laura on the airplane (chapter four). God had proven to me dozens of times before that He actually does give the right words at the right time for every circumstance when I proclaim His love to others. But I still feel a lump of fear swell up in my throat when God's mission is right before me. Only as I draw close to Him and remember His promises can I follow through and repeat the words He speaks to my soul.

God's response to Moses is so gracious and forceful at the same time, *"Who has made man's mouth? Or who makes him mute or deaf, or seeing or blind? Is it not I, the Lord? Now then go, and I, even I, will be with your mouth and teach you what you are to say."* (Exodus 3:11-12). Can you sense God's passion in His response? God promised to be with Moses' mouth and to give him the words to say while on this mission to deliver the Israelites.

No matter what Moses' weaknesses may have been or how he perceived himself, God would work with him and give him success. How could Moses possibly make a mistake with those guarantees? As we saw throughout the Gospels in the previous chapter, God continues to make the same promises to us. He will give us the words to say that none of our opponents will be able to contradict or refute in their souls.[14]

Despite God's response, Moses allowed his fear to press him further, *"Please Lord, now send the message by whomever You will."* (Exodus 3:13). In other words, "God, please send someone else!" Like we so often do, Moses resisted God's mission. Moses was still living in fear instead of being fearless with God's power and purpose. At that point, God became righteously angry with Moses.[15]

But in an amazing act of grace, God worked to relieve Moses' fear even further. God encouraged Moses by allowing his brother, Aaron, to help on his assignment to deliver the Israelites. Aaron spoke fluently[16] which should have taken away Moses' recurring fear–filled excuse to not obey God's directives. God added that He would be with both Moses' mouth and Aaron's mouth. He promised to teach the two brothers about the task and even what they were to say once they faced Pharaoh.[17] This finally gave Moses the comfort he was looking for. He then began the journey back to Egypt to fulfill all that God had directed him.[18]

From Fearful to Fearless

The story continued in Exodus 4–7, as Moses repeated his excuse that he was unskilled in speech.[19] No less than four times, Moses reminded God that he didn't know what to say and couldn't address the Egyptians. Each time God promised He would be with Moses and would give him what he needed. Whether Moses honestly was unable, or terrified, or just stubborn, God didn't change His plan to use Moses. He still gave him the assurance of being given the right words for each interaction throughout his mission.

In Exodus 7:7, we learn that Moses and Aaron both spoke to Pharaoh. God came through on the promises He made to Moses. Finally, Moses chose to carry out the mission God had given him at the burning bush. God is absolutely for us and wants our success in verbally carrying out His mission.

The purpose in walking through this long interaction between Moses and God at the burning bush is to highlight the *consistency* of God throughout the Scriptures. God declares to make us 100% successful, 100% of the time when we speak His message to those He directs. The closer we draw to His heart, the more alert we become to the opportunities He gives us.

Over time, I have learned to be more fearless in these interactions by practicing obedience: to repeat what God speaks. My obedience to the opportunities given by God is strengthened as I become more intimate with Him. The more I trust what God puts in my mouth, the more I prove to myself that He does come through in brilliant ways. My fear keeps shrinking, and I become more fearless in sharing God's love and words with those He graciously and strategically places in my life. It really is a journey of learning that begins with trust. It leads to the action of obedience in repeating what He speaks, and the joy of recognizing God's faithfulness to His promises.

Fresh and Fearless

A few short weeks after becoming a Christ–follower, I attended a seminar on evangelism and noticed an information table set up by a group called Ex–Mormons for Jesus in the lobby of the church. After listening to their stories and passion, I chose to join them on one of their adventures to share the truth of Jesus with Mormons. A week or so later, I found myself in a home Bible study with leaders from the Ex–Mormons for Jesus, learning about how to effectively share Jesus with Mormons. I was so excited to know Jesus and to obey what He called His followers to do; to become fishers of men![20] I had very little knowledge of the Scriptures, but the people in that home Bible study embraced me as part of their 'tribe.' They encouraged me to go and tell Mormons about the true Gospel. A few days after our training session, we met at a Mormon Ward (meeting place) to hand out information about the Jesus of the Bible and how He is different from the Jesus of Mormonism. I thought that because some of these people had gone door to door telling people about their Jesus that they would be warm to us as we came to tell them about the Jesus of the Bible.[21] I quickly found out they were not receptive.

I was assigned to hand out flyers from the middle of a driveway to cars both entering and exiting the parking lot. It was as dangerous as it sounds. Cars were coming from every direction and I was distracting them as I urged them to take the material. I could have caused an accident, but I wasn't thinking about the risks. I was concerned about these people's souls!

Several minutes into this activity, a man stopped his car in the middle of driveway. He held up traffic, but he did not care and he was not happy. As he exited his car, it was strikingly obvious he was a big man, probably 6'8". He was middle–aged with a fitted compression glove that covered his hand to his elbow. He began yelling at me even before he opened his car door. He demanded that I get out and stop handing out our information. When I respectfully told him that we had as much right to distribute information at his meeting place as he had to hand out information at my house, rage boiled in his eyes. He raised his gloved hand in the air and threatened to smack me. My mind raced as I thought about how to defend myself. "Do I kick him between the legs or just stand there and endure a beating like the Apostle Paul?" Instead of those options, the Lord put His words in my mouth and I began to say over and over again, "Jesus loves you and died for your sins." After the fifth time repeating the mantra Jesus gave me, the man lowered his hand, got into his car and parked...without another word.

As I handed out more flyers to the cars coming and going, three men dressed in suits headed straight for me. The men called me to come and speak to them and so I did. The oldest gentleman introduced himself as the bishop of the Ward and the other two young men were elders. They began questioning me about what we were doing and why we were doing it. I was unashamed of the truth about Jesus and answered their questions with the words God promised to give me when I obeyed his command to speak. I could hardly believe it when the bishop called me a "moron" and then turned and walked away.

My faith was so fresh, and my passion for spending time with Jesus and knowing His Word were so strong, that I believed I could do anything for Christ.[22] Risk is not as hard when we are convinced Jesus is with us! I have heard stories and personally experienced this strong desire to live fearlessly for Christ–this is how sparks of wildfires spread! The more we love Jesus and allow our lives to be fully His, the more His passion and purpose ooze from our being. The richer our relationship with Jesus becomes, the more we seem to understand the need of mankind to know Him. In essence, we have found the cure for having an unfulfilled life[23] and we want the world to know! Why would we ever choose to remain silent about Him?

Come and Go with Jesus

This chapter has focused on the simultaneous call of God on each person's life to draw close to Him and to go out for Him (Exodus 3–7; Mark 3:13–15). God wants our hearts to be fully His, which will always equate to being on mission for Him, encouraging people to place their trust in Jesus Christ. Moses was called to draw near to God and immediately given the task of going to Pharaoh to deliver the Israelites from Egypt. I was freshly called to live out trust in Jesus when He sent me to the Mormon Ward and shared the truth about the Jesus of the Bible. There are many other Biblical examples of God calling people to be with Him and simultaneously sending them out on mission for Him.[24] One of the best Biblical examples of this truth is found in Mark 3.

*"13 And He went up on the mountain and summoned those whom He Himself wanted, and they came to Him. 14 And He appointed twelve, so that they would be with Him **and** that He could send them out to preach, 15 and to have authority to cast out the demons." Mark 3:13-15 (emphasis mine)*

The story of Jesus calling the twelve apostles takes place only a few short months into His public ministry. Over the weeks leading up to this passage, Jesus had been walking through the region and inviting people to come along with Him. After spending some time with them, He decided to appoint twelve of them to be His apostles. Apostle simply means, "sent ones." Jesus had spent the previous night in prayer,[25] seeking the Father for wisdom to make such an important selection.

The twelve that Jesus chose were ordinary men. Many were fishermen and at least one was a tax collector. Ordinary men who Jesus wanted to spend time with so they could become like Him, imitate Him, and share His Gospel with the world. Another aspect that I notice is that these men really had little idea what they were getting themselves into. What did it mean for them to obey Jesus' command to "Follow Me,"[26] or to become fishers of men?[27] Jesus chose these rookies to be the ones who would share His Good News with the world. He wants to use you to start wildfires throughout your lifetime as well.

Jesus called these twelve men to carry out three important directives which apply to every believer.

The *first* action Jesus called His twelve apostles to was to **BE** with Him. We are to invest in getting to know Jesus better throughout our lifetime. Being with Jesus requires time, sacrifice and even murky times of wondering if we are really growing in our faith or even hearing the voice of God. Spending time with Jesus through prayer, straining to hear His voice through the Word and with a community of believers are all essential practices. These practices help us to know His heart, ways and customs as we engage the world. It is through the consistent investment of getting to know Jesus that we cultivate a mature faith-life Drawing close to Christ is vital to becoming familiar with His voice and following it wherever He leads us.

The *second* action Jesus called His twelve apostles to was to **GO** for Him. All throughout the time that Jesus spent with these twelve men and many others, we see the normal pattern that Jesus sent people out often and even before they were ready.[28] This seemingly pre-mature sending of people out to speak for Him actually had the benefit of causing his new followers to ask more questions, be primed to learn and developed a sense of boldness and fearlessness for the future. Jesus is a genius! Over time, our message does mature as we get to know Him more intimately.[29]

In the Mark 3 passage, Jesus tells these brand–new followers to go and preach. Jesus sends newbies out to do what many would consider a very important task of the church; preaching or proclaiming the Gospel message. We might think that Jesus is crazy, but it is more likely that we are the crazy ones when we don't follow the example set by Jesus Himself.

The *third* action Jesus called His twelve apostles to was to **DAMAGE** the enemy's plans. Jesus gives His followers His authority over demons to damage the enemy's plans to destroy our souls. This sending out His followers simultaneously to calling them to Himself is consistent for Jesus.

In Matthew 10, we read that Jesus sends His followers out as *"...sheep in the midst of wolves."* (Matthew 10:16). In Matthew 16:18, Jesus tells Peter that the church will be built by Christ Himself and she is to be in the world attacking the gates of hell. This can mean nothing else than every believer infiltrating the dark places of the world to bring light. As we enter dark places of sin and suffering, God calls us to share that the Kingdom of God is among them,[30] offering a truth many have never heard nor experienced.

New believers often find out that no one thinks they are capable of going on mission for their King. From a human perspective, this makes sense. There are few areas of life where people are naturally capable of accomplishing big things immediately. However, the spiritual realm is not the natural realm, and the rules are entirely different, even opposite. Notice the thread of spiritual truths taught by Jesus that are 180° opposite of how the world operates.

Fearless is Unique for Each Person

My friend Ron once shared the story with me of how God started convicting him about evangelism. Ron had been a drug user for decades before he came to know Jesus as his Savior. He was scarred by years of abuse, and had been used by people most of his life. Of course, he was grateful that God had cared enough to save him, but like many others, he was not sure about giving the same blessing away. That was for other, more experienced Christians or evangelists.

Then, one week, Ron was convicted into action. He had been passively sitting in the house church. His mind was wandering when the conversation became livelier. He tuned back into the conversation to hear what all of the excitement was about. As he listened, Ron found himself sliding to the edge of his chair as passionate stories were told about sharing the good news of Jesus in work places, coffee shops, and homes. Ron knew that he had not been active in sharing the good news of Jesus, but Jesus was speaking to his heart through the stories he was hearing.

Throughout the next week, Ron prayed that he would have stories of his own to share with his friends in his house church. God began to increase a craving to share the love of God that he had received and enjoyed. Due to Ron's more private approach to his relationship with Jesus, he tried to shake the feeling or explain it away, but God would not leave him alone, He was actively answering Ron's prayer. He decided that he needed to tell his house church about God's nudging to share Christ. He wanted to be fearless but knew he needed accountability. Ron spoke up one day in the group and promised that he would share Jesus with someone before their next gathering.

During the next week, every day that went by reminded Ron to follow through on his commitment to find opportunities to share the love of Jesus. It was in a checkout line at the local grocery store that God broke through in Ron's mind and heart. In front of Ron was a man in his 20's, waiting for his turn to pay for his items. God nudged Ron to tell the young man that Jesus loved him. But that felt too much like the cold turkey evangelism Ron was against. Eventually, Ron opened his mouth to strike up a conversation that went something like this:

Ron: "How are you doing today?"

Man: "I'm doing good thanks, how about you?"

Ron: "Things are going good, but I want you to know that Jesus loves you."

Man: "Hey, thanks for letting me know."

Then the conversation ended, and they moved on. Now you might think this example is not very fearless, but I say it is powerful. It certainly was a cold turkey approach, but Ron was obeying what he knew Jesus was asking of him. Why did Ron speak at that time, on that day, in that line, to that man with those words? Just to keep his word to his church? Maybe, but I suspect there was much more.

Ron met with his church a couple of days later and shared his encounter with the man in the checkout line. His church encouraged him and prayed for the young man. Ron told me he knew he obeyed God and he knew he was effective. His heart, mind, and expectation was for the love of God to roll more and more freely off his lips to friends and strangers.

Being fearless will look different for each person. God wants to move each of us forward in following His unique promptings to share His love. Evangelism should be creative and unique to each person because each person is vastly different in their needs, personality, intellect, conversational skills, etc. There is no point in comparing our efforts in sharing the grace and truth of Jesus to another's efforts. God works with each of His children, right where they are. He moves them forward as they grow in Him, at their own pace. Even the smallest of steps forward in following the nudges of Christ matters! It may be just sharing that "Jesus loves you" or it may be a month–long conversation about deeper questions of life. Either way, the Gospel is proclaimed,[31] and we should rejoice, and encourage each other. When we encourage obedience in following the nudges of God, fearlessness grows.

And the more fearlessness grows, the more seeds will be sown. When this happens, the Scriptures promise that an abundant harvest is on its way![32]

Fighting Against Fear is Forever

I love to see people's eyes brighten when they learn some new or encouraging truth. I'm hoping that the subsection title, "Fighting Against Fear is Forever" is that kind of truth in your life. It can sound discouraging at first. "You mean that I'll be fighting fear about sharing the gospel for the rest of my life?" My answer to that question is, "Most likely!" I hope this is actually encouraging.

No matter how often I have seen God come through with the right words for the right situation and see God move someone forward towards faith in Christ, I still get doubts about sharing God's words. Many of the boldest believers still fight against fear and worry when they have a chance to share the truths of Jesus. This is a spiritual battle raging; the enemy wants us to be silent, not confidently vocal for God's Kingdom.

> *"18 With all prayer and petition pray at all times in the Spirit, and with this in view, be on the alert with all perseverance and petition for all the saints, 19 and pray on my behalf, that utterance may be given to me in the opening of my mouth, to make known with boldness the mystery of the gospel, 20 for which I am an ambassador in chains; that in proclaiming it I may speak boldly, as I ought to speak."*
> *Ephesians 6:18-20*

Paul encourages us to be in prayer at all times in the Spirit for other believers regarding the sharing of Jesus' good news. As much as possible, we should discipline ourselves to be in tune with the Spirit's leading in our lives. It is a strong belief of mine that the Spirit is constantly active in our lives, drawing us closer to Christ and more engaged with pointing people in the direction of Jesus. As our spiritual ears become more sensitive to the voice of the Spirit, our prayers will increase and so will the answers.

The last half of verse 18 calls us to be alert with all perseverance and petition for all the saints. We need to be in daily prayer for our sisters and brothers to persevere and to be alert to the Spirit's activity regarding our sharing the mystery of the gospel. Being alert to the Spirit is vital as our lives align with Christ's.

Then, in a surprisingly transparent moment, Paul said that he needed a dose of fearlessness!

Paul even admitted that he was dependent on the Spirit to give him the right words at the right time. This was the great church–planting, miracle–working, dead–raising apostle Paul; he needed boldness and the right words to speak to people about the gospel?

Fear can lurk throughout our lives, no matter how successful we may seem to be. We have to fight to believe Jesus and "...*not worry about what to say or how to say it.*"[33] Paul admits that whether he spoke in powerful ways in the Acropolis to King Agrippa[34] or when he addressed Herod[35] or when he chose which Scriptures to share in a synagogue, he was reliant on God to give him the words. Maybe Paul's secret to spreading so many wildfires was that he only spoke what the Lord gave him to speak. What else could make such a transformation in the life of a stubborn Pharisee who hated Jesus and Christians?

Paul not only asked for prayer to be full of God's words to speak, but for a big dose of boldness. Paul asked for prayer, "...*to make known with boldness the mystery of the gospel...that in proclaiming it I may speak boldly, as I ought to speak.*" Like many of us, he may have sometimes wondered if he was actually hearing God's voice in what he was to speak. But his heart's desire was to walk in the fearlessness of God as he proclaimed the gospel wherever Jesus led him.

I pray you are comforted as you read the above couple of paragraphs. The apostle Paul is just like you and me when it comes to sharing the gospel. If he didn't know what to say, he asked for the right words to come from God to his lips; if he was tempted by fear, he asked for boldness to proclaim as he knew he should. Fighting against fear is a life–long endeavor, but it is worth it as we become stronger in our faith walk.

Some find themselves arguing with God about their abilities to share the good news like Moses. Some are fresh in their faith and are ready to take large risks for the King. Still others are stuck in fear like Ron was before following the nudges of the Spirit. No matter where we are today, the answer is for us to take off our sandals, as Moses did, and interact with God. Allow Him to expose your heart, your questions and fears about sharing the love of Christ with others. There will come a time when you will say "yes" to the Lord and follow through on spiritual opportunities in your path.

As you follow through on the chances given to share the truth of Jesus with others, boldness will begin to rise. Sometimes you will be able to see that people are deeply affected by what you share; sometimes you won't see much visible results. But either way, constant obedience will help your trust grow. The Lord wants us to be unified with Him so that we can produce much fruit.[36] Let's move forward by learning from people who fearlessly engaged with their culture to see the Gospel spread rapidly.

CHAPTER 6: FRUITFUL

When a lot of people do a little, much is accomplished - Juan Isaias

It is So Simple

A faithful sower + good seed + good soil = harvest! Jesus told us it is that simple. The good seed is the Word of God (Mark 4:14). The good soil is a person who hears the Word of God, accepts the Word of God and allows it to grow and bear fruit; some 3,000%, some 6,000% and some 10,000% (Mark 4:20). This is a fruitful equation and it is uncomplicated; a faithful sower + good seed + good soil = fruit!

I recently planted winter grass in my backyard. Having lush green grass throughout the winter is a benefit of living in the desert of Arizona. The equation for a lush green yard all winter is also simple, a faithful sower + good seed + good soil = lots of green grass!

Over the past several years, I have learned a few practical advantages to getting the best amount of grass possible when I plant the winter rye seed. In the first years of planting winter grass, I cut my grass and threw some seed on top of it. It was quick and easy, but my yard was not as thick and lush as my neighbor's yard. I ended up asking my neighbor what his secret was to having luscious green grass. The next year I followed his instructions.

I cut my grass as low as my mower would go. This turned my lawn from green to a mixture of yellow and brown, but there was more to the cultivation process. The next step was to 'dethatch' what was left from the yellow and brown grass. This thinned the existing grass out even more to provide more room for the new seed to germinate in the ground. Once I dethatched the grass, my yard was mostly brown dirt and ugly. The third step was to aerate the ground by using a machine to punch holes in the soil. Aeration allows air, water and nutrients to go deeper in the ground. This allowed the roots of the new grass to produce a more vigorous winter lawn. The final step was to sow abundant seed on the cultivated ground. A faithful sower + good seed + good soil = green grass.

Every September, when I plant winter rye grass, there are areas on my lawn that are not as cultivate as well as other areas. In these less cultivated areas, I notice more birds eating more seed because the ground is not able to accept the seed easily. The birds enjoy the feast.[1] There are some areas in my backyard where seed lands but it is beyond the designated lawn area and is full of rocks and shallow soil. When seed lands there, it does reproduce, but dies out rapidly.[2]

In Mark 4:1–20, we find Jesus telling His disciples and others the parable of the soils. Understanding this parable of the sower, seed and soil is foundation according to Jesus. In Mark 4:13 Jesus said, "Do you not understand this parable? How will you understand all of the parables?" Because this is the foundational parable according to Jesus, we must understand what this parable is about.

As an evangelist, when I look over the parable of the soils (Mark 4:1–20), I automatically see the principle of indiscriminate sowing. To sow seed indiscriminately means to plant the story of Jesus everywhere I go and to anyone who will listen. The surest way to know the quality of soil is to plant seed and observe if grows and reproduces fruit.

When we find reproducing good soil, we should invest more time and energy there to develop a reproducing mindset. When we find people (good soil) who show interest in knowing more about Jesus, we should give them our full attention. People who are interested in knowing more about Christ are usually an entrance point into a whole new relationally connected group where wildfires can begin. We must sow a lot of seed in order to find good soil and enjoy a large harvest. Remember, Jesus said this parable is foundational to understanding all of the parables (Mark 4:13).

When we understand this parable, we are on our way to grasping the rest of parables that He used to teach us His truth. There are two important parts of this parable that I want to highlight: cultivating and sowing.

Cultivating

The first highlight from Mark 4:1–20 is that we need to learn how to cultivate the soil of souls around us. Good seed needs good soil to germinate and be fruitful. So how do we cultivate souls toward becoming good soil? How do we prepare and 'aerate' souls? Here are three suggestions to launch you in learning how to cultivate the people around you to become good soil as they receive the Word (seed).

Prayer: Nothing can prepare a person to want Jesus and His truth more than the Spirit of God. In John 16:8 we learn that the Spirit of God will *"...convict the world concerning sin and righteousness and judgement...."* In cultivating, we must begin to pray for the people we have a relationship with. Ask God to soften their hearts and prepare them to become good soil. Here are some suggested daily prayers to offer to God for your not–yet–believing friends:

- For God to draw your friends to Himself (John 6:44, 65).

- That they will seek to know Jesus (Acts 17:27).

- For them to hear and believe the Word of God (1 Thessalonians 2:13).

- For their souls to be guarded from Satan blinding them from the truth (2 Corinthians 4:4, 2 Timothy 2:25-26).

- For them to change their minds and to follow Christ (Acts 17:30-31, 1 Thessalonians 1:9-10).

- That they will put their trust in Jesus as Lord, grow in faith and bear fruit for God's glory (Romans 10:9-10, Colossians 2:6-7, Luke 8:15)!

Engagement: Most believers want to see the plentiful harvest Jesus spoke about.[3] They pray about the harvest, hear messages about the harvest, have conversations about the harvest and even plan events at their church buildings in hopes of a harvest. But the harvest seems to rarely come. If you ask an average believer in the West just a couple of questions, the reason why a harvest is rare becomes obvious.

What are some of these questions? "What are the names of the six neighbors closest to your house?" or "Who are your closest not–yet–believing friends? When was the last time you had not–yet–believing friends over to your house for a meal or coffee?" The answers are often silence. If we want to encourage souls to place their trust in Christ, we need to befriend not–yet–believers. As we engage not–yet–believers, we must <u>not</u> see them as projects to get them into the Kingdom. We must genuinely love them through the process of their spiritual journey.

Jesus said the harvest is plentiful but there are not enough believers who are willing to work in the fields of souls.[4]

Our mission begins where God has already placed us in the world; our work places, neighborhoods, family and other third places.[5] As we engage with people recreationally,[6] our words, character, desires, activities and priorities will tell a story of invitation for them to consider engaging the Christ they see in us.

As we engage them, we are modeling for them how they are to move forward in doing the same to the next generation of not–yet–believers. That is multiplication! This also begins the discipling process before they place their trust in Jesus as their savior. Like Jesus did with His twelve followers, you begin to disciple them before they are actually believers!

Serving: Few things grab people's attention more than service. In our crazy, busy world, service and humility are rare commodities and people are drawn to us when we serve them. In my neighborhood, our trash cans go out on Wednesday night for

Thursday pick up. If I see one of my neighbors forget to put their trash can on the curb, I'll take it out for them. If they forget to bring their trash can in on Thursday night, I bring it in for them. This sort of help is easy, takes almost no time and yet it startles people. Serving often softens souls, and shows them there is more.

On Saturday mornings, I meet with two other believers for accountability. We discuss our Bible reading for the week, confess our sins, and pray for not–yet–believers to place their trust in Jesus. Our favorite place to meet is Fair Oaks Cigar Lounge; we have a purpose there. But when we first started meeting at Fair Oaks, we were a little put off by how dirty the lounge was when it opened. The ash trays were not cleaned, the floors had not been swept, and the windows and counters were dusty. We made comments about the untidiness of the place but continued on with our agenda. A few weeks into our getting together on Saturdays, we began praying for Scotty, the manager of Fair Oaks.

A couple of us had been sharing with Scotty about our trust in Christ and what He meant to us. Over time, we learned that Scotty had grown up going to a church. As a young boy, Scotty came to Sunday School with questions about evolution; a topic he had been learning at school. According to Scotty, his Sunday School teacher dismissed his questions and told him to stop asking. Only the Bible and the teacher's views were allowed in class. The claims of science had no place there; the Bible was to be believed without question. Not long after, Scotty quit going to church and never went back.

One day we decided that instead of immediately sitting down and chatting, we would show Scotty love by cleaning. We grabbed paper towels and Windex to clean the ash trays, windows and counters, and soon that became part of our Saturday morning routine. Scotty was surprised and touched, that we were willing to do all that for him. He felt obliged to return the favor and offered us free cigars. We told him that we were not cleaning up the place to get something in return. We were simply showing Scotty our love. We also said that we enjoyed following Jesus' example of serving others. Scotty's response was bittersweet to hear; he said we were the first Christians he had met who lived out what they believed.

Our story of our tidying up Fair Oaks on Saturday morning began to spread as Scotty told others in the lounge. The regulars at Fair Oaks have since nicknamed us "The God Squad." We now see others doing similar things throughout the week. Our serving the manager has now spread to others and the attitude at Fair Oaks is shifting, becoming more positive. Our serving is softening many hearts and the gospel is spreading there in both obvious and subtle ways.

Prayer, engagement and service are three simple ways to begin cultivating the soil of souls. If we want to experience an abundant harvest, we must also be sowing an abundant amount of seed on the cultivated soil around us. The book of Acts is full of stories of sowing and reaping by believers!

Sowing

The second highlight from Mark 4:1–20 is that we need to learn the principle of abundant sowing.

The worship center in the church I was speaking at was silent; except for the sound of my fingers snapping rhythmically every second. After sixty snaps, I said, "Every second, one person somewhere in the world dies and goes to hell." My fingers continued to snap every second. "That is 86,400 people every day, going to hell. Two million, five hundred thousand, every month die and go to hell." My fingers kept snapping with every tick of the second hand on a clock. "Thirty–one million people this year will die and be forever separated from God. One person for every second of every day."

I had picked up this illustration somewhere, and it seemed like the people in the room were as convicted by it as I had been. The only way to reduce this overwhelming number of people heading to a Christ–less eternity is to sow more seed.

One of the laws of the harvest is that an abundant harvest comes from an abundant sowing.[7] Fruitfulness does not happen spontaneously. All believers are to be speaking or sowing the truth of the Bible throughout our lives.[8] When we speak the good news of Jesus to others, the truth of God's Word begins to transform them. As more people are connected to Jesus, they can share the same message with others, affecting future generations. This is multiplication and the expansion of the Kingdom of God!

The key to the gospel expanding rapidly is the total mobilization of all believers to be sowing seeds of the gospel.[9] This can happen in natural ways and settings as God directs with freedom and fearlessness.

The Book of Acts

The story of the book of Acts took place over a period of about 30 years (33 A.D. to 63 A.D.). It begins in Acts 1:15 with 120 people crammed into a room waiting for the Holy Spirit. They anxiously waited, but had little clue of what to expect. We learn in Acts 21:20 that there were tens of thousands of believers. This swelling number included Jerusalem and everywhere the gospel had spread. It certainly is an estimate on Paul's part, but it indicates just how rapid the expansion was.

The growth from 120 to tens of thousands in just thirty years is astounding! One of the keys to this expansion is the sowing of the Word of God wherever people went. Let's track their movement and see what we can apply to our lives to realize this type of fruitful multiplication in the church today.

In Acts 1:8, we find Jesus meeting with His Apostles for the last time. At this last meeting, He gave them their marching orders to expand His good news to the ends of the earth. You can imagine the weight of this final interaction with their risen Lord. Here are Jesus' final words recorded to His closest friends.

8 "...but you will receive power when the Holy Spirit has come upon you; and you shall be My witnesses both in Jerusalem, and in all Judea and Samaria, and even to the remotest part of the earth." Acts 1:8

After Jesus went up to Heaven, the Apostles gathered with others in an upper room in Jerusalem where they stayed, prayed and worshipped.[10] But the story doesn't end tamely there; it continues in Acts 2.

Several days later, the Holy Spirit suddenly came from heaven as promised, and filled the believers with His power and presence. They began to speak in other languages so those around them could understand what was being said in their own languages. This was so unexpected that a large crowd gathered to see what was going on.

Peter stepped up and preached about the death and resurrection of Jesus. Approximately 3,000 people placed their trust in Christ. These new believers joined the others and met daily to enjoy meals, pray, discuss the apostles' teaching, share their resources and enjoy each other's company. But this didn't happen in isolation; we read that every day more people placed their trust in Jesus Christ! A wildfire spread in Jerusalem.

I'm convinced that this multiplication happened because the new believers engaged their friends and neighbors with the good news of Christ they had believed. There is a power in the flow of relationships and conversations as we live our lives among others.

The wildfires kept burning as believers obediently shared the love and truth of Christ. In Acts 3, Peter and John healed a lame man at one of the temple gates. This caused such a stir that Peter gave another talk, inviting people to place their trust in Jesus.[11] Acts 4 tells us that the Jewish leaders became so disturbed by their teaching about Jesus as the Messiah that they put Peter and John in jail. These men knew it was dangerous to speak out boldly about Jesus and yet no risk or loss was too big. Eternal outcomes are more important than temporary safety or comfort.

Peter and John's fearless proclamation of the good news in Acts 4 resulted in about 5,000 men being saved.[12] This number was only men and did not include any women or children. It is often true that when there is an attempt to squash the gospel, that the Spirit of God causes an amazing expansion of people placing their trust in Christ.

After being arrested and questioned, Peter and John were released and found their way to the believers who were having a prayer meeting on their behalf. When the two apostles were reunited with the praying believers, they recounted to them all that had happened while in jail. The believers were so encouraged that prayer erupted again as they worshipped and made a grand request to God that they would have even more confidence to be bold for the gospel.[13]

In their corporate prayer, they asked the Lord to take note of the threats against them and to grant the believers the supernatural ability to speak the gospel with all confidence![14] These believers knew that proclaiming Christ would mean more confrontation and persecution, but the souls of people were more important than their comfort. Their prayers asked God to keep on allowing them to see healing, signs and wonders through the name of Jesus[15] despite the surrounding opposition. What would happen if we imitated this in our own lives?

When they had finished praying, *"...they were **all** filled with the Holy Spirit and began to speak the word of God with boldness." Acts 4:31(emphasis mine).*

As we think about sowing seeds of the gospel, notice that the Holy Spirit did not fill only the Apostles or evangelists but ALL the people! When we are filled with the Spirit, He saturates us so we can do things His way and for His purposes. When we surrender to the saturation of the Holy Spirit, one of the results will be a boldness to speak the truth.

Boldness to speak the truth is something God wants for all of His believers. We see this in Acts 1:8 when Jesus promised that when the Holy Spirit came on believers, that they would receive power to be a witness to the good news of Jesus. Power and boldness go together. Like those believers in the first century, we can ask God for His confidence and boldness to speak His word. Who knows what could happen!

The Gospel Expands

The spread of the gospel continues in Acts 5 with the story of Ananias and Sapphira who had lied to the Holy Spirit about money and were struck dead. This startling event caused a strong fear of God amongst the believers and all who heard about it.[16] Some probably stayed away from the believers, but many were drawn closer towards placing their trust in Jesus.

The Apostles performed many other signs and wonders among the people and there was a growing sense of unity as they met for worship and equipping. Because of all these wildfires being sparked, *"...more believers in the Lord, multitudes of men and women, were constantly added to their number..."* (Acts 5:14).

The impact of the gospel was gaining momentum. In Acts 2 and 4 we learned about 3,000 and 5,000 people being saved; by Acts 5, we read that there were "multitudes of men and women." There were so many that they could no longer be counted! Not only were large numbers of men and women saved, people *"...were constantly added to their number."* (Acts 5:14b). Just a few verses before, we learned that ALL of the believers were filled with the Spirit to speak the gospel boldly. These followers of Christ were active among the crowds communicating the message of Jesus to those who were seeing the signs and wonders performed by the Apostles. This is the mobilization of believers on many levels. The impact on Jerusalem was amazing at this point, but the wildfires was just starting! I imagine that the people of Jerusalem couldn't ignore what was happening among the brand–new believers.

From Addition to Multiplication

*"The word of God kept on spreading; and the number of disciples continued to increase greatly in Jerusalem, and a great many of the **priests** were becoming obedient to the faith." Acts 6:7 (emphasis mine)*

There are two important things to notice in the verse above. This is the first report we have that things had shifted from *addition* to *multiplication*. This is a significant shift. Up to this passage, all of the descriptive words had to do with addition and wider growth. In this passage, we see a more expansive growth. The spread of the gospel was so invasive that it could no longer be measured or tracked. It was also spreading beyond ordinary people. The religious leaders of the Jews were affected, and many of the priests placed their trust in Jesus Christ.[17]

Multiplication is always more rapid and expansive than addition. While addition is good, it is often manageable. When things begin to multiply exponentially, manageability is lost to the speed of the momentum.

The church today needs to get comfortable with a lack of manageability, so there is more space for multiplication. When we insist on micro–managing the church, we automatically limit growth. The more we try to control the church, the more we limit multiplication. When God is in control, all things are possible. When we look at the first–century church in Jerusalem, we see wildfires could not be controlled by the Apostles or by anyone. It could also no longer be ignored by the religious leaders of Jerusalem.

Beyond Jerusalem

Acts 6 begins with some logistical problems of food distribution in the church. Eventually, the believers prayed and chose seven godly men to be responsible for the daily distribution of food to the needy. We are introduced to Stephen, one of the believers in Jerusalem.

Stephen was one of the seven chosen to help manage the daily distribution of food. Acts 6:8 tells us that he was full of grace and power, and God had led him to perform some amazing miracles. This caused a confrontation with some of the Jewish religious leaders. As the religious leaders attempted to argue with Stephen they found themselves outwitted. This was not because of Stephen's intellectual ability. It was because they could not cope with the wisdom of the Spirit that was giving him the words to speak. Here is an example of the promise about being given words that no one could refute (Luke 21:12–15).

The seventh chapter of Acts records a long talk given by Stephen to the Jewish religious leaders about their need to place their trust in Jesus Christ. The power of the Spirit was so strong on Stephen in this encounter that all the Jewish leaders could do was to repent or to stubbornly fight. They chose to fight.

The end of Acts 7 tells the story of Stephen as he became the first recorded Christian martyr, stoned by the people around him. The Spirit and his love for the people was so strong that as the rocks dealt blows to his body he cried out, *"Lord Jesus, receive my spirit...Lord, do not hold this sin against them.* "[18] As he died, he imitated his Lord by using similar words to the ones Jesus used when He died on the cross. Jesus said, *"Father, forgive them; for they do not know what they are doing."* [19] May our lives imitate Jesus as Stephen's did! Are we willing to believe enough in eternity to tell the story of Jesus with boldness, no matter the risk? Or will we cling to our comfort and safety?

Everything that we have looked at about the gospel fire spreading from Acts 1–7 took place in Jerusalem. It was an amazing adventure of spiritual fires growing, expanding, adding and multiplying followers of Christ. It affected many levels of society.

If we think back to Acts 1:8 and Jesus' last words to his followers, He had clearly told them, "...but you will receive power when the Holy Spirit has come upon you; and you shall be My witnesses both in Jerusalem, and in all Judea and Samaria, and even to the remotest part of the earth." They, and all the people who placed their trust in Christ, would be witnesses for the gospel of Jesus Christ. Jesus was also clear that their being witnesses was to begin in Jerusalem and spread to Judea, Samaria and to the uttermost parts of the earth. Up to this point in Acts, only Jerusalem had been affected. It was time to move out to Judea and Samaria.

Acts 8 introduces the world to Saul of Tarsus, who later became the Apostle Paul and wrote much of the New Testament. But before he came to know Jesus personally, he hated Christians and set out to destroy them because they were threatening the Jewish religious system. As Stephen was stoned to death, Paul was watching and approved.[20]

Stephen's death marked the beginning of the anti–Christian movement in Jerusalem. It was such a broad and strong persecution that believers *"...were all scattered throughout the regions of Judea and Samaria..."* (Acts 8:1). The pressure was too strong for the believers to live freely in Jerusalem. We have already seen in Acts 4 that persecution of believers had a radical effect. Instead of persecution stopping the expansion of the gospel, it often caused the gospel to spread broader and faster.

And so, this expansion happened in Acts 8.

This may seem like the beginning of the end, but it was the only the beginning! Followers of Christ were forced out of Jerusalem and into the regions of Judea and Samaria, the same regions Jesus had mentioned in His instruction in Acts 1:8.

"Therefore, those who had been scattered went about preaching the word." Acts 8:4

Imagine packing up as many of your belongings that would fit in your car and taking off to live in places you had never been before. You would have no income, limited resources, and no place to stay. You would have to focus on survival, finding a way to make money, locating a place to sleep and eat. With all of those pressures, these displaced believers still *"...went about preaching the word." (Acts 8:4)*. Why is it that we don't follow this example of sharing the gospel wherever we are? Most of us live in comfort and safety but rarely share our faith. The Jerusalem believers had to focus on survival, and still they were completely committed to telling others about Jesus and His good news.

What we can learn from this story is that while we work, play or wash our car, we can always have the concern of God for His creation to hear the good news. We don't have to do more. We simply need to have God's heart for those around us and look for the chances that He creates for us in the moment.

In the passages we have looked at so far, the Apostles have played a very central role in seeing people come to Jesus. It would be easy to assume that without the Apostles, there would have been no rapid expansion of the church in Jerusalem. As we discussed in previous chapters, we often expect our modern pastors, deacons, and church staff to take responsibility for making new followers of Jesus. We find something very different and surprising in Acts 8.

*...they were <u>all scattered</u> throughout the regions of Judea and Samaria, **except the apostles.**" Acts 8:1 (emphasis mine)*

The apostles remained in Jerusalem while the other, 'ordinary' believers fled. That meant that the major growth of the church beyond Jerusalem was done without any of the Twelve Apostles! The word for apostles simply means "sent ones." The Bible gives them this title because they were _sent_ by Christ to start spiritual wildfires to the uttermost parts of the world.

It is ironic to note that in Acts 8:1, it was the common believers who spread the gospel to Judea and Samaria,[21] not the 'sent ones.' I believe God is making a strong yet subtle statement that He sees all of his followers as being sent. Since most people won't think they're sent, the apostle's job is to equip other believers to also identify as being sent.[22] Jesus wants to mobilize His army of saints to fearlessly and continuously spread the gospel.

Multiplying Communicators, Not Listeners

Many churches today think of evangelism as gathering larger groups of people in one place so they can hear a crafted message that invites people to place their trust in Christ. I'm all for these kinds of events but they do require a level of resources and expertise that most do not possess. The important issue is to not to be limited to one method, but that the gospel is spread by all believers.

Much of the evangelism we see in Acts 1–7 was in the context of preaching to large groups (Acts 2:41, 4:4, 5:14). We also see ordinary believers sharing the good news in relational ways resulting in expansion (Acts 2:44–47, 4:32–35, 5:42). However, things changed after Acts 8 to a more *decentralized* movement of people into the world to live out and speak for the way of Christ.

The pattern we see throughout the rest of Acts and in the New Testament is that ordinary people are usually the ones through whom the gospel is spread.

Apostles and missionaries often spearheaded new efforts, but ordinary believers spread the most wildfires. This is a huge contrast to our modern western church, where many believers feel incompetent to share their faith. We rely on large group settings and church meetings to share the gospel of Jesus. This takes us back to Jerusalem and a centralized form of evangelism which is not evil, but certainly not as powerful or influential. It has caused the church to be stagnant rather than expanding. The effectiveness of programs and events is waning, but we still feel dependent on them as the main source of evangelism.

While gathering people to a location to hear the gospel is good, sending people out to impact their surroundings is best. Any time we can multiply the number of communicators, more people will be engaged with the gospel message. *God has given every believer everything they need to be effective at sharing the Gospel.*[23] *The church needs to equip believers to understand that the Bible teaches that they are able to communicate eternal truth adequately.*[24]

We repent all the time in different ways. We repent when we realize we have some habit that needs to be changed, or when we are convicted about our spending habits. *Repent* is a good, healthy and maturing word. Repentance means that we are acknowledging that some of our ways are not in step with Jesus' ways of doing things. When this is true, we simply agree with Jesus and change, following His ways, instructions and invitations. That is repentance; an internal resolve to turn from a sinful direction and to align with Jesus' direction. Our dependence on professional evangelists and church programs is something we need to carefully consider; is this an area we need to repent of as well?

When we equip and send out masses of believers to share the gospel naturally, every corner of society is touched. Most people honestly would not be interested in visiting a large group to hear a talk given by someone they have never met. Those same people, however, would enjoy having a drink with a friend and talking about life. If we are that friend, we can be the light of the gospel to them in our words and actions. This is mobilization; *when a lot of people do a little, much is accomplished.*

In Acts 8, rapid multiplication began as persecution scattered the believers. Philip was one of those who were forced out of Jerusalem by persecution. Like Stephen, he had been one of the seven chosen to distribute the food fairly in Acts 6. We read that

Philip made his way to Samaria, where he was preaching and performing signs and wonders. There was much rejoicing in that city.[25] After Philip and his companions had spoken the word of Jesus to many villages in Samaria, they were headed back to Jerusalem, their home town.[26]

Philip and his companions trusted the Holy Spirit to keep the message pure and reproducing in Samaria, even though they were brand new followers of Jesus. They had seen many amazing spiritual events, from physical healings to personal salvations. I imagine they were homesick by that point. As they set off to return to Jerusalem, God again moved to keep the expansion of the gospel going.

An angel of the Lord spoke to Philip and told him to go south to the road from Jerusalem to Gaza.[27] We are not told how long Philip traveled, or if he knew why God wanted him to be on that road, but at some point, he encountered an Ethiopian eunuch in a chariot. This eunuch was a court official and treasurer of Candace, the queen of the Ethiopians. The eunuch was returning from Jerusalem where he had been worshipping.[28] A conversation with a person of this caliber could be intimidating, but it could also impact Ethiopia's royalty.

Philip may have noticed this dignitary reading a scroll, but he likely had no way of knowing what the eunuch was reading or who he was. He might have guessed that the eunuch was important, based on the chariot and possible guards. In Acts 8:29 we read, *"Then the Spirit said to Philip, 'Go up and join this chariot."* If there were any bodyguards or soldiers, running up to the chariot of a dignitary without invitation could be seen as a threat. Philip obeyed anyway.

By then, Philip at least had an idea of why the Holy Spirit had sent him to the desert road. As he approached the chariot, he heard the eunuch reading out loud from the book of Isaiah. This encounter lead to a conversation about Jesus.

> *[34] The eunuch answered Philip and said,*
> *"Please tell me, of whom does the prophet say*
> *this? Of himself or of someone else?" [35] Then*

Philip opened his mouth, and beginning from
this Scripture he preached Jesus to him. ³⁶ As
they went along the road they came to some
water; and the eunuch said, "Look! Water!
What prevents me from being baptized?" ³⁷
[And Philip said, "If you believe with all your
heart, you may." And he answered and said, "I
believe that Jesus Christ is the Son of God."] ³⁸
And he ordered the chariot to stop; and they
both went down into the water, Philip as well as
the eunuch, and he baptized him. Acts 8:34–38

This is another reminder for us to be sensitive to the Spirit's
leading and follow His pull on our hearts. When we do obey, we
will move people towards Christ. When we do not obey, we will
never know how the Spirit wanted to use us. The more we obey,
the stronger and more rapid our response will be. Obedience
leads to a maturing in our ability to recognize the Spirit and a
boldness to follow through, even when our plans are suddenly
changed like those of Phillip.

God wants to multiply communicators of the gospel. Because
of Philip's obedience, the gospel message moved to another
country, which is a partial fulfillment of Acts 1:8 to the uttermost
parts of the world! If the Ethiopian eunuch had traveled to
Jerusalem to worship, I imagine that he loved the God of the Old
Testament. On that desert road, he learned about salvation
through Jesus Christ and was baptized. We can only wonder
about the conversations he had with his queen and others when he
returned.

As soon as the eunuch emerged from the waters of baptism,
Philip was "snatched" away by the Spirit and miraculously found
himself in the city of Azotus.[29] Although I think he would have
been even more homesick by then, Philip kept on preaching the
gospel in all the cities he traveled through on his way to Caesarea,[30]
which is not on the way back to Jerusalem.

God multiplied communicators throughout Samaria and
Ethiopia and fulfilled His prophecy,[31] and the wildfires kept
expanding! *Sometimes the spreading of the gospel is more in*

beginning wildfires than how far they spread. The results, as we learned earlier, are up to God. Our role, responsibility and privilege, is to start spiritual wildfires, follow the Spirit's prompting, and trust that God will take care of changing hearts for His glory!

Multiplication of Churches

As more communicators launched out to spread the good news of Christ, different levels of impact and multiplication were reached. By Acts 9, we read that there were several thousand 'ordinary' people displaced from Jerusalem because of persecution. As they settled into new places, they became missionaries to the world, spreading the gospel truth. The momentum was unstoppable.

Early in Acts 9, Saul of Tarsus became a follower of Jesus Christ on the road to Damascus and immediately began to proclaim Christ.[32] One pattern we see is that people who come to Christ in the book of Acts immediately share what Christ had done for them. Of course, this describes the experience of the believers of Acts, and is not necessarily a command for all believers. That being said, when we see a pattern like this in the Bible, we should ask if our contemporary experience is different, and why. Why do we not encourage new believers to share the gospel widely and wildly? When and why did we start to think that new believers are not capable of sharing the gospel on their own?

> *"So the church throughout all Judea and Galilee and Samaria enjoyed peace, being built up; and going on in the fear of the Lord and in the comfort of the Holy Spirit, it continued to increase." Acts 9:31*

By this time, the church had jumped into Judea and even Galilee! Acts 1:8 was being fulfilled. It's important to remember that the Apostles were still in Jerusalem at that point.[33] The multiplication of disciples happening in Judea, Samaria and beyond (Galilee and Ethiopia) were all accomplished by 'ordinary' believers. In other words, ordinary people were making disciples and trusting the Holy Spirit to mature them, fulfilling the prophecy by Jesus in Acts 1:8. This pattern evolved as ordinary believers took the initiative to openly share their love for Jesus and His gospel.

In Acts 9:31, we learned that churches were multiplying. No longer are we talking about individuals multiplying but churches. This multiplication was taking place in many regions. When the ordinary followers of Christ are empowered, decentralized, and released into their communities from the beginning, they are a powerful force for Jesus!

Wherever the gospel goes and is shared fearlessly, we see wildfires emerging. As the story of Acts continues, the scattered believers continued to spread out and make disciples. This resulted in more new churches emerging. Acts 11:19 informs us that the gospel reached Phoenicia, Cyprus and Antioch. In Acts chapter 2–10, we read about Jewish believers from Jerusalem sharing the good news with other Jews in these areas.[34] That was about to change.

> *"20 But there were some of them, men of Cyprus and Cyrene, who came to Antioch and began speaking to the Greeks also, preaching the Lord Jesus. 21 And the hand of the Lord was with them, and a large number who believed turned to the Lord...and considerable numbers were brought to the Lord." Acts 11:20-21, 24b*

These believers made a radical change; they broke away from only witnessing to the Jews and began to cross ethnic lines to share with Gentiles (non-Jews). We can gather from this verse that believers (ordinary believers, not apostles) planted the first Gentile church. Cross–cultural missions broke out and the mobilization of ordinary people played a large part in this new breakthrough.

> *"5 So the **churches** were being strengthened in the faith, and were **increasing in number daily**...19 After he had greeted them, be began to relate one by one the things which God had done among the Gentiles through his ministry. 20 And when they heard it they began glorifying God; and they said to him, 'You see, brother, how **many thousands** there are among the Jews of those who have*

believed, and they are all zealous for the Law...'" Acts 16:5, 21:19-20 (emphasis mine)

In this last excerpt from Acts, we learn that churches multiplied and many thousands[35] of Jews came to know the Lord. This report did not include the Gentiles that placed their faith in Christ. All of this happened because the ordinary believers took seriously the truth that Jesus Christ gives eternal life to any who will trust Him for it. These new believers understood it was their responsibility to actively and regularly share that truth.

God wants every believer and every community of believers to be fruitful. Jesus wants His church to thrive![36] When lots of seeds are sown in good soil, we see good harvests springing up. We need to empower, release and decentralize believers to go into the world under the Holy Spirit's direction. A faithful sower + good seed + good soil = a large harvest. The Holy Spirit in us is our source of power!

God's Power, Plan and Program

God's **power** is at work when the Holy Spirit fills believers. As we rely on Him to guide us and give us the approach and the words to speak, we will be successful every time.

God's **plan** is to use every believer to be a witness for Jesus Christ in unique and natural ways. When believers understand how God freely equips us, we will become more fruitful and impact generations to come.

God's **program** is to see the gospel spread throughout the whole earth. We can begin locally, but our vision needs to include the world. God may send you to a foreign land or He may bring people from foreign lands into your life. We must pray beyond our "Jerusalem" to the whole world because that is the heart of God.

God wants His people to fulfill His prophecy of reaching the whole world. This task is not limited to a few gifted ones but is done best when a lot of people do a little. The book of Acts clearly shows that God uses ordinary people to impact whole countries,[37] individuals,[38] religious leaders[39] and all parts of society. God wants to use you and me to continue spreading His gospel and fulfilling His prophecy.[40]

The key to being fruitful is multiplication as opposed to addition. Addition requires a gifted few to spread the gospel by multiplying listeners. Multiplication requires a lifting of control and allows the wildfire of souls to spread without limits.

We have to encourage risk in sharing the gospel. We can trust the Holy Spirit, more than our education or experience, to keep the integrity of the message. When believers feel free to creatively share the gospel, it can spread through levels of society beyond where a typical church or evangelist can reach.

The church in the book of Acts exploded throughout the known world in a short burst of 30 years. Today Christianity struggles to expand in many parts of the world. In the first century, there was heavy persecution in many areas where the gospel went. Today, persecution continues heavily in some areas but in the Western world, most persecution is limited.

We have many more resources than the church of the first century had (internet, printed material, audio material, easy travel, more money, more people etc.). *And yet we see much less ground being taken by the gospel than 2,000 years ago.*

So, what is the reason for this lack of expansion? If we have better resources and the same marching orders with the same Holy Spirit, what is the problem? I think the problem begins with me...and you!

Let's keep exploring what it might look like to share the gospel as we go through life. When we follow the Spirit's lead, we see the oxygen increasing around the wildfires, causing it to roar and bring more souls into the Kingdom of God.

PART 3 - WILDFIRES NEED OXYGEN

The Wind –the Holy Spirit, blows wherever He pleases (John 3:8) and we should follow Him to experience the power of His passion. The Holy Spirit provides the fresh air needed to empower ordinary people to fight forward in the battle for souls. As we learn to leave our agendas behind and follow the Wind, the wildfire will spread until the whole world hears of our great King and we meet Him face to face.

CHAPTER 7: FOLLOW THE SPIRIT

"The Wind blows wherever it pleases." John 3:8

I burst through the laundry room door into the garage and raced to the car. Backing out of the driveway, I noticed Jim and Sarah in my rear–view mirror walking hand in hand down the street. After navigating around the basketball pole and the trash can by the curb, I put my car in drive and stepped on the gas pedal. As my eyes moved to the end of our street, preparing to turn right, I saw Sarah and Jim waving at me. In that split second, I remembered that Jim started chemo this week to treat his brain cancer. For him to be out walking was impressive. I noticed Jim and Sarah were not just greeting me; they were trying to flag me down to talk. I stopped, surrendered my plan to the Holy Spirit and opened the window.

"Hey Ed, how are you doing?"

"I'm fine. How are you?"

I listened as they told me about Jim's chemo progress, latest MRI results, and treatment plan. Then came the question they had been wanting to ask, "We will be celebrating our 25th anniversary in a couple months. We were wondering if you would be willing to renew our vows in our home?"

Jim and Sarah knew that I love Jesus, but they had not seemed very interested in spiritual conversations. I was amazed. God was opening the door to a deeper friendship and the opportunity to have eternal discussions as we planned for their renewal ceremony. I had been caught up in my plans, but the Spirit of

God had a different agenda. This one conversation became a defining moment in our friendship that led to many spiritual discussions about Jesus, the Holy Spirit, and eternal life.

God does have a sense of humor. I was in a hurry and He wanted to slow me down. Listening to the voice of God and following the Spirit is more important than accomplishing what seems urgent at the time. Too often I find myself handcuffed to agendas I've created, instead of loosely holding them in my hand for Jesus to rearrange. Following the Spirit is a lesson that I learn over and over.

Jim battled brain cancer valiantly, but the cancer won in the end. A few months after his death, Sarah asked me to organize a memorial service. It was a holy event, held in their home with dozens of friends and family, some who had witnessed their vow renewal a few months earlier. I was able to share with the group about the spiritual conversations between Jim and I.

A few weeks after the memorial, a few family members and close friends invited me to the mountains to spread Jim's ashes. During the hours we spent in the car together, the gospel was shared as questions were asked about life after death. The spiritual conversations with the family members continue.

My interaction with Jim and Sarah was a supernatural event, led by the wind of the Holy Spirit. Conversations about Jesus are always God–inspired events.

I was not focused on Jesus when Jim and Sarah flagged me down to talk. I was not thinking about sharing Jesus or even praying about sharing Jesus. I was on an errand that was unimportant in light of eternity, but God was creating an opportunity. From a human perspective, I was not ready for talking about Jesus or following the Spirit. God knew I was not "in the game" on that day, yet He created a window of opportunity for me.

God wants to develop our sensitivity to the Holy Spirit so we will follow His nudges into situations and conversations to share His gospel. Following the Spirit is a discipline that few people seem to practice, or even talk about. Following the Spirit is certainly a spiritual art form; the more we practice it, the more comfortable we become.

One way of developing our sensitivity to the Spirit is simply to repeat what we think the Holy Spirit is saying to us in any given conversation that is focused on sharing the good news. As we develop this spiritual art form of listening and repeating, it's important to test these thoughts with the Scriptures.

All of this hearing from the Spirit and testing what we hear against the Bible happens internally and often in flashes of time. The more familiar we are with the Scriptures, the easier this becomes. Practicing these suggestions over time makes the art form of hearing from the Spirit more natural.

As we saw in the last chapter, relying on the Spirit of God is crucial to being fruitful. We saw how the Spirit filled believers to proclaim the gospel, changed their agenda so they would follow His, and allowed persecution so the gospel would spread.

The same happens today, and, in each situation, His intention is to help us learn. He wants us to follow His voice as our default mode, especially when it comes to evangelism. My default mode in sharing the gospel is an approach that I am comfortable with or that I have used in the past.

Many believers have a default mode of rarely speaking the good news to others; they expect professional pastors and leaders to do the real work of evangelism. In contrast, the default mode of believers should be a strong dependence on God to lead us into relationships with not–yet–believers.

We should expect and even want God to give us the approach and words to use in conversations about the good news of Christ. This default mode is not just for young, zealous believers; it is for everyone. When a variety of people, from new believers to seasoned veterans, begins to hear the voice of the Spirit for themselves and follow it, something unique begins to emerge corporately.

A Corporate Evangelism Story

A few years ago, I was involved in a house church that has

since multiplied several times. Two of our families had sons on the local high school's wrestling team. Over time, our house church adopted the wrestling team as a place to serve together. We wanted to be an encouragement to the team, the parents and the coaching staff. Our goal was to actively share our excitement for the team and to show the love of Christ in tangible ways.

One of the moms in our house church, who had a gift for organization, became the team mom. I had wrestled in high school so I volunteered to help the coaching staff. Others in our house church prayed for the team and coaching staff, and came to cheer at the wrestling matches and tournaments. Everyone in our church helped out with various tasks of hospitality, providing rides for some of the wrestlers, or keeping score during tournaments.

The Spirit of God led some people to sit in the stands and develop relationships with parents, others felt more comfortable connecting to the wrestlers. Others helped out with the high school girls that kept the score. I hosted the team at my home a few times during the season; we provided pizza, had a party, and I shared some thoughts from the Scriptures. Throughout that season, we all contributed a little and were proud of "our team" whether they won or lost. When a lot of people do a little, much is accomplished!

A sense of family developed, and we saw several young men place their trust in Christ. A few of the parents from the team joined us in prayer for the team and became more engaged with the behind–the–scene organization. The family of one of the wrestlers became part of our house church on a regular basis. The wife of this family placed her trust in Jesus, then both of her children, and today many of her grandchildren now have a relationship with Christ.

Following the lead of the Spirit brings unity, teamwork and a multifaceted approach to bringing the good news of Christ to people on various levels. These events happened several years ago but the fruit of that investment continues today with the head coach and many of the wrestlers and their families.

Hearing the voice of God requires an ongoing, intentional development of a relationship with Christ. As our relationship with Jesus deepens, our sensitivity to the voice of God is heightened and our obedience to His voice becomes quickened.

Remember that as we draw near to Jesus and follow Him, our relationships with others will also grow. Friendships with not–yet–believers are the natural result of becoming closer to Christ. I believe that a person who claims to be close to God but does not have many friends who are not–yet–believers has to question how close to God they actually are! To put it another way, can we be close to God but not engaged with not–yet–believers?

Throughout the New Testament, we read a variety of stories where whole cities, families, and regions were affected by the good news of Jesus. These levels of impact are only possible as we develop a sensitivity to two areas; the needs of the community and voice of God.

The Needs of the Community

If we want to know the needs of a community, we need to have a relationship with people in it, whether they seem near or far from the Kingdom of God. We have to be good listeners to hear their pain and see their needs. Then we can see chances to shine the light of Christ into those situations.

One way to do this is to find ways to cheer on accomplishments. Many people are hungry for recognition in our competitive, self–serving world. When you speak encouragement to a thirsty soul, you can see the light go on in their heart. Encouraging people is an easy way to spread the love of God to the others. As you train your soul to hear the voice of the Spirit, words of insight and encouragement will flow[1] to you from the Lord. God can use these for small and large breakthroughs for current and future conversations. God is about drawing the listener close to His heart and He wants to walk with you to reach out to them.

As I shared in earlier chapters, God nudged me to hang out with my son at a local cigar lounge called Fair Oaks. As I visited Fair Oaks, I talked with men who seemed to be there every day.

One day I was relaxing in the nearly–empty lounge, when I noticed Steve and said hi. Steve put down his phone and looked straight at me and said, "There's a rumor about you going around."

Surprised, I asked,

"Oh yeah? I hope it's a juicy one."

"Rumor is that you are a preacher."

I smiled.

"Well, I do help lead a network of house churches."

Still staring at me, Steve said,

"What in the he*l is a preacher doing in a cigar shop?"

That was exactly why God wanted me to be there, I thought.

"I enjoy cigars," was my response to Steve.

As Steve and I got to know each other better, I learned that his father was a preacher and Steve wanted little to do with the church. His life was fine without it, he said. In the ensuing months, I had other conversations with Steve about Jesus, faith and living for God. The movement in Steve's heart seems slow to me, but I know that my love and conversations with him has an eternal affect that will only be fully measured in the future. It is always the right time to love. It is always the right time to engage others in conversations; following the lead of the Holy Spirit to nudge others towards choosing to follow Jesus.

In my conversations with some of the men at Fair Oaks, I've discovered that I'm not the only Christian–or the only pastor, who hangs out there. I am praying with several of them for the hearts and souls of the men there who do not know Jesus. We have begun a few discipleship groups and have seen many men begin a journey to Christ while others are reconnecting to Him.

Several believers have organized breakfasts on Sunday mornings during the football season. Our purpose is to serve and love these guys in tangible ways. We want them to know that we are serious about living out our faith in their midst. The network of house churches that I am a part of regularly prays for the men at Fair Oaks. Several of the men from our network now visit Fair Oaks, which means more chances to make a difference and encourage our new friends there to know Jesus.

You can learn a lot about people at any place where the only agenda is to relax and interact. One day I found myself sitting in a circle of chairs talking with some men as we glanced at our phones and tablets. One man mentioned that Chad had had a liver transplant. A bit later, my son told me that Chad had told him a very spiritual story about his transplant. Chad was hoping to talk to me about his story too. What was God up to?

"Hey Ed, I have a story to tell you. You will not believe it!" I was standing at the cash register at Fair Oaks when I heard Chad's voice. Chad paid for his 'stick' (cigar), cut it and lit it. Before he told me the details of his story, he said he was nervous that I would think he was out of his mind. I assured him that I had heard many supernatural stories and had experiences myself that some would think impossible. As we settled into the deep brown chairs, Chad began to tell me his story.

In his twenties, he contracted Hepatitis C after being pricked with a dirty needle someone had left in a couch at a house he was visiting. Chad had never used drugs in his life but learned years later that he had contracted the liver–killing disease.

Several months after receiving his first liver transplant, Chad was back to work and playing golf. Life was good again for him. He was feeling healthy, but the Hepatitis in his body was silently taking over again. He became more and more sick, until doctors placed him on a new liver transplant list.

Chad's wife was driving him down a freeway when he received a call from the hospital where he was getting care, informing him that they had a new liver for him. He had to make his way to the hospital immediately. As he met with the doctor, he learned the news that the liver he was to receive had sclerosis. "What would you do, if you were in my place?" Chad asked the doctor. "You've only got a short time left," the doctor said. "I would take it, if I was you."

Without this transplant, his life expectancy was months, not years. After thinking it over, Chad agreed to receive the liver with sclerosis…but he never did receive that liver. During one of the last tests for compatibility, the team decided it was not the perfect match for Chad so the surgery was cancelled. There were no options left.

In a miraculous move of God, another liver became available to him before he had even left the hospital. As he lay in his hospital bed in severe pain, Chad told me of an out of body episode he experienced. He found himself floating to the ceiling of his hospital room. As he looked around the room, every inch of the walls was covered with the heads of bald men, gnashing and grinding their teeth. Worried, he tried to convince himself that he had lived a good life and was a good person. Certainly, a good person like him was not headed towards hell.

As his panic rose, he looked back down and saw a man in a white gown standing over his body. He saw Him wave his hand over his body from toe to head and heard a voice tell him he would be fine. The next thing Chad knew, he was awake in a hospital bed, in recovery from the transplant. He was able to be put on a trial drug for Hepatitis C, and by the time he told me the story, it had been years since his transplant. "And now I'm as healthy as ever," he finished. The hepatitis was gone from his body.

Chad looked at me and said he had told very few people about his experience. "You are a preacher, Ed," Chad said to me. "What do you make of that experience?" What a wide–open door to share the love and grace of the gospel!

After our conversation, Chad said he did believe that the person who waved his hand over his body was Jesus and that he wanted to put his trust in Christ. He certainly did not want to end up in the hell the bald men were beckoning him towards. Chad and I have had an ongoing conversation that includes following Jesus, golf, and cigars. He has joined a few of us in spiritual discussions and is searching for deeper ways to connect to God. It has been a slow process, but I and other believers at the church at Fair Oaks are praying for his spiritual journey.

Chad said he shared his experience with my son and me because he knows we are men who love Jesus. We in turn encouraged Chad to tell others his story, and he told us that we could share it as well. Chad knows Jesus is the one who saved his life and I believe Christ is nudging Chad into deeper fellowship with Him. I can walk with him on his faith journey because I have taken the risk of becoming part of the Fair Oaks family, and because I wanted to be his friend and listen to his story.

How can you find ways to engage with not–yet–believers and listen to the needs of your community? I suggest making a list and brainstorming ways you and other believers can hang out with people the way Jesus did. *This doesn't mean you need to do more; it means you can do things differently.*

If you like coffee, show up at your local coffee house and meet new people. If you become a 'regular' by showing up frequently, or visiting around the same time or day, it will be easier to fall into conversations with people there. If you like to jog or hike, join a local club or meet up with new friends. If you like to watch sporting events, hang out at a local sports bar and cheer on your team. The idea is to use your passions and gifts to connect with your community, not add more to your schedule. You will be a breath of fresh air to your environments and have a positive impact. This is what new believers did in the book of Acts. They connected with their community, met needs, and the Lord gave them fresh opportunities!

> *"...and they began selling their property and possessions and were sharing them with all, as anyone might have need...having favor with all the people. And the Lord was adding to their number day by day those who were being saved." Acts 2:45 & 47*

We can't meet the needs of people around us when we don't know their needs. The people in our neighborhoods and workplaces are stressed and hurting. They deal with financial pressures, relational pressures, work related pressures, familial pressures, emotional pressures, identity pressures. When we share a cup of coffee or a chat by the mailbox, God may open doors for us to make a difference. We just have to be willing.

The Voice of God

The second area where believers need to become more sensitive is to the voice of God. For many, the subject of the voice of God is a touchy one. I want to be clear that I firmly believe that the Scriptures (all sixty–six books) are the inspired, infallible, and final authority on faith and practice from God to His creation.[2] We are told not to add to or take away from the Scriptures.[3] But God still speaks today to His children in everyday life. He guides us through the indwelling of the Holy Spirit to engage the world. He gives us spiritual gifts, as well as the words and actions to be successful in sharing the gospel.[4]

As we identify the needs of our community, it's crucial to listen to the voice of God if we want to move beyond our own intellect and abilities and flow with His. Too many people trust in their own ideas of how to present the gospel instead of depending on the Lord to direct them. God knows what each person needs to hear, and what they need to hear is His Spirit that lives in us as believers. The connection between God's insight and our hearts makes evangelism simple.

Here are four factors to think about when we want to understand the voice of God.

The Sense of His Presence (The Voice of God; Factor #1)

In previous chapters, I have spent some time sharing the reciprocal equation between loving God and sharing His message. The more we love Jesus, the more we will share His message and the more we share His message the more we will love Him. This continues to be vital throughout our lives. There is no short–cut to a deep fellowship with Christ; time for prayer, Bible reading and study are vital.

It is also important to train and discipline ourselves to go through our days asking Jesus to give us His eyes for what is happening around us. We may feel a nudge to pray for a co–worker who looks stressed, or to ask the person in front of us in a line how their day is going. This may end up encouraging a person or be the beginning to a new friendship. God uses these small adjustments in our attitudes and actions to help us align

148

more with His heart or to start spiritual wildfires when we connect with people God leads across our path.

When you are tempted to make a snarky comment to a co–worker, what goes on in your head? Do you take the idea to Jesus and ask Him what to do? Do you just blurt out what is rolling around in your mind? Do you think about why snarky or negative comments may be quick to jump through your mouth? When someone offends you, do you choose to give the cold shoulder or a glare? Or do you say, aloud or silently, "I forgive you"? The answer may lie in your default mode. Is your default mode your own sense of what is needed, or it is a surrender to what Christ *knows* is needed? Having a default mode that is full of God's presence will make a radical difference.

When I think of believers who were full of God's presence, I think of Stephen, a believer in the New Testament, and one of the chosen seven of Acts 6. The Scripture describes Stephen as a man full of faith and of the Holy Spirit, and full of grace and power.[5] We also learn that when Stephen was confronted by religious leaders about his message and the miracles he was performing, they were unable to answer the wisdom in his words.[6] Stephen was following the Spirit and the Spirit was speaking through Him just as Jesus promised.[7] At the end of Acts 6 verse 15 we read about Stephen, *"And fixing their gaze on him, all who were sitting in the Council saw his face like the face of an angel."* God's presence was obvious through the words Stephen spoke, as well as in the way he looked and acted when on trial.

A few chapters earlier, in Acts 4, Peter and John had also been arrested and were confronted by the priests and high council. Peter, filled with the Spirit,[8] spoke boldly to this prestigious group. When he was done presenting the gospel to the Jewish leaders, they couldn't believe the confidence these uneducated and untrained men had. It was obvious to everyone there that they had been with Jesus despite their lack of credentials or spiritual training.[9]

When our hearts default to Jesus' way of doing things, our lives will also be obviously different. When we love and forgive instead of hate and hold grudges, people are inspired. When we are kind and humble instead of bragging and prideful, people are intrigued. As we become more and more like Jesus, our lives shine like a city on a hill.[10]

Certainly, living like Jesus may also bring persecution, misunderstandings, or even anger. Peter reminds us that not everyone is attracted to the ways of Christ. Here is how Peter wrote about this,

> [13] *Who is there to harm you if you prove zealous for what is good?* [14] *But even if you should suffer for the sake of righteousness, you are blessed. And do not fear their intimidation, and do not be troubled,* [15] *but sanctify Christ as Lord in your hearts, always being ready to make a defense to everyone who asks you to give an account for the hope that is in you, yet with gentleness and reverence;* [16] *and keep a good conscience so that in the thing in which you are slandered, those who revile your good behavior in Christ will be put to shame.* [17] *For it is better, if God should will it so, that you suffer for doing what is right rather than for doing what is wrong.* 1 Peter 3:13–17

The Value of the Present (The Voice of God; Factor #2)

What is happening right now in your life is most important. When it comes to following the Spirit, many people are stuck in the pain or glory of yesterday, or, they may be dreaming about what could happen in the future.[11] As we have learned, the Spirit guarantees to give us the what and the how of evangelism in the moment of the encounter. This should alert us to be living in the present.

Valuing the present is not a very Western characteristic. In our Western culture, we often spend our days racing off to the next meeting or event. We lose the value of the right now too easily. People and events around us are only objects blocking our forward progress to the next event. This cultural habit affects our ability to follow the Spirit. God may want to begin a spiritual wildfire right where you are, but you may miss it if you are too focused on where you are headed or the pain from your past.

Recently, I boarded a plane, headed to a week–long writing retreat and I wanted to get started on the plane to maximize my time away. But after my experience with Dr. Laura (chapter 4), I wanted to be open for conversations with the people around me. I had a window seat, and a man in his forties moved into the seat next to me. As we settled into our seats, my seat partner put on his headphones, turned on his tablet and began watching a movie. I had wanted to introduce myself and at least say hello, but he was quick to get isolated, surrounded by the hundreds of people on the plane.

As soon as the plane hit 10,000 feet, I pulled out my laptop, put in my own headphones and began writing. Every now and then I would glance over to my seatmate, hoping to begin a conversation but it never seemed to be the right time. In all honesty, I was glad for the opportunity to work and not have to talk ...but I also wanted to experience the value the present of this seat assignment. I had a feeling that God was up to something and I needed to keep my spiritual ears open to His nudges.

After landing and arriving at the gate, the seat belt sign went dim and everyone began to deplane. At this point, I assumed I had either missed an opportunity or my spiritual intuition was way off. The man seated next to me pulled down a bag from the over–head compartment that said, "Ehler's Estate Wines."

My cousin worked for that company in Napa Valley, California for several years and I wondered how this man was connected. Or had the bag just been a gift? As we waited in the aisle, I said, "Can I ask where you got your bag?" "Oh, I work at Ehler's Estate," he answered. "My cousin Maria works there, do you know her?" It turned out that he did. We exchanged names and chatted for a while on our way off the plane. We even asked the flight attendant to take a picture of us. I sent it to Maria who couldn't believe the coincidence...or was it a coincidence? Did I miss out on a prime opportunity to live in the moment by focusing on my writing? Was the nudging of my heart to connect with this man just a habit, or was it the Holy Spirit?

As I said goodbye my new acquaintance Armand, I told him I would be in Napa next year and we agreed that maybe we could meet up for dinner some time. Several days later, in the middle of my writing retreat, I needed a change of scenery and some good coffee. I drove from where I was staying to the other side of the city and found a new coffee shop where I could sit and write.

After finishing a paragraph, I looked up and there was Armand, looking at coffee mugs, waiting for his drink. I could hardly believe my eyes. How was it possible, in a city this big, to meet the same person I sat next to on a flight a few days earlier? I greeted Armand and he almost jumped out of his skin. "How funny that we are in the same place at the same time!" we agreed. The value of the present is a mindset that takes time to develop especially for those of us who live a fast–paced life. Developing a regular practice of being aware that God is constantly active in our lives allows us to have one finger on the pause button for the encounters God creates around us. I believe this sensitivity caused me to look up and notice Armand instead of continuing to press the letters on my computer's keyboard.

I sensed in my soul that God was up to something, but I didn't know exactly what the next step looked like. I responded to our bumping into each other by saying, "I guess God must really want us to be friends." Armand only smiled.

We chatted about traveling for business and how much he flies each year. He commented that when he flies, he would often give up his seat to help another couple sit closer together. He said it was good karma for him! He then mentioned that my cousin, Maria had texted him about our meeting. She told him that I traveled some internationally. I told him I was on a writing retreat, believing he would ask me what I was writing about so I could tell him about Jesus, but he remained silent.

Armand needed to leave for a dinner engagement so we started to say our goodbyes. Then the Spirit of God whispered to my soul that now was the time. *"What should I say?"* I asked God. *"Ask, 'Is there anything I can pray for you about?'"* was God's response to my soul. I repeated the question to Armand, and the look of surprise on his face told me he was not very spiritual. He

152

stammered a bit and said that there wasn't anything to pray about because his life was so good that he needed nothing. I sensed the Spirit of God telling me to let his own statement hang in his mind. I shook his hand and just said I looked forward to dinner in Napa in a few months.

There is no right way or best way to discipline yourself to be more alert to the value of the present. One easy way to begin is to take a five or ten–minute walk around your neighborhood, park, mall or work environment and just be alert to the Spirit's promptings. You do not need to act on them, just begin to notice them. When you see someone, look into their eyes for a moment and offer up a prayer for their soul. As you pray, listen in your spirit for the Spirit of God to nudge you with words and interactions. Don't feel pressured to act on all the nudges, but be aware of them. This simple exercise primes your spiritual ears to be aware that God is speaking, and that He does care about the people around you. He wants you to enjoy the process of inviting them to take one more step down the road of knowing Him in simple, natural ways on your part.

Being aware and alert to the promptings of the Spirit is something you would not want to miss. It brings adventure into your faith. I find myself driving down the street, talking to the Spirit. I ask Him if I need to stop and talk to anyone in particular, or if I should stop and help a person fixing a flat tire. Even now I'm sitting on a beach writing and asking God if He wants me to strike up a conversation with someone. It is not every time, nor all the time, that He nudges me. But when it is the time to speak, it is a joy to know that I was obedient and God was working out His eternal purpose in that interaction

> *"1 Therefore if you have been raised up with Christ, keep seeking the things above, where Christ is, seated at the right hand of God. 2 Set your mind on the things above, not on the things that are on earth. 3 For you died and your life is hidden with Christ in God." (Colossians 3:1-3)*

Here, the Apostle Paul is clear that the focus of every believer's life is to set our minds on things of Christ. It is too easy to get our priorities reversed. The pressures and priorities of the world hold top position in our lives, while spiritual disciplines often take a minor role. Work and commitments win out over being open to the value of the present. We certainly need to do our work with all our effort, but keeping our spiritual minds and ears open to God is crucial if we want to see wildfires spread.

The Dimension of Friendship (The Voice of God; Factor #3)

When we look at stories throughout the New Testament, we see that many of the evangelism moments flow out of invitation or relationship. Modern–day evangelism is often explained as a process to get people to abandon what they believe in short conversations with little relationship. The church seems, as a whole, to be retreating from relationships with people who are different than they are. When a more mechanical evangelism is the norm, coupled with this expectation that a 'good believer' looks a certain way, you have a perfect recipe for a stagnation of souls. Our souls long for adventures.

Many approach evangelism by listening for what someone believes, then immediately arguing against those beliefs and stating that Jesus is the only way. While Jesus is the only way, it's important to respect others, since they are made in God's image. We can do this by developing a relationship and opposing any wrong beliefs they may have as God directs. The following examples of evangelism in the Bible seem to be lacking relationships: Philip and Ethiopian eunuch (Acts 8:26–40) or Jesus' interaction with demoniac of Mark 5 or even Paul and Silas witnessing to the Philippian jailor which began by their worship songs in prison and then through conversation (Acts 16:25–40). But even in these examples of 'stranger evangelism' in the Bible, there was some kind of request from the non–believers to hear about the good news of Christ.

Helping our friends to understand the good news of Jesus happens over time, over coffee and in the flow of relationship. I fully understand the passion to move people from where they are to placing their trust in Jesus quickly, but not many things in life happen quickly that require transformations of various types. We don't get degrees from educational institutions without years of work. We don't lose weight without diet and exercise. Loving relationships develop over time spent together.

Instead of cold–turkey evangelism, we can take a generous approach to sharing the gospel with friends. After a relationship and conversation has developed, I often ask people to tell me the story of their spiritual journey. As I listen respectfully, they usually let their spiritual guard down. People love telling their stories, but most believers are too busy to ask or listen.

A generous approach allows the love of Jesus to peek through your eyes, actions, questions and words. As you develop new relationships, always keep your spiritual ears open to follow the wind of the Spirit. He knows how to adjust the sparks of your words to meet the need of your friend(s) so that spiritual wildfires become ignited.

When people do quickly get convicted that their long–held belief system is no longer valid, this is often the culmination of God's moving in their life for some time. In my experience, these conversations almost always happen when they have been invited to tell their story. Sometimes a positive response comes from a realization that what they have been trusting in drains their soul dry and leaves them thirsty for something more. That something more is Jesus Christ.

We need to get back to befriending the world. This doesn't mean we should share the sinful activities and priorities of the world.[12] It means we should befriend people who are sinners! Isn't that what Jesus did[13] and aren't we supposed to be like Him?[14] The New Testament holds several verses that guide us in our interactions with not–yet–believers.

"Behold, I send you out as <u>sheep in the midst of wolves;</u> so be shrewd as serpents and innocent as doves."
Matthew 10:16 (emphasis mine)

"18 As He was getting into the boat, the man who had been demon-possessed was imploring Him that he might accompany Him. 19 And He did not let him, but He said to him, "<u>Go home to your people and report to them what great things the Lord has done for you,</u> and how He had

mercy on you." 20 And he went away and began to proclaim in Decapolis what great things Jesus had done for him; and everyone was amazed. Mark 5:18-20 (emphasis mine)

"46 Day by day continuing with one mind in the temple, and breaking bread from house to house, they were taking their meals together with gladness and sincerity of heart, 47 praising God and <u>having favor with all the people</u>. And the Lord was adding to their number day by day those who were being saved." Acts 2:46-47 (emphasis mine)

"14 I have given them Your word; and the world has hated them, because they are not of the world, even as I am not of the world. 15 <u>I do not ask You to take them out of the world</u>, but to keep them from the evil one. 16 They are not of the world, even as I am not of the world. 17 Sanctify them in the truth; Your word is truth. 18 <u>As You sent Me into the world, I also have sent them into the world</u>. 19 For their sakes I sanctify Myself, that they themselves also may be sanctified in truth." John 17:14-19 (emphasis mine)

9 I wrote you in my letter not to associate with immoral people; 10 <u>I did not at all mean with the immoral people of this world</u>, or with the covetous and swindlers, or with idolaters, <u>for then you would have to go out of the world</u>. 1 Corinthians 5:9-10 (emphasis mine)

How did we ever get away from thinking that we are not to be friends with people of the world? As your friendships grow and expand, you'll find out that some friends will accept your faith and some will not. Some will be open to spiritual conversations, and some will not be. Neil Cole,[15] a friend of mine, has come up with a simple illustration to show the difference. When you walk into a dark room and turn on the light; you'll see cockroaches run away from the light and the moths fly to the light.

Turning on the light is a metaphor for you sharing in some way that you follow Jesus. It may be when you mention you go to church, that your prayers were answered, or that you will pray for something that is shared in a conversation. God will give you the words! Once the light of Jesus is on, you will notice that some people move away or change the subject (cockroaches). Those are the people who aren't interested in spiritual things at the moment. Don't go chasing after them, but do pray for them to be drawn to Jesus. Other friends may seem interested when you mention God, or at least open to talking about spiritual things (moths). Those are the people you want to hang out with to see where Jesus may take the friendship and conversations.

As you develop and deepen friendships, they may spread into areas you could not have created yourself. One day, I was having coffee with some friends as we discussed the Scriptures. I noticed a middle–aged man leaning our way to listen in on our conversation. I didn't know him (yet), but the light of Jesus was turned on and he was attracted to it. We were discussing a particular Bible passage when I abruptly began telling the story of how I came to know Jesus. My two friends, who had heard the story before, looked at me in confusion.

Eventually the stranger joined our conversation, and we found out that his name was Jerry. That was the first of many conversations we would have over coffee. I shared about my life and work, and he shared about his, including that he had had cancer but had fought it successfully through the medical circuit. I invited him and his wife over for dinner, and he invited me to parties at his house. Years passed, and our individual sets of friends soon became shared friends. Jerry, and his wife Bette, visited our house church sometimes, but nothing deeply spiritual seemed to take root.

One day, Jerry found out that his cancer had come back. Near the end of his life, some mutual friends and I went to visit him. When Jerry noticed me in the room, he mustered up his strength and commanded everyone's attention. He looked around the room at his friends. "Ed and I have had a lot of talks over the years. You all need to listen to him and what he says about God." It was an opening I could only thank God for.

A few weeks later our group of friends drove up to a secluded place to have a memorial service for Jerry at his favorite place to camp. It was somber and joyful at the same time, it was also full of spiritual conversations for the several hours we were together. Many wildfires were started that day as we remembered Jerry.

As followers of Jesus, we need to imitate His example of loving the people of the world deeply and sharing the truth of the gospel strongly. Ask God to help you become more outgoing and make fresh friendships often. You don't have to be an extrovert; you do need to be yourself and follow the Spirit. At times this will involve some risk and discomfort, but if you are tuned in to the Spirit, you will experience a surprising, new dimension to friendships.

The Power of Spontaneity (The Voice of God; Factor #4)

What if when you woke up this morning, God told you about all of the divine encounters He had for you? What if He said you would have three chances to talk about His Son? One opportunity was to be with your neighbor, because her teenager has same–sex attractions; another opportunity was to be with supervisor at work because of some gossip; and another opportunity with your best friend because he can't seem to get a handle on his emotions? You might have a panic attack if you knew what was about to happen!

God is graciously spontaneous with our evangelistic endeavors. God wants us to follow the Spirit, and the opportunities He creates for these things will often take us by surprise. These spontaneous opportunities reinforce our complete dependency on the Lord in all areas of life, but especially when it comes to knowing what to say to people who need Jesus. It's tempting to think up strategies so we can control the when, where and how of evangelism. God wants us to relax in Him so He can create the when, where and how for us.

The third chapter of Acts has an amazing story of the power of spontaneity in the lives of Peter and John. These two followers of Christ had an afternoon routine: every day around 3:00 p.m., they passed through the Beautiful Gate on their way to the Temple to pray. It so happened that a lame man, crippled from birth had a routine of his own; every day he was brought to the same gate to beg for money so he could buy food.

In Acts 3:3, the two routines suddenly intersected. Peter fixed his gaze on the begging man and said, "Look at us!" Peter and John wanted this man's undivided attention, but why that day? Why not the day before, or week or month before? Maybe it was God nudging them.

The man turned his attention to Peter and John expecting to get something from them. I can imagine Peter and John praying silently, "Ok, now what, Jesus?" Then Peter told the man, "I do not possess silver and gold, but what I do have I give to you: In the name of Jesus Christ the Nazarene - walk!" Why did Peter start a healing ministry right then? It may have been something Peter had done before, or it may have been supernaturally infused in Peter's mind. Peter then reached out his hand, seized the man and lifted him up. Immediately the man's feet and ankles were strengthened and he leaped for joy throughout the temple. A wildfire had begun!

This healing led to the opportunity for Peter to give a sermon inviting people to place their trust in Christ. Over five thousand men responded to the message by placing their trust in Christ. Peter and John were arrested for causing a disturbance, which led to yet more people coming to Christ. All of this happened because of the power of spontaneity.

I doubt that Peter and John began their walk to the temple strategizing about what to say to the lame man, or whether they should heal him. We do know that Peter and John had a sense of God's presence in their life. And they had seen first-hand how Jesus interacted with the people He met in unexpected ways, as the Spirit led Him.

Allowing the Holy Spirit to create and customize chances for every believer turns evangelism from a sterile presentation to a surprising adventure. As we follow the Spirit's lead, we may find ourselves making new friends who may curse, smoke, eat or drink too much, and make other life choices we don't agree with. What matters is whether we choose to trust the urges God gives us, no matter where we are or who we are with.

Branching out to develop new friendships as we seek to discover who the moths are in our lives is risky and obedient. The gospel has always spread faster through the connections of relationships. Whether you are an introvert or extrovert, God can start wildfires through you. As you learn to trust Jesus in these new friendships, you will see His hand at work which will increase your faith.

Always be on the lookout for those spontaneous moments where God's nudges meet people's needs through you. The power of spontaneity, like lightning, can start a wildfire as we become willing to move as He leads.

Every follower of Christ is <u>called</u> to share the good news.

Every follower of Christ is <u>chosen</u> to share the life of Christ in them.

Every follower of Christ is <u>sent</u> to be a light to the world.

The more convinced we become that God creates the opportunities for us, the more we will understand that He really can use ordinary people to do extra–ordinary things. Let's explore how God has always sent believers out to be successful before they believed they were ready to do so.

CHAPTER 8: FISHERMEN AND OTHER ORDINARY PEOPLE

"Follow Me and I will make you become fishers of men." Mark 1:17

J esus was a revolutionary. One of the most revolutionary changes Jesus addressed was the equipping, empowering, and releasing of ordinary people to do great things. Jesus' closest friends were fishermen, villagers, and tax collectors. And yet they have impacted the entire world for over 2,000 years. The genius behind this revolution of releasing the ordinary is the potential size of the army; unlimited!

Jesus also set the stage for quick expansion by keeping the principles He passed along simple.[1] When things are simple, they are easy to put into practice. When a lot of people do a little, much is accomplished! The oxygen needed for wildfires to spread rapidly is a movement of ordinary believers equipped by Jesus to be on His mission of reproducing His followers. When ordinary people are equipped and empowered, more expansion is possible.

In John chapter one, John the Baptist was telling large crowds about someone coming who was greater than he was.[2] As Jesus was walking by, John called out, "Behold the Lamb of God!" John was basically saying, "Hey, here is the man I have been telling you about!" John's task was to prepare the Jewish people to be on the lookout for the Messiah. Once the Messiah was revealed, two of John's disciples did what they had been prepared to do: they left John and followed Jesus (John 3:25–36).

One of the two disciples who left John to follow Jesus was Andrew. Andrew and the other disciple asked to stay with Jesus and He agreed. After they had spent an evening interacting with Jesus, Andrew was so excited that he set out to find his brother Simon and told him, "We have found the Messiah!" Simon went back with Andrew to meet Jesus. As they talked, Jesus gave Simon the new name of Cephas, which can be translated as Peter. Jesus had such an impact that in a few short hours at least three people were connected to Him.

The next day as Jesus and His new followers headed out, Jesus saw Philip and said, "Follow Me," so he did. Philip immediately went and found Nathanael and he came and followed Jesus as well. This is simple multiplication.

Jesus Sends People Out Before They are Ready (Mark 3)

Several weeks into Jesus' public ministry, many were following Him. Anticipating what was to come, Jesus spent a whole night in prayer[3] before choosing twelve men to be His students, His disciples. In Mark 3 we can learn why this rapid expansion was taking place.

> *"13 And He went up on the mountain and summoned those whom He Himself wanted, and they came to Him. 14 And <u>He appointed twelve, so that they would be with Him and that He could send them out to preach, 15 and to have authority to cast out the demons.</u> 16 And He appointed the twelve..." Mark 3:12-16 (emphasis mine)*

Jesus appointed these twelve men to be with Him; to learn from Him, to watch Him, to be equipped by Him and to become close and intimate friends. They set aside their work and their old lives so they could follow Jesus full–time. In Israel at that time, it was not uncommon for people to put aside their normal life in order to follow a Rabbi for a period of time. Many families encouraged relatives to leave for a while to gain knowledge, insight, and respect as they followed a Rabbi. It was a great honor, and disciples of Rabbi's would later return to their old lives equipped with what they had learned.

Jesus not only wanted to influence the Twelve He had chosen as He spent time with them and equipped them, Jesus also sent them on mission immediately. When Jesus released the twelve in the passage above, it was with simultaneous authority to proclaim His gospel and to disturb demonic influences. Distributing this type of authority to new followers is part of how rapid multiplication happens.[4] Jesus trusted these ordinary men from the beginning to do great things, even though they were certainly rookies.

When people today choose to follow Jesus, I am convinced that He gives them permission and responsibility to do similar important tasks, like making disciples. When leaders today follow the example of Jesus and release people on mission immediately, ownership of the mission and expansion of disciples take place.

Releasing new believers is not easy for many leaders. It carries the risk of mistakes and missteps with lasting consequences. But there are also risks in not releasing people to proclaim the gospel and to cause spiritual disturbances.

One of these risks is that new believers learn they are not able to make a difference for God, at least not yet. Most of the liabilities caused by not releasing people quickly is that many tend to have a more passive faith. When people learn to be more passive in their faith they become dependent on the organization or leader, instead of dependent on the One who called them into service (Jesus).

Believers often hesitate to share or serve from the beginning of their following Jesus because of their understanding of what church is and does. I challenge leaders to follow the example of our Shepherd who constantly sent people out before they were ready. When leaders dare to do the same, new believers develop a more rugged trust in Christ from the very start. This teaches the follower that they are able to do whatever the Master inspires them to do.

From the beginning, Jesus sent out His twelve apostles to make a difference. He did not require them to mature before being given responsibility. In fact, it's impossible to mature without being in action for our King!

Jesus equipped, released and taught them to be fishers of men while giving them on–the–job training.[5] This is profoundly missing in the church today. It would have world-wide consequences if churches today would follow our Lord's example of equipping and releasing people quickly. When we read the Gospels, we learn that Jesus often sent people out before they were ready. Or at least before they were fully ready by our standards with experiences, knowledge and skills. His disciples made mistakes and had learning curves.[6] After spending over three years with these men, equipping, training and releasing them, some still doubted before His ascension![7] This should comfort us when the people we are mentoring to begin wildfires have doubts and slip back at times. Leaders must provide grace and encouragement as their doubts emerge.

Jesus Teaches Deeper Insights on Being Sent (Mark 4)

Shortly after inviting His disciples to "be with Him and that He could send them out," Jesus opened their minds further on the topic of what it meant to be sent on mission for Him. He shared three parables with His disciples on principles for reproduction.[8] This is a very important subject that our Master Teacher wants all of His followers to understand. He taught these parables from a boat a little way out from shore.[9]

The first parable He taught, had to do with a farmer sowing seed in four different soils (for more detail on Mark 4, refer to chapter 6). Each soil had varying degrees of results.

The first soil where seed fell was hard and un–welcoming. Satan came and plucked the seed off the ground. There was no reception in this soil. The soil rejected the seed which is the Word of God (Mark 4:12).

The second soil received the seed (the Word) with joy, but was full of rocks and shallow. The roots of this seed were not deep and when problems and pressures of life arose, they quickly fell away or found relief by going back to the way they once lived. These people (soil) did not reproduce or pass on their faith.

The third soil also received the seed and grew quickly. This soil was full of weeds or distractions from the cares and concerns of life. Without a trust that God will provide, the soil was not fruitful. There was no second generation of fruit in this soil.

The fourth soil was rich and deep and received the seed and grew and reproduced. This soil type allows for continued growth and reproduction for generations to come.[10]

I believe that Jesus wanted His disciples to learn some valuable lessons from the parable of the four soils: to sow the word (tell people about God's story), to sow it indiscriminately (tell His story to anyone who will listen), and to remember that not all soils (souls) will receive or reproduce, however, we should focus on the soil that does reproduce.

The soil that reproduces will have a harvest of 3000%, 6000% or 10,000%! This does not mean that a church will see 3,000 to 10,000 new people. It actually is communicating something much larger. It is about multiplication. When a person receives the word of God so they become seed–sowers themselves, multiplication takes place. The 3,000%, 6,000% and 10,000% represent generations of future believers that come into being from sowing in good soil. We must believe the seed and the principle of multiplication when we find good soil.

The second parable[11] demonstrates the simplicity that good seed in good soil will produce crops automatically.

> 26 And He was saying, "The kingdom of God is like a man who casts seed upon the soil; 27 and he goes to bed at night and gets up by day, and the seed sprouts and grows—how, he himself does not know. 28 "The soil produces crops by itself; first the blade, then the head, then the mature grain in the head. 29 "But when the crop permits, he immediately puts in the sickle, because the harvest has come." Mark 4:26–29

The farmer had sown seed and went about his life and carried out his responsibilities. All the while, the good seed in the good soil produced crops all by themselves. This parable emphasizes the fourth or good soil from Mark 4:1–20.

When the crop was ready, the farmer harvested the crop. Here we learn that we are to be active in sowing and reaping. We are also to be aware that God is the one who does the growing in people's lives. Growing happens automatically when good seed is sown in good soil. Growing is God's responsibility, not ours. This is a difficult concept for us to grasp or accept, but Jesus taught it with deep clarity.

The third parable[12] is about what happened when the word of God was sown in a soul.

> *30 And He said, "How shall we picture the kingdom of God, or by what parable shall we present it? 31 "It is like a mustard seed, which, when sown upon the soil, though it is smaller than all the seeds that are upon the soil, 32 yet when it is sown, it grows up and becomes larger than all the garden plants and forms large branches; so that the birds of the air can nest under its shade." 33 With many such parables He was speaking the word to them, so far as they were able to hear it. Mark 4:30–33*

It may have been a small mustard seed of truth, but in the right or good soil it grew large and touched many. With these three parables, Jesus illustrated to His followers how to trust the seed of God's Word to grow when it is placed in good soil. Jesus then decided to take His disciples on a field trip to see these principles put into action.

Jesus Teaches the Parables of the Seed and Soil in Real Time

After teaching these principles to His disciples, they took the boat Jesus was teaching from and set off to the other side of the lake.[13] As they were making their way across the lake, a fierce storm kicked up and became so strong that water was filling the boat. The disciples, some of whom were seasoned sailors from their fishing profession, became afraid of capsizing and drowning.

Jesus, however, slept during the storm. This reminds me of the second parable, when the farmer rested no matter what happened outside (Mark 4:16–29).

> 38 "Teacher, do You not care that we are perishing?" 39 And He got up and rebuked the wind and said to the sea, "Hush, be still." And the wind died down and it became perfectly calm. 40 And He said to them, "Why are you afraid? How is it that you have no faith?" Mark 4:38–40

Jesus then scolded His disciples for lacking faith, highlighting their lack of trust in Him. The disciples' lives were full of distractions at this time in their lives,[14] just like the second soil of Mark 4:1–20. The experience of calming the storm taught the disciples the authority Jesus had and that they could trust Him in the midst of confusion. This experience tied the truth of His previous parable together with what they were about to witness as they landed on the shore across the sea.

They landed in the Gerasene region, which was an area full of Gentiles. Jesus was beginning to teach His followers that He came not only for the Jews but for all people.[15] He wanted them to know that they needed to sow indiscriminately into all people they encounter. As soon as Jesus got out of the boat, a man with an unclean spirt approached Him.

Mark, the writer of the gospel, went into great detail about this man who was so troubled. He was an outcast who lived among the tombs. He was a problem and an embarrassment to the community. He would scream and cut himself with stones. He had no friends, he had no clothes and he was possessed by demons to the point that even chains and shackles could not contain him. I imagine no one dared visit the area where he roamed. He was probably treated more like an animal than a human being.

As a Gentile, this man likely had no concept of a Messiah, but the demons who were tormenting him certainly knew who Jesus was. As he ran up to Jesus he cried out, *"What business do we have with each other, Jesus, Son of the Most High God? I implore You by God, do not torment me!"*[16] Jesus began saying to Him,

"Come out of the man, you unclean spirit!" and then He asked *"What is your name?"*[17] The man replied, *"My name is Legion; for we are many."*[18] At this point Jesus sent the demons out of the man and into a herd of 2,000 pigs who immediately ran over a cliff and drowned in the sea. You can imagine the relief of the demonized man, and the horror of the herdsman who had just witnessed their livelihood destroyed.

As the man was cared for by Jesus and His disciples, the herdsmen ran to the city and countryside telling the Gerasene residents what had happened. When the Gentile residents heard the story, they went to the scene of the incident to find out what had happened for themselves.

As they approached Jesus and His disciples, they recognized the man previously demonized. He was relaxed, seated, in his right mind and clothed. This caused them to be afraid. Instead of rejoicing that this man was delivered from a tortured life, fear overcame them. As the residents of that region recognized what had happened, they begged Jesus to leave their area. Their response and their hearts matched the hard soil[19] in the first parable Jesus had told them the evening before. The disciples saw first–hand how people with hard hearts could quickly reject the Word in their midst. The birds of the air (Satan and his demons) were plucking the seed right off the hard soil.

Instead of pressing on, Jesus respected the request of the residents of the Gerasene region. Jesus and His disciples got back in the boat to leave the area. Then the previously demonized man asked Jesus if he could go with Him.

The formerly demonized man was an object lesson in real life for the disciples of good soil.[20] He had placed his trust in Jesus and was ready for what was next. It was obvious from his response that the man wanted to be a disciple of Jesus and follow Him.

Jesus' response to His request seems startling. Jesus said a straight–forward, "No." The master disciple–maker of the world denied the man the opportunity to spend more time with Him. Why would Jesus do something like this? After all, this man was ready to leave everything behind to follow Him, exactly what He asked the twelve apostles to do. Jesus was ready to culminate His teaching to His disciples about the simplicity of good seed in good soil and how that will reproduce automatically.

Instead of allowing the man to come and be with Him, Jesus sent him on mission…immediately! Jesus told him to go to the ten cities of that region and tell them the great things Jesus had done for him and how He had mercy on him. This man could not have been relieved from the torment of the demons for more than a few hours at best and yet he was being sent back to his region to share his story with all who would listen.

How could this man be remotely ready to go on such an important mission? He had no training! His audience had little or no context for a Messiah! He had no resources! The only thing he had was a reputation. Everyone in the region had probably heard about the crazy demon possessed man. He was instructed to tell one message; what Jesus had done for him and how He had mercy on him. And the man obeyed.

"And he went away and began to proclaim in Decapolis what great things Jesus had done for him; and everyone was amazed." Mark 5:20

The whole region of ten cities marveled at him and his story. His immediate obedience to Jesus' instructions was a real–life example of the parable we find in Mark 4:26. A farmer sowed his seed, and went on with his life until the crop was ready for harvest. How it grew, the farmer did not know, because the soil produced crops automatically. As the disciples passed fields throughout the years, I imagine their Teacher's example came back to them, reminding them to keep sowing, even if they didn't know how (or when) the harvest would come.

Jesus trusted this previously demonized man and sent him out before any leader would consider him to be ready for such a task. *Jesus turns the world of mentoring and discipling upside down; He is a revolutionary.*

No one trusts inexperienced disciples with important responsibilities, and maybe that is why the western church today is not seeing radical expansion. Leaders do not trust most people, especially new believers with radical, important, and risky adventures. But Jesus did exactly that with his twelve disciples and with this newly saved, formerly demonized man.

Jesus masterfully taught and demonstrated to His disciples the principle of good seed + good soil = reproduction. Jesus began a new wildfire in this region with a single, brand–new Gentile follower.

A little later in the Gospel of Mark, we learn something more about the results of this formally demonized man's impact on the region. Jesus returned to the region of ten cities and the people eagerly brought Him a man who was deaf and Jesus healed him.

> *"31 Again He went out from the region of Tyre, and came through Sidon to the Sea of Galilee, within the region of Decapolis. 32 They brought to Him one who was deaf and spoke with difficulty, and they implored Him to lay His hand on him. 33 Jesus took him aside from the crowd, by himself, and put His fingers into his ears, and after spitting, He touched his tongue with the saliva; 34 and looking up to heaven with a deep sigh, He said to him, "Ephphatha!" that is, "Be opened!" 35 And his ears were opened, and the impediment of his tongue was removed, and he began speaking plainly. 36 And He gave them orders not to tell anyone; but the more He ordered them, the more widely they continued to proclaim it. 37 They were utterly astonished, saying, "He has done all things well; He makes even the deaf to hear and the mute to speak." Mark 7:31-37*

In Mark 8 we find Jesus deep within this region[21] feeding the 4,000 miraculously. This is another example of Jesus reinforcing to His disciples the principles found in the parable of the sower, seed and soil. Jesus is the Master Teacher. Remember, He told his disciples that if they did not understand the parable of the sower, seed and soil, they wouldn't be able to discern any of the parables (Mark 4:13).

Jesus was committed to the disciples understanding this vital principle of multiplication and used the Gerasene region as another example and experience for them to draw on in the future. The good news was expanding in the Gerasene region, just like the parable of the mustard seed. From a single seed in a very troubled man who was good soil, to a whole region impacted by the life and message of Jesus. This was an amazing lesson for us to learn. Good seed in good soil produces generations of influence.

If we look at it from an evangelistic point of view, the key to this passage is that Jesus sends out people before they are ready. He trusts that when good seed (the Word of God) enters good soil (a receptive obedient person) spiritual genetics takes over.

All of this began with Jesus sending out a brand–new Gentile follower on a mission that affected thousands in the region. When good seed falls on good soil, wildfires spread rapidly. We can follow Jesus' example of sending out ordinary people before they are ready. We can learn to trust the Holy Spirit to guide new believers as they sow the good seed.

Jesus' Example of an Immoral Woman Staring a Wildfire (John 4)

Typical of Jesus' revolutionary ways, he directly confronted several cultural issues of His day in a single encounter with a non–Jewish woman. We find this story in John 4.

Jesus and His disciples traveled from Judea back to Galilee, choosing a direct route through the heart of Samaria. Samaritans were part Jewish and part Gentile. Interaction with them was frowned on by most Jews. They were considered a half–breed and treated poorly by the Jewish people. When most Jews traveled they would opt to take a much longer route around the large Samaritan area to avoid any interaction with Samaritans. When Jesus decided to lead His disciples through the middle of Samaria, you can imagine the tension it likely caused.

After what I imagine was a long morning of traveling, Jesus and His disciples arrived in the southern Samaritan town of Sychar. Being tired, Jesus sat down at the town's water–well while the disciples headed into the village to get some food. While the disciples were away, a woman from the city came to the well to get some water.

It was an odd time for a single woman to draw water in the heat of the day. Culturally, her coming to the well at noon showed the village's rejection of this woman. Most women would come to the well together to get water, in the morning or evening when it was cooler. Drawing water from the well was a time for interacting and community. But this woman came in the middle of the day all by herself. She was likely an outcast because of her lifestyle choices. Rabbi's would never talk with a single woman, especially one with a dubious reputation. It was also not acceptable for man to speak to a woman without her husband present so her conversation with Jesus would really stand out to anyone who heard about it.

Jesus asked this woman for a drink of water. This was another cultural no–no. For a Jew to drink water drawn by a Samaritan would be an unclean act. Jesus knew what he was doing. He wanted to start a wildfire in the soul of this woman to touch the village of Sychar and even beyond into all of Samaria. She was yet another low–status person whom Jesus chose to invest in to see His Kingdom expand and a wildfire start.

There are several interesting things to learn from this interaction. Jesus invited this woman to place her trust in Him, and then immediately allowed her to go and tell of her encounter to the whole city of Sychar. Jesus began by asking this woman for a drink of water. Her response was, *"How is it that You, being a Jew, ask me for a drink since I am a Samaritan woman?" (For Jews have no dealings with Samaritans).*[22] This woman was not only startled by His request, she was telling Him she knew the rules and this was not culturally an acceptable interaction. Jesus' response was *"If you knew the gift of God, and who it is who says to you, 'Give Me a drink,' you would have asked Him, and He would have given you living water.*"[23] Jesus was breaking the rules and making an amazing statement that rocked this woman's understanding.

"...Sir, You, have nothing to draw with and the well is deep; where then do You get that living water? 12 You are not greater than our father Jacob, are You, who gave us the well, and drank of it himself and his sons and his cattle?" John 4:11–12

The woman could sense something was different with this man and His request. Even the fact that he was interacting with her was amazing.

Her curiosity was piqued and she turned the conversation from water to a deeper spiritual meaning. This is another example of how God gives what to say to us at the right time so that people's hearts are touched to think deeper. In His humanity, Jesus was fully dependent on the Father to share with Him how to proceed in each interaction.[24] Jesus followed her lead and took the conversation deeper into spiritual territory. Jesus' response was;

13 "Everyone who drinks of this water will thirst again; 14 but whoever drinks of the water that I will give him shall never thirst; but the water that I will give him will become in him a well of water springing up to eternal life." 15 The woman said to Him "Sir, give me this water, so I will not be thirsty nor come all the way here to draw." John 4:13–15

She was thinking about H20, but Jesus was about to share with her who He was and how He could satisfy the deepest desire of her soul.

Jesus asked this woman to go and get her husband. Jesus switched the subject from water to her life. Why? Again, I believe that the Father gave Jesus the change of subject to expose her to who He is and that she has a need for Him. He never explained that the living water is actually the Holy Spirit.[25] We have to get comfortable with God giving us what to say in the moment to meet the need of the person we are engaging with. He may even change the subject to alert the person to their need. Depending on God to guide us in conversations is vital and is why chapter 3 of this book (Furnace), is about the importance of staying close to God.

When she replied that she had no husband, Jesus told her that He already knew. He not only knew she has no husband, but He knew she had had five husbands and the man she was living with was not her husband.

Jesus didn't condemn her lifestyle, nor tell her to stop living with this man. He was more interested in exposing her to her need for Him. As her heart was drawn towards His grace, the conviction of the living water (the Holy Spirit) would draw her to consider living a life that was pleasing to Him. It is important to point people to Jesus as their primary need. Then we allow Him to move people forward in how they live as they engage with the Word, the Spirit and a faith community.

She realized that Jesus was a prophet as their conversation pivoted to spiritual things. They discussed the right place to worship and the differences between the Jews and Samaritans' understanding of worship. The woman then went even deeper and stated that the Messiah was coming and would declare all things. Jesus response goes to the core of the issue when He replied, *"I who speak to you am He."*[26]

At this point the disciples returned from getting food and were amazed that Jesus was speaking to a woman in the middle of the day at the well.[27] The woman left her water pot and returned to the city.[28] There she gathered the men together and told them, *29 "Come, see a man who told me all the things that I have done; this is not the Christ, is it?" 30 They went out of the city, and were coming to Him."*[29] The woman's story of her interaction with Jesus was so compelling that the men came to see for themselves if this man was the Christ, the Messiah.

While the woman returned to tell the city about her encounter, the disciples encouraged Jesus to eat food. He answered, *"I have food to eat that you do not know about."* He meant that he was filled by the spiritual conversation He had with the woman. The disciples were confused, but Jesus urged them to think differently and more deeply. As Jesus watched the men of the city coming towards Him to see if the woman had found the Christ, He told His disciples:

174

35 Do you not say, 'There are yet four months, and then comes the harvest'? Behold, I say to you, lift up your eyes and look on the fields, that they are white for harvest. 36 Already he who reaps is receiving wages and is gathering fruit for life eternal; so that he who sows and he who reaps may rejoice together. 37 For in this case the saying is true, 'One sows and another reaps.' 38 I sent you to reap that for which you have not labored; others have labored and you have entered into their labor." John 4:35-38

The disciples must have been amazed at what happened when the men came and talked with Jesus. The Scriptures tell us that, *"From that city many of the Samaritans believed in Him because of the word of the woman who testified, 'He told me all the things that I have done.'"* A wildfire had begun because one woman simply shared about her experience with Jesus in a short conversation at the well.

Notice the Word says that many *"...believed in Him because of the word of the woman...."* They were supernaturally drawn to Jesus because of the woman's testimony. She had placed her trust in Christ and then they believed in Him as well. Jesus uses our stories to draw people towards His love. We should never underestimate the (future) impact of our stories and the words given to us by God.

After the villagers arrived at the well, we learn that they *"...were asking Him to stay with them; and He stayed there two days."* Jesus and His Jewish apostles broke more cultural boundaries by sleeping and eating in Sychar, a place they wouldn't have willingly travelled. The disciples probably never imagined they would be eating food prepared by 'unclean' Samaritans or staying under their roofs.

At the end of the story of the woman at the well, many more believed in Jesus, not just because of the woman's story of her interaction with Jesus, but because they themselves had met the Messiah.[30]

One woman with a bad reputation began what may have been the first revival in Samaria. She was an outcast, but Jesus chose to

175

offer her living water. He exposed her need and watched her spread the good news immediately in her city. Deep transformation often leads to spiritual wildfires to those all around the transformed.

A Disabled Man Starts a Wildfire (John 9)

This is the final example of Jesus inviting and releasing low–status people to spread the gospel. In John 9, we find Jesus and His disciples passing by a man who was born blind. The disciples asked their teacher, or Rabbi, a very practical theological question that was prominent in their day. *"Rabbi, who sinned, this man or his parents, that he would be born blind?"* (John 9:2) The Jewish culture leaned toward the opinion that all disabilities or disfigurement was either a result of a person's sin or their parent's sin. The disciples were naturally curious to know who was responsible for the man's blindness, but I imagine they were shocked by Jesus' response.

Jesus answered, *"It was neither that this man sinned, nor his parents; but it was so that the works of God might be displayed in him."* (John 9:3) This man lived in complete darkness and was trapped in a life of begging and poverty. To learn that his disability was allowed so that the works of God would be displayed in him stunned the disciples. Jesus went on to say, *"We must work the works of Him who sent Me as long as it is day; night is coming when no one can work."* (John 9:4) Jesus included His disciples (and all later disciples) in the redemptive work of His mission.[31]

We need to work for the King while we have life and ability to do what He has prepared for us.[32] When Jesus spoke of the night, he was referring to death. Once our lives are completed on earth, we no longer are able to accomplish His mission. We need to be about the Father's business with diligence while we are here!

To His disciples and anyone who was listening, Jesus added, *"While I am in the world, I am the Light of the world"* (John 9:5). Then He brought light for the first time into the life of this man born blind. Jesus spat into the dirt and rubbed it on the eyes of the blind man and instructed him, ' *"Go, wash in the pool of Siloam," (which is translated, Sent)"'* (John 9:7). It is interesting that Siloam means "sent," since the man was being sent on a mission. The mission would show the crowd, the Pharisees, and the disciples what a person, any person, is capable of when they place their trust in Christ.

When the man washed his eyes in the pool of Siloam, he returned with his vision! I can imagine the joy of the man and the amazement of the crowd and Jesus' disciples. Some in the crowd argued that it could not be the same man because no one had ever been cured of congenital blindness. Others claimed it really was the same man, but he has been healed. The man born blind kept on insisting, *"I am the one."* (John 9:9). When people asked him how he had gotten his sight, the man gave them his simple testimony: it was Jesus.

There was so much controversy around this event that they brought the formerly blind man to the Pharisees. Certainly, these religious experts would be able to sort out what had just happened. To top off the revolutionary ways of Jesus, He performed this miracle on the Sabbath. According to the law, no one could work on the Sabbath and giving a man born blind his sight certainly violated this work clause. Jesus was always challenging culture.

The Pharisees interrogated the man at least four times about how he had gotten his vision. The man was so irritated by all the disbelief that he finally answered them, *"I told you already and you did not listen; why do you want to hear it again? You do not want to become His disciples too, do you?"* The Pharisees were infuriated by his question, *"You are His disciple, but we are disciples of Moses. We know that God has spoken to Moses, but as for this man, we do not know where He is from."* (John 9:27-29). The man's response is one of the simplest and shortest four-point sermons ever recorded.

"30 ...Well, here is an amazing thing, that you do not know where He is from, and yet He opened my eyes. 31 We know that God does not hear sinners; but if anyone is God-fearing and does His will, He hears him. 32 Since the beginning of time it has never been heard that anyone

opened the eyes of a person born blind. 33 If this man were not from God, He could do nothing." John 9:30-33

This man repeated back to the Pharisees what they had taught, and used it to totally undo their teaching. The man claimed that they could certainly know where Jesus is from when he outlined the following four points:

1.) God does not hear the prayers of sinners.

2.) If anyone does fear God, he does His will and God hears his prayers.

3.) No one has ever been known to open the eyes of a person born blind.

4.) Therefore, it must be that this man is from God because if He was not, he could not have opened blind my eyes.

The Pharisees were flabbergasted and enraged. Their own teaching was turned against them; he had put them in a theological corner. They had a chance to respond in humility, but instead they answered him, *"You were born entirely in sins, and are you teaching us?"* (John 9:34). Then they threw him out of the community of the Jews. As a Jewish outcast, he would be unable to associate or interact with the Jews. Excommunication meant he would not be able to buy or sell anything with Jews nor have a relationship with his family.[33] It was meant to be a devastating sentence for life. When Jesus heard what the Pharisees had done, He went looking for the man.

> *"35 Jesus heard that they had put him out, and finding him, He said, "Do you believe in the Son of Man?" 36 He answered, "Who is He, Lord, that I may believe in Him?" 37 Jesus said to him, "You have both seen Him, and He is the one who is talking with you." John 4:35–37*

Once the man understood that Jesus was the Messiah he replied, *"'Lord, I believe.' And he worshiped Him."* (John 9:38).

This man's new trust in Jesus caused a lot of turmoil in a very short afternoon. He stood his ground and proclaimed his devotion to be a disciple of Jesus. He confounded the Pharisees in short order which brought them face to face with their own theological inconsistencies. He simply told his story and it had tremendous repercussions on the Jewish community of Jerusalem.

This Could Happen in Your Workplace

When our lives are saturated with Christ and we are aware that He is keenly interested in using us to share His good news, we become aware of the opportunities all around us. In Chapter Five, I shared a story about Monica and the "white couch" moments in her office. Monica does not keep her hope in Christ a secret.

Monica is so saturated in Christ that His love, life and truth flow out of her. From Monica's desk, her conversations can be heard from almost every desk in her office. Her staff often gathers in an area near her desk to talk about life and even let off some office steam in their conversations. Now and then, Monica is prompted by God to offer a word of encouragement and even gentle words of correction. At times, the conversations near her desk turn spiritual. Monica told me, "If I hear something not Biblically accurate, the Lord pretty much compels me into action by questioning the issue and backing up my comments or thoughts with Scripture. Often, I am met with respect that surprises me. I could get a big head, but I'm always reminded that it's not I who speak, but the Lord."

As most of us do, Monica sometimes wondered if the words she spoke were actually from God or simply from her passion for Him. Both are great motivations to speak for Jesus, but Monica thought she more likely spoke from her passion than words directly from the Lord. As a way of affirming Monica recently, God used one of her co-workers to make her aware of the influence and impact her words were having–even though she was unaware of the impact.

Garth, a co-worker of Monica's, took a bad spill on his bike over one weekend. He was hurt so badly that he could not come to work for a week. The following week Garth came back to work, hobbling along on crutches. He had to pass by Monica's desk to get to his office. About his third day back, as he passed by Monica, he asked, "Monica, have you been praying for me?"

Monica was stunned. Garth was not a believer and they had never had a one–on–one spiritual conversation, but there he was, asking Monica if she had been praying for him.

What may seem like an innocent comment about prayer was really a huge step for Garth and an affirmation for Monica to continue following the leading of the Spirit! May the Lord cause many more special moments for Monica and the people she interacts with for the glory of the Lord!

Jesus called His disciples to be with Him and simultaneously sent them out to preach and have authority over demons. In this way, Jesus demonstrated to His followers (and to us) His pattern of sending out people before most leaders today would believe they were ready.

He sent the demonized outcast man of Mark 5 back to a hostile environment to tell them what Jesus had done for him and how He had mercy on him. He encouraged the woman at the well in John 4 to start the first spiritual wildfire in Samaria. He also used a formerly blind man to confound the Pharisees, which caused controversy but spread His mission.

Jesus used the outcast, immoral and disabled to spread spiritual wildfires immediately after they had come to place their trust in Him. He trusted these low-status people to handle eternal truth adequately. Jesus gave us radical examples of how things should be; sending out people to start spiritual wildfires before anyone would expect them to be ready. He wants to do the same with you and me.

Where did we learn to hold back people from sharing their faith experiences until they were ready or "mature"? What is our standard of measuring whether people are ready to share the Gospel, anyway? Jesus' standard was that they were ready when they believed in Him. His approach is to send them out quickly while the wildfire of God is hot in their souls. This sets the foundation in their souls that Jesus believes in them even when their faith is new. His standard is to trust the Holy Spirit and the seed of truth embedded in souls from the outset of their faith.

God has made every believer competent to share the gospel from the moment of salvation.[34]

CHAPTER 9: FIGHTERS

"God is not restrained to save by many or by few." 1 Samuel 14:6

Outside of Christ, I am weak; in Christ, I am strong. Outside of Christ, I cannot; in Christ, I am more than able. Outside of Christ, I have been defeated; in Christ, I am already victorious. How meaningful are the words, "in Christ"? - Watchman Nee

Inspiration is the process of moving people forward to create and accomplish things that are difficult. It is my prayer that this book inspires you to fearlessly share the gospel on a regular basis as He leads in ways that are natural for you.

Inspiration in my life to keep going when things seemed impossible has come from many sources. I've shared with you some of the challenges from my life about sowing the seeds of the gospel: Taking risks to share Jesus with Mormons on their turf when my faith was only a few weeks old; Debating with my grandfather about how to be sure of eternal life; The day I met Dr. Laura on a plane ride and learned to overcome my insecurity in sharing with intellectuals. In each of these encounters, God provided the words and ways to speak directly into these souls, nudging them towards placing their trust in Jesus.

All circumstances in our lives can have a spiritual impact. I believe God uses all experiences to develop or challenge our character to become more like His. We all have had experiences that we wish were never part of our story, but we would not be who we are without them. Christ wants to develop rugged disciples, and that is impossible outside of overcoming challenges and taking risks.

In this chapter, I want to share with you three stories to inspire you forward in becoming a fighter for our King as we start wildfires for Him. We need to learn to squeeze character and maturity out of every experience so we become more like Christ.

The world needs more determined disciples who will never give up. The Holy Spirit is the greatest inspirer, leader, and motivator; He is in the process of drawing you forward to engage the world and its darkness with His light. He has already given you all you need to be passionate for Him[1] and He promises to guide you as you share His story and yours with others.

Find the Fighter in You

Jack Harnden mentored me as my football coach at Long Beach Jordan High School. Coach Harnden believed in me like no one ever had before; he saw potential in me and called me to show it during my senior year of high school. Besides being on the wrestling team, I played football and was the captain of Jordan's defense in the fall of 1974. I played the middle linebacker position. This position was nicknamed "The Hawk." As "The Hawk", I needed to develop a keen sense of what the opposing team was doing on offense, and attempt to disrupt their planned play. "The Hawk" was the cornerstone of Coach Harnden's defense. Coach Harnden and I had a deep bond that developed during those years that I played "The Hawk" position.

In the spring before my senior season, Coach Harnden attended one of my wrestling matches. In the match Coach Harnden attended, I was 'pinned' (held down) with only seconds to go before the end of the match. My loss meant that my team lost the entire team event. I hung my head as I left. Coach Harnden met me outside the gym doors and pulled me so close to his face, I could almost taste the cigarette he had just finished. He looked me in the eye and told me to never hang my head. With a deep stare, he told me he was proud of how valiantly I fought on the wrestling mat and how excited he was to have a fighter like me as the captain of his football defense. He told me to walk in the spirit of "The Hawk."

I was amazed by his words when I had just failed. No one had talked to me like that before. He may have forgotten that conversation but it has stayed with me all my life. His influence laid a foundation of a never–quit attitude, which I could fall back on when struggles in life showed up.

Coach Harnden and our Jordan Panther football team had many times of losing together in my senior year. We were 0-9 that season but he never gave up on us. He never let us coast and always believed we could win the next game. We never actually won a football game, but our experiences taught me how to win at life by never giving up. I am grateful for the fighter mentality God called out in me during a season of losing. I no longer play on a football team, but I still carry the spirit of "The Hawk" in my soul.

Ministry, or loving people to be more like Jesus, is hard. Sometimes it brings risk to our souls. Everyone faces times where the temptation to quit rises. People disappoint us. God disappoints our expectations of Him. Plans fail, and we are often misunderstood. It is in times like these that we need to draw upon the truth of God's faithfulness that we have experienced in our lives.

On a crisp morning walk to a meeting of church planters in New Mexico, I was thinking about the disappointments of loving people. My friend Paul Kaak and I were discussing the difficulties of church planting. My family had recently relocated to Phoenix to plant churches and we were not seeing the type of growth we thought God wanted. I must have sounded a bit discouraged when Paul asked me a simple question. "Ed," he said, "What makes you want to quit?" After taking a moment to think about his question I responded by saying, "That word is not in my vocabulary." That answer flew out of my experience of God's faithfulness through the years.

185

This question from Paul was significant to me. It inspired me to keep going even when the situation was difficult, and to switch my perspective from my ideas of success to God's call on my life, no matter the results. As God tests and trains us through life's storms, the Scriptures are packed with important principles to keep us moving forward and following King Jesus' instructions.

The following are three principles from three passages of Scripture that I hope will inspire you to find the fighter within you.

All believers will face strong storms in our lives for the purpose of developing our strength and character. We may be tempted to quit, but instead, we should persist and fight on!

> *1 Therefore, having been justified by faith, we have peace with God through our Lord Jesus Christ, 2 through whom also we have obtained our introduction by faith into this grace in which we stand; and we exult in hope of the glory of God. 3 And not only this, but we also exult in our tribulations, knowing that tribulation brings about perseverance; 4 and perseverance, proven character; and proven character, hope; 5 and hope does not disappoint, because the love of God has been poured out within our hearts through the Holy Spirit who was given to us. Romans 5:1–5*

We are to be committed to not losing heart in all we do for the Lord.

> *Let us not lose heart in doing good, for in due time we will reap if we do not grow weary. Galatians 6:9*

We are to press on for our King so we will mature in our pursuit of Jesus.

> *12 Not that I have already obtained it or have already become perfect, but I press on so that I may lay hold of that for which also I was laid*

hold of by Christ Jesus. 13 Brethren, I do not regard myself as having laid hold of it yet; but one thing I do: forgetting what lies behind and reaching forward to what lies ahead, 14 I press on toward the goal for the prize of the upward call of God in Christ Jesus. 15 Let us therefore, as many as are perfect, have this attitude; and if in anything you have a different attitude, God will reveal that also to you; 16 however, let us keep living by that same standard to which we have attained. Philippians 3:12–16

We are to be fighters for our King with the goal of pointing men and women to Christ. I challenge you to look for times in your life where God has prepared you to become a fighter for the King.

Great Fighters Who Didn't Know How to Quit

Grit, is that hard to quantify quality that pushes us to keep moving on challenging paths towards completion of a goal. Throughout history, there have been many people with goals who met opposition and yet pushed through with grit. The following is a list of people who faced difficulties and failures and went on to impact people for generations. While we may often face the temptation to quit, staying the course is a way to develop perseverance.

Demosthenes was a great orator of the ancient world who used to have a stuttering problem.

Julius Caesar suffered many mini strokes in his life.

Beethoven and Thomas Edison were deaf.

Homer was thought to be blind.

Babe Ruth struck out 1,330 times. In between his strikeouts, he hit 714 home runs.

Abraham Lincoln failed twice as a businessperson and was defeated in six state and national elections before being elected the sixteenth president of the United States.

R. H. Macy failed in retailing at least four times before his store in New York became a success globally.

Louisa May Alcott, the author of Little Women, was encouraged by her family to find work as a servant or seamstress rather than to write.

Theodor S. Geisel's first children's book was rejected by 23 publishers. The twenty–fourth publisher sold six million copies, using Geisel's pseudonym of Dr. Seuss.

When we remember that we are ambassadors to share the message of the King, no matter what our circumstances may be, we can be used by Him to start a wildfire that can affect an entire nation. It only takes one. Will you be one?

It Only Takes One...Little Girl (2 Kings 5)

> *Now the Arameans had gone out in bands and had taken captive a little girl from the land of Israel; and she waited on Naaman's wife. 2 Kings 5:2*

In 2 Kings 5, we learn about a little slave girl who was captured. This captured Israelite had a small role and yet a large impact in expanding and spreading respect for the One True God of Israel in the country of Aram.

Naaman was the captain of the army of the king of Aram and was respected as a great man, *"...but he was a leper."* The Arameans had been raiding the Israelites villages, and 2 Kings 5:1 informs us that *"...the Lord had given victory to Aram."* It may be disturbing to learn that God sometimes allows His chosen people to lose battles. Because of the Israelites' constant disobedience, God was giving Israel's enemies victory over their villages. One of plundered villages was where this little girl lived. The Scriptures tell us that this unnamed young girl was assigned to wait on Naaman's wife.[2]

We have no idea how long the interval of time was between this young girl's capture and the details of this story. It's probable that enough time had passed for her to learn the Aramean's language and customs. We can also imagine that she was

188

traumatized after being ripped away from everything she had known, and could have easily had a deep anger towards her captors. Since her master was a leper, it would be easy to imagine her praying for his nose and fingers to fall off!

Instead of praying for Naaman's physical demise, we find this conversation between the slave girl and the wife of her master. *"I wish that my master was with the prophet who is in Samaria! Then he would cure him of his leprosy."* Once Naaman was told what the slave girl from Israel had said, he reported it to the king of Aram. The king quickly sent Naaman to the king of Israel, along with gifts and a letter asking for the prophet to cure Naaman from his leprosy.

The king of Israel responded by tearing his clothes in anger, convinced that the king of Aram was trying to start a war. Where the servant girl held on to faith despite her slavery, the king in his palace let himself doubt and fear.

Shortly after the letter and entourage arrived at the king of Israel, Elisha the prophet heard about it. When Elisha heard that the king had torn his clothes, he scolded the king and asked why he would do such a thing. Then he boldly requested, *"Now let him come to me, and he shall know that there is a prophet in Israel."* Naaman traveled to Elisha's house with his whole entourage, along with the gifts of silver, gold and clothes. I imagine Naaman seated proudly in his chariot waiting for this great prophet to pronounce his healing so he could return to his own home whole and healed.

Instead of Elisha coming out and giving Naaman the red–carpet treatment, he sent a messenger out to him. The messenger told Naaman, *"Go and wash in the Jordan seven times, and your flesh will be restored to you and you will be clean."*[3] Naaman was furious at this message and left Elisha's house. It was clear that Naaman expected to be treated like royalty, not like a villager with some problem. *"Behold, I thought, 'He will surely come out to me and stand and call on the name of the Lord his God, and wave his hand over the place and cure the leper.'"* This was not going as Naaman had planned. His servants approached him and begged him to go and do as Elisha had instructed. Naaman finally gave in and went to the Jordan river.

The scene at the river must have been startling. The great leader of the mighty army of Aram had to go down to the river's edge, take off his robes and regalia, and enter the waters of the Jordan. I imagine his face twisting in disgust as he went up and down in the water. The last and seventh dip saw him emerge with *"...the flesh of a little child and he was clean."*[4]

Picture the amazement of everyone who witnessed the miracle! I imagine that they started celebrating even before Naaman had put his clothes back on. Naaman returned to Elisha and said, *"Behold now, I know that there is no God in all the earth, but in Israel..."*[5] Naaman insisted that Elisha take the reward that was brought for his healing but Elisha refused. Naaman went on,

> *"...for your servant will no longer offer burnt offering nor will he sacrifice to other gods, but the Lord. In this matter may the Lord pardon your servant: when my master goes into the house of Rimmon to worship there, and he leans on my hand and I bow myself in the house of Rimmon, when I bow myself in the house of Rimmon, the Lord pardon your servant in this matter." 2 Kings 5:17-18*

What a mighty change of events in the life of Naaman. Once a leper and worshipper of false gods, he vowed to only worship the God of Israel. All of this took place because of the faith of an unnamed servant girl. She chose to speak up for the God of Israel and He responded with a miracle. A wildfire began in Aram.

We don't know what the conversation was like between Naaman and the King of Aram once Naaman returned home. I can imagine the King's heart was nudged towards looking to the God of Israel instead of the god of Rimmon after hearing Naaman's stories. Because one girl chose to be different, souls were transformed.

I want this story to encourage you to speak up for the Lord as He gives you the words to say. His desire is to develop your character and trust in Him. You are just as competent to share about God as this unnamed girl. Will you be one that believes the truth of the Word of God? If so, you will make an impact on the world around you, whether you see it or not. It only takes one to start a wildfire.

It Only Takes One…Person of Courage (2 Kings 18)

"Thus Ahab did more to provoke the Lord God of Israel than all the kings of Israel who were before him."[6] There were some terrible kings in Israel before Ahab[7] but Ahab was arguably the most evil king. He fully committed himself to selfishness, the worship of idols and was ruthlessly opposed to those who challenged his evil ways. It is with this backdrop that God sent the prophet Elijah the Tishbite. When Elijah came before King Ahab, Elijah told the King, *"As the Lord, the God of Israel lives, before whom I stand, surely there shall be neither dew nor rain these years, except by my word."*[8] Once the dire prediction was delivered, God sent Elijah away to be safe from King Ahab.

During his exile, Elijah experienced several miracles from the hand of the Lord to strengthen his faith.[9] About three and a half years later, God told Elijah to deliver the message to Ahab that rain was on its way.[10] Meanwhile, the drought had become so bad that Ahab and his right-hand advisor, Obadiah, personally traveled around Israel looking for any springs or valleys that might have water and grass to keep their livestock alive.

While Ahab surveyed the land for water and grass in one place, Elijah met Obadiah on the road in another place. Elijah told him to go to King Ahab and tell him that Elijah was there.

For the past three years, Ahab had been searching for Elijah to force him to stop the harsh drought in Israel (and then, likely, to execute him). Obadiah knew that God had protected Elijah's location and wanted to know that Elijah would keep his word and actually show himself to King Ahab. If King Ahab showed up and Elijah had disappeared, it could mean death for Obadiah. So, Elijah gave Obadiah his word and Obadiah found King Ahab and passed on the message. Elijah, true to his word, waited until the king arrived.

Ahab greeted Elijah with, *"Is this you, you troubler of Israel?"* Elijah, answered, *"I have not troubled Israel, but you and your father's house have, because you have forsaken the commandments of the Lord and you have followed the Baals."* Elijah's bold proclamation to the face of the King of Israel came from a heart focused on the justice of God for His people. To stand strong in the face of an evil king took a deep trust, but Elijah wasn't finished. *"Now then send and gather to me all Israel at Mount Carmel, together with 450 prophets of Baal and 400 prophets of the Asherah, who eat at Jezebel's table."*[11] Directed by God, Elijah called out those who had been opposing God and misleading Israel for years. God was about to establish a wildfire in Israel through one man's bold obedience.

King Ahab gathered all the sons of Israel together along with the prophets as Elijah had requested. Once the people were assembled at Mount Carmel, Elijah set a question before the people; *"How long will you hesitate between two opinions? If the Lord is God, follow Him; but if Baal, follow him."* The people stood silent. They could have shouted their allegiance to the Lord but they didn't. They were torn between Baal and God.

When Elijah saw the people hesitate, he called the prophets of Baal to a showdown to prove who was actually God. He commanded that two oxen be brought forward to be offered as sacrifices; one to God and one to Baal. Elijah told the 450 prophets of Baal to cut up their oxen and place it on the wood but to not light a fire. Elijah did the same. He then told the prophets of Baal to call on the name of their god and he would call on the Lord and *"... 'the God who answers by fire, He is God.' And all the people said, 'That is a good idea.'"*

The 450 prophets of Baal took their ox and prepared it for a sacrifice as Elijah had instructed them. The prophets danced about the altar, cut themselves and called on Baal to light the wood on fire to burn up the offering. They passionately called up their god by yelling and mutilating themselves according to their custom with swords and lances. Their blood flowed to incite Baal to action but nothing happened. *"When midday was past, they raved until the time of the offering of the evening sacrifice; but there was no voice, no one answered, and no one paid attention."*

Now it was Elijah's turn and he called all the people to come near to him to see what God would do. Elijah repaired an ancient altar on that spot where the children of Israel had long ago offered sacrifices to the Lord. He took twelve stones, one for each of the Israelite tribes, to add to the altar. He then dug a trench around the altar and placed the wood under the altar. He then had water poured on the ox that had been cut into pieces so that the trench was filled with water all around the altar. Once the ox was drenched and the trench filled with water, Elijah prayed a simple prayer, one time.

> *"36 At the time of the offering of the evening sacrifice, Elijah the prophet came near and said, "O Lord, the God of Abraham, Isaac and Israel, today let it be known that You are God in Israel and that I am Your servant and I have done all these things at Your word. 37 Answer me, O Lord, answer me, that this people may know that You, O Lord, are God, and that You have turned their heart back again." 1 Kings 18:36-37*

Elijah's desire was to see the people of Israel turn their hearts back to the Lord God of Israel. As soon as he spoke his prayer, the fire of the Lord fell on the sacrifice and consumed the ox, the wood, the stone, the dust and all of the water![12] When the people saw this miracle, they fell on their faces and said, *"The Lord, He is God; the Lord, He is God."* Elijah then had all of the prophets of Baal brought down to a nearby brook and killed them.

He then prayed for the Lord to cause rain to pour on the land to bring relief from the drought. The rain came, the drought was broken. Elijah was a fighter for the Lord his God. The faith of one courageous man caused the people to turn their hearts back to the Lord. Elijah chose to trust the Lord to guide his footsteps and his words so that the message of God would be heard throughout the land.

Are we fighters who will begin wildfires wherever we go? Is our faith in God and His Word rugged enough to obey, risk and sacrifice under His direction?

It can be tempting to think that this type of amazing life is only for a few special people, but this is what the book of James has to say about Elijah.

> *"17 Elijah was a man with a nature like ours, and he prayed earnestly that it would not rain, and it did not rain on the earth for three years and six months. 18 Then he prayed again, and the sky poured rain and the earth produced its fruit." James 5:17–18.*

We need to deconstruct the idea in our minds that God only uses "super Christians" to do amazing things for Him. Elijah was a human just like me and you. Elijah believed God wanted to call people to Himself through his words and actions and he followed through. If you want to increase your faith in Christ, take more risks. Living in safety stifles faith. Taking risks by following the King enlarges our faith.

A Consecrated Few Can Change the World

The book of Joshua opens by telling us that Moses had just died. It was time for farewells to the tenacious leader who had guided Israel through the wilderness for more than 40 years. The camp of about one million Israelites had only one river to cross in order to enter the land God had promised Israel to be their own. Who would lead them now? God spoke to Joshua, Moses' second–in–command, telling him that he was the one to take up the mantle of leadership.[13]

God surely knew that Joshua needed a supernatural resolve to pick up where his mentor had left off. The responsibility was huge, and Joshua was still a rookie when it came to leadership at this level. So, God told Joshua,

> *"Every place on which the sole of your foot treads, I have given it to you, just as I spoke to Moses…No man will be able to stand before you all the days of your life. Just as I have been with Moses, I will be with you; I will not fail you or forsake you. Be strong and courageous, for you shall give this people possession of the land which I swore to their fathers to give them… "Have I not*

*commanded you? Be strong and courageous! Do
not tremble or be dismayed, for the Lord your God
is with you wherever you go." Joshua 1:3, 5–6, 9*

Joshua sent the officers of Israel through the whole camp to
tell the people that in three days they would cross the Jordan and
*"...go in to possess the land which the Lord your God is giving
you, to possess it."* This encouraged the people while they
mourned for Moses. They responded by saying they would obey
Joshua just as they had obeyed Moses.

With the people supporting him as their leader, Joshua sent
two spies to do reconnaissance on the city of Jericho which was
located just across the river Jordan. Once the two spies returned
and gave their report, Joshua readied the people to cross the river
and enter the Promised Land.

*"Consecrate yourselves, for tomorrow the Lord will
do wonders among you." Joshua 3:5*

"Consecrate yourselves" was a command for the Israelites to
set themselves apart for the Lord's work. It was the Lord who
would lead them to cross the Jordan, conquer Jericho, and finally
enter the rich land ahead. As a consecrated people, they would
dedicate themselves to follow God completely, with all their
hearts, all their passion, and all their obedience. After all, this is
what they had been waiting forty years to enjoy. This part of their
journey was to be something very holy and required them to be
fully focused, following all of the Lord's instructions.

As the Israelites crossed the Jordan and entered the Promised
Land, the fortified city of Jericho was a huge obstacle in their
way. Joshua 4 tells us that Israel was ready for war. They had
40,000 men ready for the battle with Jericho (Joshua 4:13).
Instead of starting a normal war, God had the people do
something that was very unconventional.

The Lord revealed to Joshua alone how they were to conquer
the city of Jericho. For each of the first six days, the people were
to march one time each day around the city without saying a
word. On the seventh day, they were to march around Jericho
seven times. Upon completing the seventh time around Jericho,

Joshua gave the order for the horns to be blown and the people were to shout loudly. When the horns and the shouts took place at Joshua's command, the walls of Jericho fell upon the people in the city, and the army destroyed all who remained. It was an amazing victory for Israel. The conquering of the land had begun.

God kept His promise to Joshua that *"Every place on which the sole of your foot treads, I have given it to you."* This promise is not necessarily meant for us today, but the principles found in this story do have application to our lives. All believers today are part of Christ's church and He came to seek and save the lost. He gave all of His followers His instruction to go through life with a focus to be making disciples. We are to consecrate ourselves for this purpose. As we are set apart to fully follow the Lord, we will see the Lord work in amazing ways as He draws boys and girls, men and women to Himself. God will woo souls to Himself (John 6:44, 65) through our faithful sharing of the Gospel.

It is my firm belief that God wants believers today to have a holy fixation on taking the land. That land is our neighborhoods, work places, coffee houses, sports bars, and neighborhood watch groups. God wants wildfires to be spreading wherever we go.

We are to ignite the flames of His truth and glory, so souls can choose to follow Him by placing their trust in Jesus Christ. This takes a holy consecration of our lives. We are to see that whatever we are doing in life, there are souls He wants to come to Him all around us. Whether we are on vacation, at work, in our neighborhoods, or at our gyms, God is drawing people to Himself.

God is going before you, preparing people to hear His gospel and place their trust in Him. It is our holy and consecrated mission to say, as the people of Israel said to Joshua, that we will obey the Lord.

Will we set ourselves apart to do the work of the Lord? Will we fight as the Lord leads us in the battle for the souls of people we find all around us? Will we sacrifice in order to fully follow Christ? Will we do all that He speaks to us, even when it is unconventional?

The battle is the Lord's. The Lord is our King. Our King desires to expand His Kingdom over the whole earth. For the Kingdom to expand, He calls, equips, and sends every believer in the world to start wildfires of His great good news. Will we be a consecrated few and follow Him as fully as we can?

The Lord is Not Restrained to Save by Many or by Few

Jonathan was tired of waiting for something to happen. This is often true of young warriors who are full of energy to get things done. While Jonathan's father, King Saul of Israel, was staying under a pomegranate tree,[14] hiding with his soldiers from the Philistine army, Jonathan and his armorbearer came upon a Philistines group of soldiers. I'm sure adrenaline pumped through Jonathan and his armorbearer's veins as they approached this fierce fighting garrison of soldiers.

As they got closer to the enemy, Jonathan said to his armorbearer, *"...perhaps the Lord will work for us...!"* This was a huge risk on the part of Jonathan. The armor bearer and Jonathan against a whole Philistine garrison. Jonathan had faith that God could do amazing things through this risk...... Jonathan then added, *"...the Lord is not restrained to save by many or by few."*

When we venture out in the name of the Lord to start wildfires in the enemy's camp, it positively affects the people around us. The armorbearer's response was *"Do all that is in your heart; turn yourself, and here I am with you according to your desire."* Stepping out in faith to take ground for the Lord can nudge the people around us towards a deeper faith in God.

Jonathan and his armorbearer defeated the enemy. This victory caused chaos in all of the Philistines camp. God sent a panic on all the Philistine warriors. The confusion was so strong that the Philistines began to fight and kill each other. This emboldened the Israelites so that even those who had hid themselves in the hill country came out and pursued the remainder of the Philistines in battle. The Lord delivered Israel that day and rallied those who were weak in faith all because of Jonathan's risk and trust in the Lord for victory.

Ordinary believers and small bands of consecrated people, willing to fight for the spread of the gospel, are one of God's favorite ways to increase His kingdom. God has always been about multiplying communicators, not simply attracting large crowds of passive listeners. When a few will commit themselves to listen to God's voice, obey His directions and repeat His words, wildfires will break out uncontrollably.

The large crowds gathering to hear charismatic leaders looks effective, but not much is accomplished once the crowds scatter. These crowds are certainly inspired, but they are often not equipped to move out to spread the gospel themselves. Small bands of sold–out soldiers for King Jesus have a much bigger impact as they can infiltrate all levels of society. Wildfires of individuals and small communities of believers can invade culture in ways large crowds never have.

In this chapter, we have seen how God develops fighters out of common people to impact entire nations, dignitaries and ordinary individuals. You can have a similar story as you invest in listening to the King and following His leading. Staying safe and secure breeds complacency. Taking risks and going on adventures while following Jesus develops strong disciples and strong movements. Wildfires most often begin with a single spark, then spread as the Holy Spirit (The Wind) drives them to capture the souls of others.

In the last chapter, we will discuss what it takes to "Finish Well" as we allow the Wind of God to move us to start wildfires throughout our lives.

CHAPTER 10: FINISH WELL

"Well done, my good and faithful servant." Jesus Christ

The Church at Fair Oaks

One of my friends at Fair Oaks is Steve. Steve is a quiet networker who knows everyone and is known by everyone. I had noticed that he was a very observant person who likes to laugh and poke fun at people when they have made a faux pas, but he is very private about his own life. I did learn that he had been involved in a church when he was younger, but had seen too many things in the church that left him feeling disillusioned with church.

Over the next several months, Steve and I continued to build a friendship. During one of our conversations, I found out that Steve had his hours at work cut and he and his wife were struggling to pay their rent. As we were chatting, I messaged the house church I am part of, asking my friends if we could use some our funds to help Steve and his wife pay their rent. I also texted some other believers who are part of the church at Fair Oaks. The response by all was an immediate "yes".

When I told Steve that we would like to help his family with their rent payment, he could not believe it. I told him there were no strings attached or expectation of repayment. He objected, and stalled, but eventually agreed. Steve has moved towards reconnecting with Christ ever so slowly…but he is moving. The church at Fair Oaks is gaining a positive reputation of love, care and authenticity in their belief in Jesus.

I started showing up at Fair Oaks to make friends and see what the Holy Spirit would stir up. Over time, I started seeing results that God had been orchestrating behind the scenes and through the rumor mill.

Pete is an older contractor who would often hang out at Fair Oaks. I noticed that when some of my friends and I would be having discussions about Jesus, Pete would move from sitting in one area to a leather chair closer to the conversation. One day he asked if he could join our conversation. We welcomed him by pulling his chair into the circle.

Pete would add his opinions and comment on different parts of the Scriptures we were discussing. It seemed obvious that he had some spiritual hunger and experience. We invited Pete to share his story with us. That began several weeks of conversations about his various connections with churches. Some of the churches he had been a part of were pretty liberal while others were very conservative in their theology. Not surprisingly, Pete was very confused about what was required for him to have a relationship with Jesus.

Pete told us about his marriages, divorces and how some of the churches had dismissed him due to his two divorces. He was spiritually broken but wanted desperately to know God and to know that God would accept him and allow him to have a place in heaven. Through the weeks of conversation, Pete explored the grace Jesus offers to anyone who comes to Him with a believing heart.

One day, in the middle of a deep talk, Pete broke down. He willingly admitted that he had been trusting in what he saw as his own goodness. He realized that he needed the grace of Jesus and asked if he could pray with us to put his trust in Christ. Since that time, Pete has continued to meet with us at the church at Fair Oaks. He even invited a couple of friends to join us. None of them chose to keep meeting with us but Pete keeps reminding them of the grace he found in Jesus. Pete now helps lead a small house church gathering.

The church at Fair Oaks cigar lounge is growing. Some reading this book may question how there can be a church in a cigar lounge. We have people in this place who gather at various times and believe Jesus has called us out as a spiritual family. This spiritual family, under the leadership of Jesus, wants us to see Fair Oaks as one of our mission fields. He actually wants us to accomplish His purpose in this place and beyond. His purpose is to see women and men come to place their trust in Him.[1] Because of these principles found in the New Testament, we see ourselves as a church. Unconventional, yet fully a church for the glory of the Lord.

Several discipleship groups have started meeting at Fair Oaks, and sometimes there are get–togethers for worship and prayer. The men who are part of this church (believers and not–yet–believers) have put on breakfasts and lunches for the men who visit Fair Oaks. We have collected money and gift cards for our friends who have gone through medical issues or hit hard times. The atmosphere is changing in that business.

I weekly have someone strike up a short or long spiritual conversation, ask for prayer for themselves or a family member. We have even held an ordination exam and ceremony for one of the men. The ceremony was complete with a signed ordination certificate from the church at Fair Oaks. Several spiritual wildfires have started and are spreading at Fair Oaks. Why not stop right now and pray for the people at Fair Oaks to place their trust in Christ? Also, pray for your own set of friends who need Christ.

Lord, I pray right now for those reading this, that they would find those places where you are working and engage those dear souls with Your love and passion. Bring those people into relationship with you; convict them concerning their sin, Your righteousness and judgment. May new churches pop up in all types of businesses and locations for Your Kingdom building pleasure. Amen!

Stay Hungry

Hunger has a way of motivating a person to satisfy the knot in their stomach…or their soul. As we wonder how to work out our salvation[2] and to finish well the race set before us,[3] we need to remember how desperate our souls are for God. If we want to be adventurous in our faith, we need to connect daily with Jesus. As we understand our need for Him every moment of our lives, our grip on Him becomes stronger and we understand just how firm God's grip is on us. When we allow our hearts to wander towards the less important things of the world, our passion for Him lessens.[4]

Physical hunger can be reduced in two ways. One is to not eat. Eventually your hunger pains go away. It may take a while, but eventually the urge to eat shrinks, even though your body needs the nourishment. The best way to reduce hunger is to eat!

The same is true with our spiritual hunger. If we starve ourselves spiritually by focusing our lives on other things, our desire for intimacy with Christ will shrink even though our souls are shriveling. Feeding our souls with a steady diet of the Word of God, hanging out with Christ–followers and sharing the gospel satisfies us at deeper levels than we often understand. Our capacity to love and share life with others is expanded. Engaging in spiritual disciplines is vital to our being sensitive to the Holy Spirit's promptings to share the love of Christ and sparking wildfires wherever we go.

There is a comprehensive effect of spending time with God consistently. No one day makes a huge impact, however, the total cumulative effect of spending time with God and growing our faith is unquantifiable and undeniable.

One day, my friend Timothy and I came back hungry for breakfast from an early morning hike. We had climbed to the top of a mountain to pray for our city, and had covered several miles on our way up and down the mountain. We decided to try a new place for breakfast, but I regretted it once we sat down. With my stomach growling, I was ready to have the food appear instantly. Instead we had to wade through the new menu, chat with our waitress, place our order and wait.

As the friendly waitress brought our coffee and water, I asked her what her name was. "Molly," she answered. After ordering, I silently prayed for Molly, asking the Spirit to share with me how I could encourage her and even introduce her to Christ.

As Timothy and I carried on our conversation, Molly brought the food to our table. The Lord prompted me to ask her to tell us more about the café. As she finished giving us a short history lesson, I complimented her on her smile, and asked, "Molly, what are you passionate about?" Her immediate answer was that her child was the inspiration of her life. She told us about her child's age and energy before she left to serve other customers. When she checked back in with more coffee, I asked her if there was anything we could pray about for her. She seemed stuck for a second, but then answered that her life was going well and she was fine. As we finished our breakfast, I told Molly that I prayed for her and that I would bring my wife someday to eat because the food and service were wonderful. She smiled and we left.

Unknown to me, Timothy and his wife, Cynthia, went out to dinner that night. Timothy had been inspired by our interaction with Molly earlier that morning, so he thought he would try the same thing with their server at dinner. At some point in their meal, Timothy asked their server what he was passionate about. Soon they were having a good conversation, and their server even took a short break and sat down with them. A short spiritual conversation took place in that moment. Was another wildfire about to spread?

The purpose of these short stories is to encourage you that you can start wildfires, not know the results, and still be 100% successful, 100% of the time. I was able to connect with Molly on a spiritual level, and without knowing it, I started a wildfire in Timothy, who then took a risk and had a spiritual conversation with his server later that evening. When we stay connected to Jesus, deep discussions with friends and even strangers happen naturally. Finishing well begins with our staying hungry for Jesus.

Remember Jesus Christ

Paul's last letter in the New Testament is 2 Timothy. In his last letter, he urges his closest disciple, Timothy, to finish well. In 2 Timothy 2:8, Paul tells Timothy to *"Remember Jesus Christ…"*. In the first chapter of 2 Timothy, Paul says, *"I remind you to kindle afresh the gift of God which is in you…".* The gift is either his trust in Christ[5] or the gift of power, love and discipline.[6] Paul also urges Timothy to *"…continue in the things you have learned and become convinced of…which is in Jesus Christ."* In the last chapter, 2 Timothy 4, Paul exhorts his disciple to *"…be sober in all things, endure hardship, do the work of an evangelist, fulfill your ministry."* Paul understood the need for Timothy and all believers to be encouraged to finish well.

The fight with darkness is brutal. The enemy wants to discourage and disqualify believers from being all they are meant to be for the King.[7] Paul's remedy to the wounds of spiritual warfare is to remember Jesus Christ, and focus on the life He gives us and His leading.

Paul knew that it was vital for Timothy to keep his love fresh for Jesus, if his young friend wanted to finish well.[8] One way to do this is to take an honest inventory of our heart for Christ. Has He become a routine in our life, or is He is the reason we live? Paul knew it would be a struggle for Timothy (or any follower of Christ) to not be distracted by the battles for our affection and attention. We can fight discouragement with a confident focus on the One who loves us so much. We can choose to believe that what He has said is true about us, instead of listening to old stories of who we once were before we believed.

It's important to remind ourselves of all Christ has done for us throughout our lifetimes. It is healthy to tell the gospel to ourselves as we share it with those we walk with in our faith. I daily remind myself how much I need Jesus, that He has redeemed me, that this who I am in Christ; I can move forward through His strength in me. By realizing who I was, and reminding myself who I am in Christ; I can ignite wildfires where ever I go. I can tell that I'm on the road to finishing well when conversations about Him roll freely off my lips.

Continuing in Christ is a discipline to be taken seriously. Hardships against our faith in Christ[9] will certainly come. Being in a close community of believers who keeps the Missio Dei, the Mission of God, at the forefront helps us stay strong during the hardships.[10]

When my discipleship trio meets up every week, we know it's not just for cigars and chatting about sports. We ask the hard questions about faith and life, even when it is uncomfortable. The first question we ask when we get together is, "Have you been a testimony to the greatness of Jesus Christ by your words and actions?" Knowing I will be asked this question each week helps me stay alert to opportunities to share my faith in Christ. Some people might bristle at being asked this kind of personal question, seeing it as too formal and performance–based. For me, it's a challenge, and a positive reminder that God provides chances to serve Him in my conversations and actions every day. It reminds me that I exist to worship and serve Him until my last breath.

Finishing Well and Future Rewards

After encouraging Timothy to stay sober, endure hardships, do the work of an evangelist and to fulfill his ministry,[11] Paul explained that he had done these things himself.

> *6 For I am already being poured out as a drink offering, and the time of my departure has come. 7 I have fought the good fight, I have finished the course, I have kept the faith; 8 in the future there is laid up for me the crown of righteousness, which the Lord, the righteous Judge, will award to me on that day; and not only to me, but also to all who have loved His appearing. 2 Timothy 4:6-8*

In essence, Paul was saying he knew the cost of finishing well. Paul experienced what it was like to have his life spent (poured out) on serving, loving and mentoring others. This is part of what is required to finish well and God has equipped us to do so.[12]

To finish well, we will need to die to our own agendas and trade them in for Christ's.[13] We need a maturity that will treat others as more important than ourselves.[14] It also includes intentionally passing on our faith to others through making disciples of Jesus.[15] In 2 Timothy, Paul knew that his life was going to end soon. When he wrote his final letter, he was in jail, awaiting execution. As he looked back over his years of serving Jesus, he knew had finished well...but he wasn't always so convinced.

In 1 Corinthians 9, Paul makes a very startling statement about the course of his life. In verses 24–26, Paul is encouraging the Corinthian believers to keep going in their faith. He urged them to run the race of faith so that they would win the prize.

22 To the weak I became weak, that I might win the weak; I have become all things to all men, so that I may by all means save some. 23 I do all things for the sake of the gospel, so that I may become a fellow partaker of it. 24 Do you not know that those who run in a race all run, but only one receives the prize? Run in such a way that you may win. 25 Everyone who competes in the games, exercises self-control in all things. They then do it to receive a perishable wreath, but we, an imperishable. 26 Therefore I run in such a way, as not without aim; I box in such a way, as not beating the air... 1 Corinthians 9:24-26)

The encouragement from this passage is to live our life focused on Jesus and His agenda, not our own. The reason to focus on Christ is so we will win the prize.

If we want to win the prize, we must compete with self–control in all things. And here Paul calls us to live in that way. He begins the call by committing himself to do whatever is necessary to win some to Christ. Cultivating our hearts and minds to be on the hunt for the opportunities God places in our paths is fundamental to living a life that is pleasing to the Lord.

As Paul wrote these words, he was very concerned that his life would be pleasing to Jesus. If Paul, with all his accomplishments and impact had this concern, how concerned should we be with how we live? We are to run in a such a way that we will win the prize. Part of living this way is to discipline ourselves to make choices to engage the world around us with the love, action and words of gospel.

Paul makes another startling comment in this passage in 1 Corinthians;

*27 ...but I discipline my body and make it my slave, so that, after I have preached to others, **I myself will not be disqualified**. 1 Corinthians 9:27 (emphasis mine)*

At this point in his life, Paul was unsure he would finish well; *"...after I have preached to others, I myself will not be disqualified."* What was Paul concerned he might be disqualified from? Certainly, he was not worried about his entrance into heaven. This could not be the case because our justification[16] is secured 100% by Jesus Christ Himself. Once we place our trust in Christ[17] and His work on the cross and His resurrection, we are fully His forever. The love of God cannot be earned and cannot be lost. We are brought into relationship with Him as his daughter or son and that cannot be taken from us because it is initiated, secured, and fulfilled by Christ alone! Our relationship with God is not based on how we live, but by Christ's work alone!

What Paul *was* concerned about is found in the context of this passage. He was concerned about receiving the imperishable winner's wreath awarded when he would meet Jesus after his death.[18] This is a good reminder for us as well. Paul knew that how we live and where our life's focus is matters. It affects our intimacy with God now, as well as the recognition we will receive when we stand before Him in the end. A life spent in pointing people towards Jesus is part of our reward.

Keep Disciplined and Stay Alert

This morning I had breakfast here in Phoenix, Arizona, with a friend of twenty years. Throughout our friendship, I helped John place his trust in Christ, and saw him grow in his faith. I watched him baptize some of his children and I walked with him through a divorce. At breakfast, we were discussing what it takes to stay the course of following Jesus for the long haul and how we can help others to do the same in organic and holistic ways.

When our waitress, Jackie, asked us about coffee, water and our order, I knew God was up to something. Jackie informed us that another waiter, John, would be helping her as he was in training. As both Jackie and John kept us comfortable with our drinks and food, I sense the Lord nudge my spirit to ask Jackie to tell us what she was passionate about. Jackie quickly said she was passionate about training others to serve and that she wanted to become a police officer. Her goal after becoming a police officer was to become a trainer of policer officers. We had some fun banter between Jackie and John, which made their job more pleasant and alerted us to be listening to the Spirit of God and speaking the words He gave us. It was so natural for both my friend, John, and myself.

We must have been the source of some conversations in the back room because not only did John and Jackie visit us often, but Jackie brought another waitress, Bri, over to chat with us. At one point when Jackie and Bri were at our table, I told them I was a spiritual person and believed God answered our prayers. I asked them if there were any issues in their lives that we could pray for during the week ahead.

Jackie told us that she was hoping she would get the chance to change jobs and interview to become a police officer. Bri asked that we pray about an upcoming custody court hearing with her ex–husband. She was frustrated about how the judge would not allow the court date to be switched to one of her days off. This meant she would have to lose a day's pay to make her court hearing and that missing a day's pay would be a burden to her. I promised them we would pray, as well as come back for breakfast periodically and see how God was answering our prayers.

A few minutes later, Bri came over to check on our coffee. I boldly asked her if she would be comfortable telling us what she earned each day as a waitress. She did not hesitate to say she made about $100.00 per day serving people. The Lord then had me tell her that our church would give her the $100.00 she would lose in order to make her court date. Tears began to flow from her eyes and she gave both John and me a hug.

As we made our way to the cashier counter to pay our bill, John asked if he could buy a pie from their dessert case to take home. John pulled out his credit card only to hear Jackie say that the pie was free today. Apparently, she was so excited about our care for Bri that she wanted to give the pie to John.

This encounter over breakfast wasn't something we could have imagined ahead of time. I certainly never planned on offering our waitress $100.00! But when we saw the opportunity, we told Bri that God cares about her and wanted to show His love to her in a very tangible way. Were we successful in sharing the love of Jesus with her? She has not yet placed her trust in Christ as far as I know, but I feel certain that she will. As I engaged Bri in conversation, Jesus directed my words to say what she needed to hear at that moment. Our ability to hear the words of Jesus in our soul comes from being aware that He wants to speak through us. We nurture our faith through hearing His voice and repeating what He speaks, in big and small moments. And this shows that we are on the course towards finishing well.

Start Wildfires Everywhere

The dream of this book is to raise up an army of ordinary believers who boldly live out and share the gospel of Jesus. As we wean ourselves from programmed evangelistic approaches and learn to rely fully on the leading of the Spirit, the gospel will spread rapidly from one soul to another.

We need to beg the Lord for His eyes and compassion to see people as He does. This will cause us to experience tears of intercession for their souls and the boldness of Christ to speak to them as He directs our hearts. All it takes is one spark, one match, one heart on fire to pass on the truth to another…then wildfires will spread. The Scriptures illustrate freedom in evangelism for believers, not dependence on 'gifted' people or professionals.

When confidence rises in our souls and we see Christ fulfill His promises to give us the words to say at the right time to impact people, global wildfires will be uncontrollable. Psalm 126 gives us a sense of this reality when embraced by believers.

1 When the LORD brought back the captive ones of Zion, We were like those who dream. 2 Then our mouth was filled with laughter, and our tongue with joyful shouting; Then they said among the nations, "The LORD has done great things for them." 3 The LORD has done great things for us; We are glad. 4 Restore our captivity, O LORD, As

*the streams in the South. 5 Those who sow in tears
shall reap with joyful shouting. 6 He who goes to
and fro weeping, carrying his bag of seed, Shall
indeed come again with a shout of joy, bringing his
sheaves with him. Psalm 126*

As believers are released from the grip of programmed
evangelism, we will be brought back to the ways Christ always
intended for evangelism to move around the world. As we depend
on the Trinity to give us the words to speak at the right time we
will have laughter, joy and store up treasures in heaven.

We will know that God is moving in our midst. We will know
that God has done great things for us and we will be glad. We
will realize just how competent He has created us to be. As we
deepen our compassion for the not–yet–believer's souls, we will
be able to choose to ignite wildfires as we live out our lives.
When we see wildfires rise and spread, our hearts will be full of
joyful shouting as we see God's Kingdom spread.

Wherever we go, we will carry a matchbook in our hearts, the
Word of God! Let's light spiritual wildfires everywhere we go
with love, boldness, and assurance. Let's stop worrying about
what to say and be confident that the Holy Spirit will give us the
right words at the right time to meet the need of the person we are
engaging. May we be convinced that we will be 100% successful,
100% of the time. The more Spirit–led conversations we have,
the more wildfires we will start until Jesus returns. May we
always be wholeheartedly involved in the adventure of God
building His Kingdom.

APPENDIX: A SIMPLE TOOL FOR SHARING THE GOSPEL

After reading this book, I want to be clear that while I am not against using evangelistic tools, I really believe they do more to limit people in sharing the gospel than releasing people to share more. Once you tell people, "this is how you share the gospel" that method has the tendency to become the default presentation in a person's life. I have to admit, I still find myself falling back to "Life's Most Important Question"[1] method simply because it was what I was told to use as a new believer.

I do realize that many believers need help getting started in sharing their faith. It is certainly important to know how to present the gospel in a simple way that communicates clearly. There is so much to learn as a Christian, but what is really essential for a person to know in order become a believer?

I like to make things as simple as possible while keeping the gospel's integrity. When things are simplified as much as possible without compromising the gospel's essence, more people will learn it and use it and tell others; which is the ultimate goal. Remember, we want to multiply communicators, not just listeners!

When Jesus taught Nicodemus what he needed to do in order to be saved, He said, *"For God so loved the world, that He gave His only begotten Son, that whoever believes in Him shall not perish, but have eternal life."* (John 3:16).

The requirement according to Jesus was to believe in Him, He gave no other requirement. When the Philippian Jailor asked Paul

211

and Silas, "Sirs, what must I do to be saved?" (Acts 16:30), their response was, "Believe in the Lord Jesus, and you will be saved, you and your household." (Acts 16:31). Again, the answer is to believe in Jesus. With that understanding, I want to give you three words that all begin with "S" to help guide through a conversation with a friend in order to invite them to believe in Jesus.

Sin

Every person who has ever lived has sinned (Romans 3:23). But what is sin and how does it affect us spiritually? The basic definition of sin is to miss the mark. What is the mark, the goal? It is perfection. Sin, therefore, is missing the mark of perfection. Sin also carries the concept of an intentional crossing of a boundary. When we sin, we violate God's standard, we are guilty and God's justice demands satisfaction.

For a person to place their trust in Christ, they need to recognize that they have sinned. They need to admit it and realize that before God, they are guilty of violating His standard of perfection. Salvation, or entrance into heaven, cannot be secured without an admission of sin. Because everyone has sinned, they are separated from God. Separation is how we are affected by sin. Romans 6:23 tells us that the *"wages of sin, is death."* Wages are what we deserve and the wages of sin is death. Death is to be understood as physical death (Romans 5:12) and spiritual death (Isaiah 59:2). This is all because everyone has sinned.

Solution

Because every person has sinned, there needs to be a solution to care for this problem. One solution is to do nothing which means that a person would physically die and eternally be separated from God which is spiritual death (Matthew 25:46). Jesus is undiminished deity (fully God) and true humanity (fully man). Jesus came to pay for our sins by offering Himself as the satisfaction to God for our sins when He died on the cross (Romans 4:25). First John 2:2 says that Jesus *"...Himself is the propitiation for our sins; and not for ours only, but also for those of the whole world."*

212

It is important to note that John includes himself and his audience (believers), but also for the *"whole world."* Jesus' death was sufficient for everyone's sins for all time (Hebrews 10:12). Jesus is the solution to our sin problem. One must understand that Jesus took your place on the cross to satisfy the anger and justice of God (Romans 3:24–26). Jesus is our substitute on the cross. Jesus paid for the sins of the whole world. Jesus is the only solution that is effective for us to enjoy life forever with Him (Acts 4:12).

Step

The last of the three "S" words is step. Once a person realizes that they have sinned against God and deserves death (physically and spiritually), and they understand that Jesus is the solution to their sin problem, they must make–a–decision. The decision is a step. One can choose to step forward in their own philosophy or thinking which would not apply the solution Jesus provides to themselves. This leaves them to fend for themselves when they are judged (Revelation 20:11–15) and they will end up forever and ever separated from God. However, if one realizes they have sinned and that Jesus is their solution and steps in His direction by placing their trust in His sacrifice, they will be given eternal life (John 3:14–16).

A Word About Eternal Security and Assurance of Salvation

I believe the Scriptures teach that once a person places their trust in Jesus, that they are fully assured and secure to spend forever with Christ. I believe this based upon the promises of God (John 3:16, 6:39, 6:47, 10:28; Romans 8:35–39; 1 Corinthians 11:29; Ephesians 2:8–9; 1 Peter 1:3–5; 1 John 5:11–13). Eternal security and assurance of salvation are not based upon our obedience, the amount of our fruit, nor on our perseverance–it is based solely on the promises of God. If our eternal life is based upon our performance, no man would be able to have security or assurance (Titus 3:3–5). The love of God cannot be earned and it cannot be lost.

BIBLIOGRAPHY

Cole, Neil. *Church 3.0: Upgrades for the Future of the Church.*
Leadership Network. San Francisco, CA: Jossey-Bass,
©2010. Kindle Edition.

———. *Cultivating a Life for God: Multiplying Disciples
through Life Transformation Groups.* Signal Hill, CA:
CMA Resources, 2014, ©1999.

———. *Organic Church: Growing Faith Where Life Happens.* A
Leadership Network Publication. San Francisco: Jossey-
Bass, ©2005.

Coleman, Robert E. *The Master Plan of Evangelism.* Old Tappan,
N.J.: F.H. Revell, 1986 printing.

Crabb, Larry. *God Calls Men to Move Beyond- the Silence [of]
Adam: Becoming Men of Courage in a World of Chaos.*
Grand Rapids, Mich.: Zondervan Pub. House, ©1995.

Easton, M. G. "Evangelist." biblestudytools.com. Accessed
September 21, 2017.
http://www.biblestudytools.com/dictionaries/eastons-
bible-dictionary/evangelist.html.

Graham, Ron. "Word Study: Evangelist." simplybible.com.
Accessed September 21, 2017.
https://www.simplybible.com/f773-word-study-
evangelist.htm

Hallowell, Billy. "He Was Researching the Decline of Churches
in America and Noticed a Parallel That Truly Stunned
Him." theblaze.com. April 28, 2016. Accessed October 4,
2017. http:// www.theblaze.com/news/2016/04/28/he-

was-researching-the-decline-of-churches-in-america-and-noticed-a-parallel-that-truly-stunned-him/.

Hodges, Zane, C. *Absolutely Free: A Biblical Reply to Lordship Salvation.* 2nd ed. Corinth, TX: Grace Evangelical Society, 2014.

Kinnaman, David. "Is Evangelism Going Out of Style." Barna.com. Accessed October 4, 2017. https://www.barna.com/research/is-evangelism-going-out-of-style/#.VFvWMFPF-yE.

Omi, Philip N. *Forest Fires: A Reference Handbook.* Contemporary World Issues. Santa Barbara, Calif.: ABC-CLIO, ©2005.

Meyers, Jeremy. "Is Crusade Evangelism Effective." Redeeming God. December, 2011. Accessed October 11, 2017. https://redeeminggod.com/crusade-evangelism-effective/.

———. "How to Get More Converts than Billy Graham." Redeeming God. December, 2011. Accessed October 11, 2017. https://redeeminggod.com/more-converts-billy-graham/.

Reiland, Dan. "Invest, Invite, and Include." cfaith.com. Accessed August 17, 2016. http://www.cfaith.com/index.php/blog/38-articles/ministry/15844-invest-invite-and-include.

Sjogren, Steve. *Irresistible Evangelism: [natural Ways to Open Others to Jesus].* Loveland, Colo.: Group Pub., 2004.

Slick, Matt. "Hinckley says that Mormons believe in a different Jesus." carm.org. December 18, 2008. Accessed March 5, 2017. https://carm.org/hinckley-says-mormons-believe-different-jesus.

Spurgeon, C. H. "Sheep Among Wolves." Spurgeongems.org.
    Accessed October 5, 2017.
    http://www.spurgeongems.org/vols22-24/chs1370.pdf.

Stebbins, Tom. *Friendship Evangelism by the Book: Applying
    First Century Principles to Twenty-First Century
    Relationships*. Camp Hill, Pa.: Christian Publications,
    ©1995.

Stetzer, Ed. "Is Evangelism Going Out of Style."
    Christianitytoday.com. May 12, 2014. Accessed October
    4,
    2017. http://www.christianitytoday.com/edstetzer/2014/m
    ay/state-of-evangelism.html?paging=off.

Stetzer, Ed. "The State of Evangelism: Are Millennials
    evangelizing more or less than previous generations?
    What is the future of evangelism?" Christianitytoday.com.
    May 24, 2014. Accessed October 11,
    2017. http://www.christianitytoday.com/edstetzer/2014/m
    ay/state-of-evangelism.html.

Whealey, Alice. *Studies in Biblical Literature,*. Vol. 36, *Josephus
    On Jesus: the Testimonium Flavianum Controversy from
    Late Antiquity to Modern Times*. New York: Peter Lang,
    ©2003.

ABOUT THE AUTHOR

Ed and his wife, Debbie have been together since high school. They have three grown children and five grandchildren. Ed has been sharing the good news of Jesus since the day he became a Christian in April of 1976. His passion for Christ and love for others has influenced many around the world. Ed has traveled globally presenting and equipping people in the principles found in *Wildfire*.

Ed helps lead ValleyLife Church in Peoria, Arizona. ValleyLife is a network of organic churches across the Phoenix valley. He is also an adjunct professor of Biblical Studies at Arizona Christian University. Ed earned a Master's degree from Grace School of Theology.

Ed loves to fly fish, spend time with his family and vacation anywhere that is warm and has a beach. You can reach out to Ed at wildfiregospelinfo@gmail.com.

219

ENDNOTES

Introduction

[1] Acts 1:8

[2] Philip N. Omi, Forest Fires: A Reference Handbook, (Santa Barbara, California: ABC-CLIO Inc., 2005), 193.

[3] John 4:35

[4] Luke 4:18–19

[5] Scott Thumma and Warren Bird, *Recent Shifts in America's Largest Protestant Churches: Megachurches 2015 Report*(Leadership Network and Hartford Institute for Religion Research, 2015), 2, http://hirr.hartsem.edu/megachurch/2015_Megachurches_Report.pdf.

[6] Because many house churches intentionally fly under the radar of research, statistics are harder to quantify. It is the author's opinion from experience that this movement of meeting in homes as a primary corporate worship expression is on the rise.

[7] Neil Cole, *Church 3.0: Upgrades for the Future of the Church*, Leadership Network (San Francisco, CA: Jossey-Bass, ©2010), 50, Kindle Edition.

Chapter 1

[1] Friendship Evangelism is the concept of befriending people who are not yet Christians with the goal of leading them to Jesus. After a friendship has begun, the Christian gains enough trust with the not-yet-believer in order to share their desire for their friend to consider the claims of Christ. There are a few books writing with this intent behind them. Some of these books are: *Irresistible Evangelism* by Sjogren and Ping, *One to One: A Practical Guide to Friendship Evangelism* by Terry Wardle, *Friendship Evangelism by the Book* by Tom Stebbins and several other books and articles.

[2] Matthew 28:16–20

[3] Acts 17:16–34

[4] 1 Thessalonians 1:5–10

[5] Alan Hirsch, "Disciplism; Reimagining Evangelism Through the Lens of Discipleship" (paper presented at the Exponential Conference, 2014).

[6] The Good News of Jesus is much more than telling people that God loves them, that they are sinners, that Jesus took their sin upon Himself to pay for it and rose from the dead. It is more than encouraging them to pray a prayer to receive this gift of grace. The Good News of Jesus is also the reversal and

renewal of all things - the Kingdom of God - His love, leadership, management, care and the order of things. Jesus is King and all things in our lives are to be submitted to Him so that we will experience the abundant life He promised to those who follow Him.

[7] We often see the gospel fly on the wings of relationship in the New Testament. Paul met Lydia at a prayer meeting where she invited Paul into her house (Acts 16:14–16). Peter was instructed to go the house of Cornelius where he found Cornelius and his family and friends gathered to hear the gospel (Acts 10). In 1 Thessalonians 1:5–10 we find these new believers impacting their whole region.

[8] Peter and John were on their way to a daily prayer meeting when God impressed upon them to engage a man born lame and saw him healed which lead to a strong outbreak of the gospel in Jerusalem (Acts 3–4).

[9] Paul spoke the gospel to Jews in Thessalonica which lead to persecution on the house of Jason (Acts 17:1–8). Paul and Silas were thrown in jail in Philippi for proclaiming the gospel, but they chose to spend some of their jail time rejoicing in prayer and singing. This led to the salvation of the jailer and his whole household (Acts 16:22–40).

[10] 1 Corinthians 12:13

[11] John 15:15

[12] 1 Corinthians 13:1–8 teaches us that without love, all that we do will amount to nothing (1 Corinthians 13:2–3). Love is the true motivation that will be effective. In John 13:34–35, Jesus teaches His disciples that they will be known by love for one another.

[13] 1 Corinthians 13:1–3

[14] Galatians 4:19

[15] Matthew 28:16–20

[16] From Barnes Notes: The idea is, that Timothy was to use all proper means to keep the flame of pure religion in the soul burning, and more particularly his zeal in the great cause to which he had been set apart. The agency of man himself is needful to keep the religion of the heart warm and glowing. However rich the gifts which God has bestowed upon us, they do not grow of their own accord, but need to be cultivated by our own personal care. http://biblehub.com/commentaries/barnes/2_timothy/1.htm.

[17] It is vital to note that there is a strong distinction between two aspects of our salvation; justification and sanctification. Justification is our coming into initial relationship with Jesus Christ by placing our trust in Jesus' life, death, burial and resurrection. This is accomplished completely and solely by Jesus Christ and it is something that cannot be lost by our poor behavior or theological shifts. It is His work alone. Sanctification is the cultivating of our ongoing relationship with Jesus through our choosing to die to ourselves and the transformation that comes from God's grace. Our daily decision to kindle afresh our faith is our sanctification to keep the wildfire spreading throughout our lifetimes.

[18] Genesis 1:27

[19] Larry Crabb, *The Silence of Adam: Becoming Men of Courage in a World of Chaos* (Grand Rapids, Mich. (Zondervan Publishing House, ©1995), page 79.

[20] Revelation 2:5

[21] Colossians 1:23; 1 Thessalonians 5:12–22

[22] 2 Timothy 1:8

[23] Romans 10:8–10

[24] Acts 1:8

[25] Matthew 10:38; Luke 9:23; John 12:24; 1 Corinthians 15:31; Galatians 2:20

[26] Luke 4:18-19

[27] 2 Corinthians 5:18–20

[28] Matthew 10:8

[29] Matthew 22:37–40

[30] 1 John 4:18

[31] Acts 1:8

[32] Romans 8:4

[33] 2 Timothy 1:7

[34] 2 Timothy 1:7

[35] 1 John 2:15-17

[36] Luke 10:1

[37] One way of doing this is through Life Transformation Groups (LTG's), small intentional accountability groups for Christians. You can find out more about LTG's at this web address: https://www.cmaresources.org/article/ltg or by doing a search for Life Transformation Groups on your favorite search engine.

[38] 2 Corinthians 5:9–11

[39] Luke 2:52; Hebrews 5:8

[40] Hebrews 4:15

[41] Hebrews 5:7–9

[42] Matthew 17:27; Mark 6:33–44; Luke 8:1–3

[43] Mark 3:19, 14:33–36

[44] Mark 3:20

[45] Luke 6:12

[46] Matthew 9:35–39

[47] Matthew 6:25–34

[48] Mark 3:13–15

[49] Luke 6:12

[50] Mark 9:19

[51] Matthew 16:8

[52] 2 Corinthians 5:18–20

[53] The message of Jesus is constant and does not shift or change with culture or from generation to generation. The amount of understanding an individual–gains throughout their lifetime of learning the Biblical Scriptures adds to one's maturity. As these truths are lived out, experience will also add to one's impact in our sharing the truths of Jesus. As our relationship with

Jesus matures, so does our obedience to Jesus increase, developing us into strong conduits of truth.

[54] 1 Corinthians 3:4–6

Chapter 2

[1] Mark 4:13

[2] Matthew 28:19–20; Acts 1:8; Ephesians 6:18–20

[3] David Kinnaman, "Is Evangelism Going Out of Style," Barna.com, accessed October 4,2017, https://www.barna.com/research/is-evangelism-going-out-of-style/#.VFvWMFPF-yE. Ed Stetzer, "Is Evangelism Going Out of Style," Christianitytoday.com, May 12, 2014, accessed October 4, 2017, http://www.christianitytoday.com/edstetzer/2014/may/state-of-evangelism.html?paging=off.

[4] Ephesians 1:3–5

[5] Ephesians 1:3; 2 Peter 1:3–5

[6] Acts 1:8

[7] There is a need for believers to take a time out from the organized church experience in order to detox from artificial environment of worship services in order to hear from the Lord in fresh ways from the Word of God. Many in churches today have experienced an atrophy of spiritual might due to the constant restraint of sitting and listening as their regular intake of preprocessed food. Instead they need to get reconnected with the heart of the Father to be active in spreading the seed of the gospel and making disciples which will in turn strengthen the church. Once this detox has taken place and a fresh emphasis is placed upon deepening their faith in Christ and making disciples (Mark 3:13–15), they can re-enter the church they took a time out from. This will actually serve to help the church to be stronger, with better disciples, than simply sitting and feeling sated with processed food.

[8] 1 John 5:13

[9] Steve Sjogren, Dave Ping, and Doug Pollack, *Irresistible Evangelism: Natural Ways to Open Others to Jesus* (Loveland, CO: Group Pub., 2004), 24.

[10] John 4

[11] Matt Matthew 23:27

[12] Luke 12:11–12

[13] Larry Gilbert, *Do You have the Spiritual Gift of the Evangelist?* https://churchgrowth.org/do-you-have-the-spiritual-gift-of-evangelism/ (accessed December 28, 2019)

[14] Christian Schwarz, *Natural Church Development* (Emmelsbull, Germany: ChurchSmart Resources, 1996), 34.

[15] Rick Rusaw and Eric Swanson, *The Externally Focused Church* (Loveland, CO: Group Publishers, 2004), 13.

[16] The gift of the Evangelist is mentioned in the following passages: Acts 21:8, Ephesians 4:11, 1 Timothy 4:5.

[17] Here is one example of how the gift of evangelism is assumed to

only belong to the gifted evangelists: https://spiritualgiftstest.com/spiritual-gift-evangelism/ (accessed June 8, 2018).

[18] 2 Corinthians 3:4–6

[19] Matthew 4:19

[20] 1 Corinthians 3:6

[21] Ephesians 4:11–12

[22] Reggie McNeal, *The Present Future: Six Tough Questions for the Church*, (San Francisco, Jossey Bass, 2003), 25.

[23] Billy Hallowell, "He Was Researching the Decline of Churches in America and Noticed a Parallel That Truly Stunned Him," Theblaze.com, April 28, 2016, wwwtheblaze.com/news/2016/04/28/he-was-researching-the-decline-of-churches-in-america-and-noticed-a-parallel-that-truly-stunned-him/, accessed August 31, 2018.

[24] 2 Corinthians 9:6

[25] Ed Stetzer and Warren Bird, *Viral Churches: Helping Church Planters Become Movement Makers,* www.christianitytoday.com/assets/10228.pdf, accessed August 31, 2017.

[26] Every believer has everything they need to be effective for the King from the moment they come to Jesus (2 Peter 1:3, Ephesians 1:3; 2 Peter 1:3).

[27] Ephesians 1:21–23

[28] Matthew 16:18 "I will build my church…" (Jesus Christ)

[29] Matthew 20:20–28 "If you want to be great, you must be the slave of all."

[30] Acts 1:8

[31] Matthew. 29:19

[32] John 13:1–17; 1 Corinthians 11:23–26

[33] 1 Corinthians 4:1; 1 Timothy 1:5; 1 Peter 2:9; Revelation 5:10

[34] For many throughout the history of the church, leading people to salvation in Jesus is a highlight of one's life.

[35] Dan Reiland, "Invest, Invite, and Include," cfaith.com, http://www.cfaith.com/index.php/blog/38-articles/ministry/15844-invest-invite-and-include. "Invest, Invite," http://franklinccc.org/invest-invite/, March 4, 2018, accessed September 21, 2018.

[36] M. G. Easton, "Evangelist," biblestudytools.com, accessed September 21, 2018, http://www.biblestudytools.com/dictionaries/eastons-bible-dictionary/evangelist.html. Ron Graham, "Word Study: Evangelist," simplybible.com, accessed September 21, 2018. http://www.simplybible.com.au/f773-word-study-evangelist.htm. From this web page; "All who preach the gospel as a vocation are "evangelists" because the word simply means "gospeller" or "goodmessenger".

[37] 2 Corinthians 5:20

[38] Acts 1:8

[39] Jeremy Meyers, "Is Crusade Evangelism Effective," Redeeming God, December, 2011, accessed October 11, 2018, https://redeeminggod.com/crusade-evangelism-effective/. Jeremy Meyers, "How to Get More Converts than Billy Graham," Redeeming God,

December, 2011, accessed October 11, 2018, https://redeeminggod.com/more-converts-billy-graham/. Ed Stetzer, "The State of Evangelism: Are Millennials evangelizing more or less than previous generations? What is the future of evangelism?," Christianitytoday.com, May 24, 2014, accessed October 11, 2018, http://www.christianitytoday.com/edstetzer/2014/may/state-of-evangelism.html, accessed September 20, 2018.

[40] In fact, I would say that if any of apostles, prophets, evangelists, shepherds or teachers (APEST) from Ephesians 4:11–12 do not spend at least 50% of their time equipping saints in their gifting, that the APEST gifted person has failed to accomplish what they have been gifted to do!

[41] 1 Corinthians 2:1–5

[42] Matthew 19:16–26

[43] John 6:67–71

[44] 2 Peter 3:9

[45] John 4:37; Matthew 9:35–38

[46] Matthew 4:19

[47] Luke 10:1ff

[48] Matthew 28:19–20

[49] Matthew 28:20

[50] Proverbs 23:7a

[51] Proverbs 24:26

[52] John 21:15–17

Chapter 3

[1] Matthew 9:35–38

[2] Luke 4:18–19

[3] John 20:21

[4] Matthew 26:39; Philippians 2:1–11

[5] Hebrews 5:7–9

[6] Genesis 1:28; Matthew 28:16–20

[7] Joshua 2 & 6

[8] Matthew 1:5

[9] Jonah 1–4

[10] Isaiah 42:1–12, 49:6, 55:5, 56:6–8; Jeremiah 3:17, 4:2; Zechariah 2:11

[11] Colossians 2:9 "For in Him all the fullness of Deity dwells in bodily form." Notice that "dwells" is in the present tense and indicates He has a continual glorified body in heaven.

[12] John 19:30; Romans3:21–25; Hebrews 2:17; 1 John 2:2, 4:10

[13] Galatians 4:19

[14] John 14:12 Jesus said "Truly, truly, I say to you, whoever believes in me will also do the works that I do; and greater works than these will he do, because I am going to the Father." Whoever believes in Jesus in any age will be completely capable of going greater works than Jesus did because He is now with the Father and has sent His Holy Spirit permanently into the hearts

of those who believe in Him. When we understand this truth and act on it confidently, we will see more wildfires spread than we ever thought possible.

[15] 2 Corinthians 5:14

[16] 2 Corinthians 5:13–15

[17] John 17:14

[18] John 17:15

[19] John 17:15–16

[20] Acts 17:1–2

[21] 1 Corinthians 4:16, 11:1; Philippians 3:17; 1 Thessalonians 1:6; 2 Thessalonians 3:7–8

[22] Robert E. Coleman, *The Master Plan of Evangelism* (Old Tappan, N.J.: F.H. Revell, 1986 printing), 116.

[23] Matthew 14:23; Mark 1:35; Luke 6:12; 41–44; John 12:27–28; 17:1–26

[24] Romans 10:1

[25] Romans 9:3

[26] Some main teachings of the Doctrine of Separation propose that followers of Jesus are to limit their interaction with the world so as not to be tainted by non-biblical worldview and practices (1 John 2:15–17), to be separated for the Lord (2 Timothy 2:19, Romans 6:1–2), to come out from non-believers (2 Corinthians 6:14–17). In this thinking, holiness is measured more by how one conforms to traditions rather than following the example of Christ.

[27] Matthew 4:19

[28] Mathew 28:16–20, Acts 1:8

[29] Matthew 5–7 The Sermon on the Mount

[30] Mark 1:21–34

[31] John 4:1–45

[32] John 4:46–54

[33] Matthew 15:21–28

[34] Mark 2:13–17

[35] Luke 7:36

[36] John 2:1–12

[37] Luke 7:1–10

[38] Luke 7:37–50

[39] Matthew 9:35–38

[40] Luke 14:25–33

[41] The primary theme of Luke 15 is more likely about relationship with God as the sheep, coin and son were all, at one time, connected to an owner. For the purposes here, I am looking at Luke 15's focus as being in relationship with not–yet–believers.

[42] Neil Cole, *Cultivating a Life for God: Multiplying Disciples through Life Transformation Groups* (Signal Hill, CA: CMA Resources, 2014, © / Church Smart (1999).

[43] 1 Corinthians 15:6

[44] Alice Whealey, *Studies in Biblical Literature,* vol. 36, Wheatley

Josephus On Jesus: The Testimonium Flavianum Controversy from Late Antiquity to Modern Times (New York: Peter Lang, © International Academic Publishers; First Edition (February 6, 2003).

Chapter 4

[1] Acts 17:26–27

[2] 2 Corinthians 3:4–6

[3] Acts 2:42–47; 4:32–35

[4] "Strong's Concordance" www.biblehub.com, accessed December 29, 2018, http://biblehub.com/greek/627.htm.

[5] Several studies (McDowell, 1999; Strobel, 2013; Geisler, 2007; Moreland, 2003; Craig, 2010; Licona, 2004).

[6] The Bible is a treasure of wisdom for believers, but we're not limited to a physical copy when we study it. Word studies, Bible commentaries, sermons, podcasts and books are a few ways for us to learn and grow in our understanding of the Scriptures. As we learn and grow, we open a door for God to bring to our mind what He knows the person we are talking to needs to hear in the moment.

[7] Philippians 1:29

[8] C. H. Spurgeon, "Sheep Among Wolves," Spurgeongems.org, accessed December 29, 2018, http://www.spurgeongems.org/vols22-24/chs1370.pdf.

[9] John 10:27a

[10] 1 Peter 4:14

[11] Isaiah 55:11; Philippians 1:15–18

[12] Luke 11:27–54

[13] Luke 12:1–3

[14] Luke 12 4–7

[15] Acts 5:1–8

[16] Luke 21:13

[17] 2 Corinthians 5:17–21

Chapter 5

[1] Acts 7:22a

[2] Hebrews 11:24

[3] "Josephus, Antiquities II," Chapter 16 footnote 22 (http://www.gutenberg.org/files/2848/2848-h/2848-h.htm#link22H_FOOT), accessed September 15, 2018.

[4] The story of Moses' origins is covered in Exodus 2–6.

[5] Exodus 3:6b

[6] Genesis 11:1ff; Hebrews 11:32

[7] 1 Samuel 17

[8] Galatians 4:19; 2 Timothy 2:2

[9] Mark 3:13–15

[10] Exodus 5:1–23

[11] Exodus 3:18

[12] Exodus 3:22

[13] Exodus 4:1–9

[14] Luke 21:12–15

[15] Exodus 4:14–17

[16] Exodus 4:14

[17] Exodus 4:15

[18] Exodus 4:18ff

[19] Exodus 6:10–12, 28–30

[20] Matthew 4:19

[21] Matt Slick, "Hinckley says that Mormons believe in a different Jesus," carm.org, December 18, 2008, https://carm.org/hinckley-says-mormons-believe-different-jesus, accessed October 5, 2018.

[22] John 14:12

[23] John 10:10

[24] In each of the following passages, God calls people to both be with Him and simultaneously send them out on mission for His purposes. Some of the following stories include less mature followers of God and some involve very mature followers. The idea is that God knows that when we draw close to Him, at that moment of movement towards Him, we become ready to be on mission as well. God calls and sends simultaneously. Joshua 1:1–5; Isaiah 1:18; Isaiah 6:1–10; Isaiah 55:1; Jeremiah 1:4–9; Matthew 28:16–20, 28:6–7, 11:28–30; Mark 1:17; Luke 24:30–35.

[25] Luke 6:12

[26] Mark 2:14

[27] Matthew 4:19

[28] See Chapter 8, "Fishermen and Other Ordinary People" for a full treatment of this principle that Jesus sends people out before they are ready.

[29] The message of Jesus is constant and does not shift or change with culture or from generation to generation. The amount of understanding an individual gains throughout their lifetime of learning the Biblical Scriptures adds to one's maturity. As these truths are lived out, experience will also add to one's impact in our sharing the truths of Jesus. As our relationship with Jesus matures, so does our obedience to Jesus increase, developing us into strong conduits of truth.

[30] Luke 10:9

[31] Philippians 1:15–18

[32] 1 Corinthians 3:6

[33] Matthew 10:16–20

[34] Acts 26

[35] Acts 12

[36] John 15:16

Chapter 6

[1] Mark 4:4, 15

[2] Mark 4:5–7, 16–19

³ Luke 10:2

⁴ Matthew 9:37–38

⁵ Acts 17:26–27

⁶ Most people have interactions with not-yet-believers at work and even eat lunch with them in the work context, but in my experience, they rarely translate this into an actual friendship outside of the work environment. There is also a deep lack of connectivity between believers and their neighbors beyond a greeting. Find creative ways to make your home the "living room" of your neighborhood. Believers should prayerfully take advantage of work and neighborhood connections and see how God draws people to Himself.

⁷ 2 Corinthians 9:6

⁸ Romans 10:8–15

⁹ Mobilization is the engagement of every believer in the mission of fearlessly spreading the gospel of Jesus. In order to see an abundant fruitful harvest, there must be the goal of total mobilization of believers on a variety of levels. In other words, a fruitful harvest is not realized by only a few people engaged in the sowing of seeds. Evangelism is the privilege and responsibility of every believer and is not reserved for a few gifted people. Mobilization engages people in worship which in turn heightens souls to spread the great love and good news of Jesus. Mobilization encourages prayer, organization, spiritual intelligence, leadership, mentoring, teaching, equipping on the subject of evangelism. Every person can and should have a roll in cultivating, sowing and harvesting the seed of the gospel so God can cause the increase. For too long the church has viewed the cultivating, sowing and harvesting as compartmentalized for a few specially gifted people. In reality, every believer has been called, anointed and sent on mission for the King throughout their lives.

¹⁰ Acts 1:12–14

¹¹ Acts 3:17–21

¹² Acts 4:4

¹³ Acts 4:31–35

¹⁴ Acts 4:29

¹⁵ Acts 4:30

¹⁶ Acts 5:5, 11

¹⁷ Acts 6:7

¹⁸ Acts 7:59–60

¹⁹ Luke 23:34

²⁰ Acts 8:1, 22:20

²¹ Acts 1:8

²² Ephesians 4:11–12

²³ 2 Peter 1:3

²⁴ At the moment of salvation, every believer is given: the authority from God to proclaim the message (Matthew 28:19–20); the power of God to proclaim the message (Acts 1:8); the mind of Christ to proclaim the message (1 Corinthians 2:16); and the words to speak from God to meet the need of the

listener in each encounter (Matthew 10:18–20; Mark 13:9–11; Luke 21:12–15).

25 Acts 8:4–8
26 Acts 8:25
27 Acts 8:26
28 Acts 8:27
29 Acts 8:40
30 Acts 8:40
31 Acts 1:8
32 Acts 9:19–22
33 Acts 9:26–27
34 Acts 11:19
35 Literally 'tens of thousands' and this does not include Gentile believers.
36 Matthew 16:18
37 Acts 8:25–40
38 Acts 10:1ff
39 Acts 6:7
40 Acts 8:1–4

Chapter 7
1 1 Corinthians 14:1–3 discusses the gift of prophecy that is available to every believer to offer security, encouragement and consolation.
2 2 Timothy 3:16-1:17; 2 Peter 1:20—21; Hebrews 1:1; 2, Jude 3
3 Revelation 22:18
4 If you are a cessationist, you are probably pulling your hair out. I fully understand as I was once where you are. There are a variety of approaches I could take to challenge your perspective but I will simply ask a line of questions for you to mull over. Most cessationists would argue that the sign gifts or God's using prophecy, dreams or other supernatural ways of communication are no longer needed because we now have the completed Canon. The questions to mull over are; When was the Canon closed and the sign gifts ceased? Was it when the last letter of the last book was written? Was it when they were compiled together? Was it when the sixty-six books were canonized? If the sign gifts and supernatural ways of communication ceased when the canon was complete why do we have instructions in the canon on how to practice the spiritual gifts? Why were these instructions needed on how to apply the gifts if they were already reading Scripture that was written to them? If a people group did not or does not have the completed canon available to them, would the sign gifts and supernatural ways of communication be needed?
5 Acts 6:5, 8
6 Acts 8:10
7 Luke 21:12–15
8 Acts 4:8
9 Acts 4:13

[10] Matthew 5:14

[11] James 4:13–15

[12] James 4:4 "You adulteresses, do you not know that friendship with the world is hostility toward God? Therefore, whoever wishes to be a friend of the world makes himself an enemy of God." This verse is talking about adopting the mindset, values and system of the world. It is not talking about being in friendship with people who are not Christians!

[13] Matthew 11:19

[14] 1 John 2:6

[15] Neil Cole, *Organic Church: Growing Faith Where Life Happens*, A Leadership Network Publication (San Francisco: Jossey-Bass, ©2005), 179.

Chapter 8

[1] Jesus taught his followers from common experiences that would touch every culture and generation until He returned. He often used farming for His illustrations, fishing, employment and other stories from life that would be able to be passed down to all generations. Every culture and generation understands the concepts of sowing, fishing, bread, wine, and celebrations. The genius behind these illustrative stories is timeless and easily passed on to the next culture or time.

[2] John 1:26–30

[3] Luke 6:12–13

[4] Cole, *Organic Church*, 134.

[5] Matthew 10:1–15, Luke 10:1–16

[6] Matthew 17:14–23

[7] Matthew 28:17 "...and some doubted..."

[8] Mark 4

[9] Mark 4:1

[10] It is best to understand the reproduction of 30, 60, 100 times as being generational rather than growing larger. No single farm or plant can be enough. Good seed in good soil will not only be fruitful, it will continue to produce a healthy harvest for future generations to come. The fruit of an apple tree is not just an apple, but an orchard of apple trees so the production of apples will continue and multiply.

[11] Mark 4:26–29

[12] Mark 4:30–33

[13] Mark 4:34

[14] Mark 4:16–17 correlates with Mark 4:38–41.

[15] I John 2:2

[16] Mark 5:7

[17] Mark 5:8

[18] Mark 5:9

[19] Mark 4:14–15 correlates with Mark 5:16–17. The people of this region had the very Word of God in their midst and they did not want anything to do with Him. It is possible that the demonic influence on the one man had

reaching effect on the whole region when truth was presented to them or it could just be the hardness of their heart both individually and corporately. Either way, the seed (Jesus) that was already in their land was not received and asked to leave.

[20] Mark 4:20 correlates with Mark 5:18--20. The formally demonized man was good soil and received the good seed which resulted in a 30, 60, 100 times return. Mark 5:20 tells us that "...everyone marveled" when they heard the man's testimony.

[21] Mark 7:31

[22] John 4:9

[23] John 4:10

[24] John 5:19

[25] John 7:38–39

[26] John 4:26

[27] John 4:27

[28] John 4:28

[29] This section is from John 4:29–30.

[30] John 4:41–42 It is also interesting to study Acts 8:4–24 when Philip left Jerusalem and ministered in Samaria. We can only imagine that impact of Jesus' ministry to the woman at the well and the city of Sychar setting the stage when Philip arrived in Samaria to again proclaim the gospel to them.

[31] "Ellicott's Commentary for English Readers", accessed January 1, 2018, http://biblehub.com/commentaries/john/9-4.htm

[32] Ephesians 2:10

[33] "Barnes' Notes on the Bible", Commentary on John 9:22, http://biblehub.com/commentaries/john/9-22.htm, accessed January 1, 2018.

[34] 2 Corinthians 3:4–6

Chapter 9

[1] Ephesians 1:3–6; Philippians 2:13; 2 Peter 1:3. These passages are a small glimpse at some of the equipment that every believer is blessed with at the moment of their placing their trust in Christ.

[2] 2 Kings 5:2

[3] This whole section comes from the story in 2 Kings 5:10.

[4] 2 Kings 5:14

[5] 2 Kings 5:15

[6] 1 Kings 16:33

[7] Jeroboam, Nadab, Baasha, Elah, Zimri and Omri all proceeded Ahab and were evil as well.

[8] 1 Kings17:1

[9] 1 Kings 17:3–7 (ravens brought Elijah his daily food), 1 Kings 17:8–16 (God keeps a jar of flour and oil replenished for three and a half years supernaturally to feed Elijah, and his hostess' family), 1 Kings 17:17–24 (Elijah raises his hostess' son from the dead).

[10] This whole section comes from the story in 1 Kings 18:1.

[11] This whole section comes from the story in 1 Kings 18.

¹² This whole section comes from the story in 1 Kings 18:38.

¹³ This is the story of Joshua entering the promised land is found in Joshua 1–6.

¹⁴ The rest of chapter is about the story from 1 Samuel 14.

Chapter 10

¹ This definition of church was first crafted by Neil Cole in his book, Organic Church.

² Philippians 2:12–13

³ Hebrews 12:1–2

⁴ Revelation 2:4–5

⁵ 2 Timothy 1:5

⁶ 2 Timothy 1:7

⁷ Ephesians 2:10

⁸ Revisit Chapter one of this book, "Fresh Fire".

⁹ Philippians 1:29–30

¹⁰ Hebrews 3:13–14, 10:24–25, 12:12–13

¹¹ 2 Timothy 4:5

¹² Ephesians 1:3, Ephesians 2:10, 3:20; Philippians 2:13; 2 Peter 1:3

¹³ Galatians 2:20

¹⁴ Philippians 2:2–4

¹⁵ Matthew 28:16–20; 2 Timothy 2:2, 22

¹⁶ Justification means to be declared righteous by God Himself (Genesis 15:6; Romans 4:5)!

¹⁷ John 3:14–16

¹⁸ 1 Corinthians 3:10–15; 2 Corinthians 5:6–11; 2 John 8

Appendix 1

¹ Life's Most Important Question Tract, http://graceconnect.us/lifes-most-important-question/, accessed December 6, 2018.

Made in the USA
Middletown, DE
25 January 2020